Thomas J. Conaty

THE CATHOLIC UNIVERSITY OF AMERICA, 1896-1903

THE RECTORSHIP OF THOMAS J. CONATY

BY

PETER E. HOGAN, S.S.J.
PROFESSOR OF CHURCH HISTORY
IN
ST. JOSEPH'S SEMINARY
WASHINGTON

WASHINGTON, D. C.
THE CATHOLIC UNIVERSITY OF AMERICA PRESS
1949

Copyright 1949

by

THE CATHOLIC UNIVERSITY OF AMERICA PRESS, INC.

21632

TABLE OF CONTENTS

ILLUSTRATIONS

Dedicated to

MARY A. HOGAN

A Mother in all but blood

PREFACE

When great figures are playing upon the stage of history, lesser, but truly important, characters are likely to be obscured. Such has been the case with Thomas J. Conaty, who lived in what was one of the most stirring periods of American Catholic history. He was not without merit of his own, but he could not, of course, be classed with James Gibbons, John Ireland, John Lancaster Spalding, Michael A. Corrigan or John J. Keane. He was a secondary figure, even though he had a creditable record as an organizer on parochial, diocesan, and national lines. Not an original thinker of particular note, he was able to give the ideas of others a practical application in spite of the obstacles put in his way. His activities were diversified but effective. An immigrant lad born in Ireland on August 1, 1847, he rose to national prominence successively as the head of the Cliff Haven Catholic Summer School, and as the Rector of the Catholic University of America. He passed from this life on September 18, 1915, as Bishop of Monterey-Los Angeles. This study endeavors to trace in as much detail as the extant sources permit, one phase of his life, together with the vicissitudes of the institution which he directed, during the years from 1897 to 1903. If at times the narrative seems to deal too much in conflicting personalities, it is because the rectorship of Thomas J. Conaty suffered greatly from these clashes. In no case have these conflicts been mentioned for themselves, but only to show more clearly the accomplishments achieved by Conaty under highly adverse circumstances. The ability of the institution to persevere and to grow in the midst of so many destructive forces, would indicate that it had a destiny to accomplish, that here was the *digitus Dei*.

It has been difficult to find terms to label accurately the opposing parties in the Church of these years. The term "liberal" has been so belabored during the last century that one specific meaning cannot be given to it. "Progressive" might be a better term, but since "liberal" and "conservative" were often employed by the parties themselves, it seems more fitting that they should be the designations given in this study. The word "liberalism", as used here, may best be understood by an explanation of conservatism as given by Roberto

Michels in the *Encyclopaedia of the Social Sciences*.[1] He gave the meanings of "love of authority and tradition" as well as "hostility to innovations in the social or moral order" as denoting the conservative elements. This description would seem to delineate the Corrigan-McQuaid wing of the American hierarchy of those days. The lack of these characteristics rather than the possession of the opposite qualities might fittingly enough designate the Ireland-Keane party. In this sense only were these bishops liberals.

The work has been based in the main upon archival sources. For that fact the writer is indebted to a number of persons. Thanks are due to the late Most Reverend Michael J. Curley and his chancellor, the Right Reverend Joseph M. Nelligan, for their generosity and hospitality while he was using the Baltimore Cathedral Archives. Most gratefully remembered also is the unstinted and thoughtful consideration of the Right Reverend John M. A. Fearns, Rector of St. Joseph's Seminary, Yonkers, New York, and of the archdiocesan archivist, the Reverend Jeremiah J. Brennan. For similar courtesies, the writer is indebted to the Most Reverend Peter L. Ireton, Bishop of Richmond, as well as to his chancellor and vice-chancellor, the Very Reverends Robert Hickman and Justin D. McClunn. A like debt of gratitude is owed to the Reverend Joseph I. Malloy, C.S.P., archivist of the Paulist Fathers in New York. It was, however, through the kind permission of the present Rector of the Catholic University of America, the Right Reverend Patrick J. McCormick, together with the co-operation of the vice-rector, the Right Reverend Edward B. Jordan, that the greater part of the sources were made available. For the permission to engage in graduate studies at the University, as well as for the understanding encouragement throughout this period of preparation, the thanks of the writer are most gratefully tendered to his former Superior General, the Very Reverend Edward V. Casserly, S.S.J.

The direction, example, kindly criticism, and above all, the unflagging interest of the Reverend John Tracy Ellis, professor of American church history, made the production of this study more than a mere toilsome fulfillment of a requirement for a degree.[2] To

[1] Roberto Michels, "Conservatism", *Encyclopaedia of the Social Sciences,* IV (New York, 1931), 230-233. Cf. also Guido de Ruggiero, "Liberalism", *Encyclopaedia of the Social Sciences,* IX (New York, 1933), 435-442.

[2] In its original form this study was a dissertation submitted to the Faculty of the Graduate School of Arts and Sciences of the Catholic University of America in partial fulfillment of the requirements for the degree of Master of Arts, May, 1948.

John T. Farrell, associate professor of American history, who read the manuscript and gave much helpful criticism, the writer extends his thanks. Appreciated also were the suggestions of Miss Anne McNamara of the Catholic University of America Department of English, the corrections of Very Reverend James Didas, S.S.J., and the generous assistance of the Mullen Memorial Library staff, especially Miss Margaret M. Donahue. For his co-operation in gathering and evaluating sources, special thanks are due to the writer's associate, the Reverend Patrick H. Ahern of the Archdiocese of St. Paul, as well as to the many other friends who gave freely of their time and interest.

In order to insure completeness of coverage of possible sources, the Archdiocese of Los Angeles and the Diocese of Springfield were contacted, but they were unproductive of any useful material.[3]

Peter E. Hogan, S.S.J.

St. Joseph's Seminary
Washington 17, D. C.
February, 1949

[3] Patrick J. Dignan to John Tracy Ellis, Los Angeles, March 30, 1946: "With reference to Bishop Conaty's papers, I have taken the matter up with Doctor Conroy, who is at present working on a history of the Archdiocese here. He says that the archives here have only sermons, clippings of accounts of celebrations etc., but no material relating to the Catholic University of America."

Timothy J. Champoux to Robert E. McCall, Springfield, Massachusetts, December 11, 1946: "As to Father Hogan's request for access to the diocesan archives, we are sorry to say we have nothing on Bishop Conaty."

KEY TO ABBREVIATIONS

AER............*American Ecclesiastical Review*.

ACQR...........*American Catholic Quarterly Review*.

ACUA............Archives of the Catholic University of America.

    CHF.........Caldwell Hall Files, records previously located in Caldwell Hall.

    FBT.........Files of the Board of Trustees.

    MMBT.......Minutes of the Meetings of the Board of Trustees.

    RRTTS......Rector's Reports to the Senate.

    RSS.........Report of the Secretary of the Senate.

    SR..........Senate Records of the Catholic University of America.

AUND...........Archives of the University of Notre Dame.

BCA.............Baltimore Cathedral Archives.

CHR.............*Catholic Historical Review*.

CUB.............*Catholic University Bulletin*.

CW..............*Catholic World*.

DAA.............Dubuque Archdiocesan Archives.

NYAA...........New York Archdiocesan Archives.

PFA.............Paulist Fathers Archives, General Files.

    PFA-A.......Paulist Fathers Archives, Americanism File.

RDA.............Richmond Diocesan Archives.

SMSA...........St. Mary's Seminary Archives, Roland Park, Baltimore, Maryland.

Chapter I

THE INSTITUTION AND THE MAN

The Catholic University of America in the year 1896 had reached a critical point in its history. For twelve years, from the first action for its foundation in the Third Plenary Council of Baltimore, through the period of its formation, and under the rectorship of John J. Keane, its existence had been precarious. In 1896, with the removal of the first rector under the cloud of liberalism, the institution seemed destined for a speedy failure. The work of John Tracy Ellis, *The Formative Years of the Catholic University of America,*[1] traced the idea of the University from its earliest days, through the plenary council and up to the realization of the idea in the opening of the doors of the institution on November 13, 1889. In this volume Ellis presented the difficulties that lay in the way of the success of the university idea as well as the courage and pertinacity of the personalities who were able to bring their plans to fruition.

The earliest mention of a Catholic university for the United States had come in 1819 when Robert Browne, in his apologetical account of the Church in the United States written to the Congregation of the Propaganda during the trustee troubles in Charleston, suggested the erection of a truly American Catholic educational institution that would fit the character of the American Catholics better than the foreign-dominated institutions of his day.[2] Archbishop Martin J. Spalding, to a great extent already responsible for the opening of the American College at Louvain in March, 1857, also desired the formation of an American Catholic university and strove to have such a project inaugurated during the Second Plenary Council of Baltimore in 1866.[3] The best that he could achieve in the council was an

[1] John Tracy Ellis, *The Formative Years of the Catholic University of America* (Washington, 1946).

[2] Ellis, *op. cit.,* pp. 41-43. Browne was an Irish-born Augustinian who became involved in the trustee difficulties in Charleston and his suggestion arose from the early Americanization struggles that were reflected in the later life of the University itself.

[3] *Ibid.,* pp. 44-50.

1

expression of the wish of the hierarchy that a university were then possible, but it left the consideration of a foundation for a later date.[4]

The idea was not abandoned after the Second Plenary Council, for periodical and newspaper articles recurrently brought the subject before the public, especially through the medium of the *Catholic World,* the *American Catholic Quarterly Review,* the *Catholic Mirror* of Baltimore and the *Catholic Advocate* of Louisville.[5] The two outstanding protagonists for a university were Bishop Thomas A. Becker of Wilmington and Bishop John L. Spalding of Peoria. Becker gradually faded from the scene but the Bishop of Peoria remained constantly active for the university project. It was through the instrumentality of John Lancaster Spalding that the first positive step towards the establishment of the University took place, for four days after the Third Plenary Council of Baltimore was opened the bishops received a letter offering $300,000 for the purpose of founding a national Catholic school of philosophy and theology. The letter was sent by Miss Mary Gwendoline Caldwell, who, together with her sister Elizabeth [Lina], had been the sole heirs of the William Shakespeare Caldwell estate and who shared with Spalding a common Kentucky background and a family friendship of long standing. The Bishop of Peoria was able to bring the matter successfully before the council, in spite of opposition from some quarters. The hierarchy accepted the gift of Miss Caldwell and set up a committee to bring about the erection of a "Principal Seminary" as expeditiously as possible.[6]

The first informal meeting of the committee took place in New York

---

[4] *Concilii Plenarii Baltimorensis II., in Ecclesia Metropolitana Baltimorensi . . . . Decreta* (Baltimore, 1868), p. 288. "Atque utinam in hac regione Collegium unum maximum, sive Universitatem habere liceret, quod Collegiorum horum omnium, sive domesticorum sive exterorum, commoda atque utilitates complecteretur; in quo, scilicet, literae et scientiae omnes, tam sacrae quam profanae, traderentur. Utrum vero Universitatis hujusmodi constituendae tempus advenerit, necne, Patrum judicio, rem totam maturius posthac perpendentibus, relinquimus."

[5] *CW,* "Shall we have a Catholic Congress?" VIII (November, 1868); "On the Higher Education," XII (March, 1871), XIII (April, 1871); "College Education," XXV (September, 1877). *ACQR,* Thomas A. Becker, "A Plan for the Proposed Catholic University," I (October, 1876); John Gilmary Shea, "The Rapid Increase of the Dangerous Classes in the United States," IV (April, 1879); "What is the Outlook for our Colleges?" VII (July, 1882); Augustus J. Thébaud, S.J., "Superior Instruction in Our Colleges," VII (October, 1882).

[6] *Acta et Decreta Concilii Plenarii Baltimorensis Tertii . . . .* (Baltimore, 1884), pp. 54-55.

2

on January 26, 1885, when a majority of the members were in the city to assist at the dedication of the Church of St. Paul, the mother church of the Paulist Fathers. Beyond taking a few preliminary steps, nothing of importance was accomplished. The first formal meeting of the committee took place on May 7, 1885, at which time the site was tentatively determined, with Washington getting the choice because of the wishes of Mary Gwendoline Caldwell, and in spite of the opposition which desired to have the University located either at Seton Hall in South Orange, New Jersey, or in Cincinnati. In the meeting on May 12, 1886, after John Lancaster Spalding had refused the offer, John Joseph Keane, Bishop of Richmond, was chosen as the rector of the proposed institution. Keane hesitantly accepted, since he felt himself to be poorly qualified for such a position, but he feared to see the project perish without someone who would be willing to devote his time to the intended University. Since he realized his inadequacy, Keane endeavored to supply for his defects by close study and observation of American and European educational institutions.

After a meeting of the committee on October 27, 1886, Keane, accompanied by John Ireland, the Bishop of St. Paul, sailed for Rome to complete the negotiations that would bring the University out of the realm of potentiality into that of actuality. The opposition of Archbishop Corrigan of New York and Bishop McQuaid of Rochester was a great hindrance to the securing of papal approval, but the interest of Pope Leo XIII had been stimulated by this American endeavor, and it fitted in so well with his desire to see a rebirth of scholasticism, that on April 10, 1887, the brief of approval was issued. At the meeting of the committee on September 7, 1887, Bishop Keane was formally appointed as rector, and from then on the major share of the work was borne by him. He devoted himself to preaching, writing and collecting for the University as well as to assembling a faculty and seeing to the construction of the building on the old Middleton estate in Washington, close by the Soldier's Home. In spite of indifference on the part of many American Catholics and opposition from others, the cornerstone of Caldwell Hall was laid on May 24, 1888, and the formal opening of the University took place on November 13, 1889.[7]

[7] Cf. Patrick H. Ahern, *The Catholic University of America, 1887-1896* (Washington, 1949), for the account of the University under the rectorship of Keane and for the assembling of the first faculty.

During the first year the rough spots were worked out of the program and the need for the students to particularize in one of the four special courses, rather than to attempt to carry all the subjects presented, was recognized. Provisions were made for such particularization by the formation of the departments of dogmatic theology, moral theology, scripture, and church history. The University began with the School of Theology, the seed from which all the other faculties were to grow. The administration pattern was put into operation; the academic senate met frequently to find solutions for the problems that were constantly arising; the idea of research rather than textbook memorization was being stressed, and the discipline and order of student life was being perfected. Internal peace and progress were maintained in the University until the School Controversy of 1891 brought friction because of the divergent opinions held by various members of the faculty on the question. The breach was widened by the Cahenslyism troubles that brought the German members of the faculty into conflict with the other professors. The final blow to the University seemed to have come in 1896, when on September 28, Keane was notified that his resignation from the University would be accepted by the Holy Father.[8]

The University had been progressing in spite of the disadvantages under which it had been laboring, for by 1895 three faculties were in operation, those of Theology,[9] Philosophy and Social Sciences. The Faculty of Theology was offering courses in sacred scripture, moral and dogmatic theology, early and modern ecclesiastical history, canon law, oriental languages and biblical archeology, as well as lectures in homiletics and ascetic theology. The Faculty of Philosophy had departments of philosophy, letters, mathematics, physics, chemistry, and biological sciences. The Faculty of Social Sciences was divided into departments of ethics and sociology, political economy, political science, and law. From the small beginning of six years previous, the true nucleus of a university had been formed.[10]

[8] Cf. ACUA, FBT, "Chronicles of the Catholic University of America from 1885," written over a period of years by John J. Keane, referred to by Ellis as the "Keane Memorial," for the report of the rector on life at the University during this period, and the difficulties and conflicts which he encountered during his period of administration.

[9] The term Faculty is used throughout this study to designate what we would now call schools, since that was the official title used in the University during the Conaty administration.

[10] *Inauguration of the Schools of Philosophy and the Social Sciences and*

The scholastic year of 1896-1897 had begun peacefully enough, for the earlier difficulties seemed to have been settled and the prospect of uninterrupted development under the direction of the former Bishop of Richmond seemed assured. On September 1, the chancellor, Cardinal Gibbons, had addressed a letter to all the members of the hierarchy, asking for their support in obtaining new students, both clerical and lay, for the institution, saying in part:

I beg leave to remark that the number, even of lay students, must largely depend on the encouragement given by the Bishops and Clergy of the country to the studious youths in their various localities to go to the the Catholic University of America for their higher and professional studies. Many hundreds of young Catholics are pursuing such studies in the non-Catholic Universities of the country. Can they not, for the future, be turned toward the Catholic University? Was not this precisely the intention of the Bishops of the country in contemplating the establishment of the University? . . . . It is very important that combined and earnest efforts should now be made by us all to build up and make thoroughly successful the University which we, with the strong encouragement of our Holy Father the Pope, have called into existence.[11]

With a promising outlook for the University it was with some surprise that the chancellor received a letter from Pope Leo XIII on September 28, to be presented to Bishop Keane and which stated:

Venerable Brother, Health and Apostolic Benediction: It is customary that they who are appointed to preside over Catholic Universities should not hold the office in perpetuity. This custom has grown up through wise reasons, and the Roman pontiffs have ever been careful that it should be adhered to. Since, therefore, Venerable Brother, you have now presided for several years over the University at Washington, in the first establishment and subsequent development of which you have shown laudable zeal and diligence, it has seemed best that the above-mentioned custom should not be departed from, and that another, whose name is to be proposed to us by the Bishops, should be appointed to succeed you in this honorable position. . . .

Given at Rome, from St. Peter's, this 15th day of September, 1896, in the nineteenth year of our pontificate.

Leo XIII., Pope.[12]

Dedication of McMahon Hall, Catholic University of America, October 1, 1895 (Washington, D. C., 1895).

[11] NYAA, G-23, J. Card. Gibbons to M. A. Corrigan, Baltimore, September 1, 1896.

[12] *CUB,* II (October, 1896), 583.

On the following day Bishop Keane humbly accepted the decision in a letter to the Holy Father, saying that,

Without a moment of hesitation I accept the will of your Holiness in the matter as a manifestation of the providence of God, and from this moment I resign into the hands of His Eminence, the Chancellor, the office of Rector, with all the rights thereto attaching.[13]

The newspapers suggested many reasons for Keane's removal. The more universal were: either he had become too liberal in his views and thus incurred the displeasure of the first Apostolic Delegate to the United States, Francesco Cardinal Satolli, as well as the conservative group of the American hierarchy as represented by Archbishop Michael A. Corrigan of New York and Bishop Bernard J. McQuaid of Rochester; or the German-Americans had secured his dismissal because of the opposition which he had gathered to defeat their plans for national church groups in the United States. One question that all the newspapers attempted to answer was that of the choice for the new rector. The Washington *Post* claimed to know from a reliable source that Thomas A. Becker, the convert Bishop of Savannah, formerly of Wilmington, would be the man chosen.[14] The choice of the *Catholic Citizen* of Milwaukee was Bishop John Lancaster Spalding of Peoria, who was "the only prelate

---

[13] *Ibid.*, p. 584, John J. Keane to Pope Leo XIII, Washington, September 29, 1896. The matter of the dismissal of Bishop Keane and the connection it had with the questions of the day will be discussed in the final chapter of this work. Keane's resignation of spirit remained with him during the trying days that followed, as may be noted in a letter written from his temporary haven of rest in California. "Doubtless you have had an anxious & weary time of it. And what a storm the press did raise for a while! It was well indeed that I was far beyond their reach, and could look down on the tumult from my hill top of solitude & peace. Though I cannot lose sight of the fact that I am *in exile;* yet no place of exile was ever sweeter, and no exile was ever more peacefully content than I. The interior calm which upheld me under the strain of those last few days at the Univ'y, has continued always. No reaction, no break of the nerves, health and strength all right." ACUA, Garrigan Papers, John J. Keane to P. J. Garrigan, San José, California, November 1, 1896. In a subsequent letter he gave the reasons why he abandoned that retirement: "Abp. Riordan has convinced me that it is my duty, for the good of religion, to sacrifice my sweet retirement in which I am so content, — go to Rome, accept the position there offered me by the Holy Father, (and which Card. Satolli said to Abp. Riordan w'd remain always open to me), — and *then,* demand an investigation of the charge of heterodoxy made ags't me by Card. Satolli, — and, thro' me, against so many others." ACUA, Garrigan Papers, John J. Keane to P. J. Garrigan, San José, California, November 19, 1896.

[14] Washington *Post,* October 8, 1896.

on the continent who can succeed Bishop Keane with a popular impression engendered that an improvement has been made." [15] This opinion was balanced by the naïve expression of the New York Democrat that the Board of Trustees "may request the Holy Father to consent to the reappointment of Bishop Keane." [16] Perhaps the wisest judgment was expressed by the New York Tribune, when it reported an interview with Archbishop John Ireland concerning this question, and quoted him as saying: "There is a time to speak and a time to be silent. That is the Scripture; you can't get around it. It is time now for me to keep still." [17]

On receiving the Holy Father's letter, the Cardinal of Baltimore called a hasty meeting of the Board of Trustees of the University for October 21.[18] On the morning of that day the Board of Trustees,[19] on the motion of Bishop Farley, accepted the resignation of Bishop Keane as Rector of the University, but retained him as a member of the Board of Trustees.[20] Certain members of the board wished to send a letter to the Pope to inform him of their sentiments:

1) that the Board accepts with filial submission His decision concerning the late Rector. 2) its regret, that because of the great commotion caused in this country, such action had not been communicated through the Board; 3) its hope that our Holy Father, knowing the high esteem with which Bishop Keane is held by this Board and his great services to the University would extend to him marks of his esteem and care for his welfare.[21]

---

[15] Catholic Citizen (Milwaukee), October 10, 1896.

[16] New York Democrat, October 11, 1896.

[17] New York Tribune, October 15, 1896.

[18] NYAA, G-23, J. Card. Gibbons to M. A. Corrigan, Baltimore, September 29, 1896.

[19] Present at the meeting were the chancellor, Cardinal Gibbons; Archbishop Michael A. Corrigan of New York; Archbishop John J. Williams of Boston; Archbishop Patrick J. Ryan of Philadelphia; Archbishop John Ireland of St. Paul; Archbishop Placide L. Chapelle of Santa Fé; Bishop Camillus P. Maes of Covington; Bishop John S. Foley of Detroit; Bishop Ignatius F. Horstmann of Cleveland, and secretary of the meeting; John M. Farley, Auxiliary Bishop of New York; Father Thomas S. Lee, pastor of St. Matthew's, Washington, and Mr. Thomas E. Waggaman of Washington, D. C. At this same meeting Patrick W. Riordan, Archbishop of San Francisco, was chosen to fill the vacancy caused by the death of Bishop Martin Marty of St. Cloud. The only members missing, besides Bishop Keane, were the two laymen, Michael Jenkins of Baltimore and Joseph Banigan of Providence, Rhode Island.

[20] ACUA, MMBT, XXI Meeting, October 21, 1896, p. 61.

[21] Ibid., p. 63.

Due to the divergent opinions of the trustees, however, no satisfactory letter could be drafted, so the matter was delayed for subsequent action.[22]

Another matter that required the attention of the trustees was that of a *terna,* a list of three men, to be submitted to Rome, from which one man would be chosen as the new rector. The minutes of the meeting succinctly report what was done.

The Constitutions concerning the election of the Rector were then read by His Eminence, the Chancellor. Names were proposed by various members of the Board. They were then read out by His Eminence as follows, Reverends Dr. Conaty of Worcester, Monsignor Mooney, V. G. of New York, Daniel Reardon [*sic*] of Chicago, Dr. Garrigan Vice Rector of the University, Dr. Brann of New York, Dr. Kennedy of Philadelphia, Monsignor O'Connell ex-rector of the American College Rome.

The vote was then taken by secret ballot and on the first ballot Dr. Conaty, Dan'l Reardon [*sic*] and Monsignor Mooney received the requisite number of votes. A second secret ballot was then taken on the order in which names should be sent to our Holy Father and resulted in the choice of Dr. Conaty for first place, Rev'd Dan'l Reardon second and Monsignor Mooney, third.[23]

Before adjourning, the board, in an attempt to quiet the rumors of

[22] That the matter was not entirely neglected is shown by a letter from John Ireland to A. Magnien, the Baltimore Sulpician and close adviser of Gibbons, St. Paul, November 19, 1896, ACUA, Bouquillon Papers. "I have read carefully the enclosed letter. In my view it will do, provided not one word is taken from it. The language is respectful; but enough is said to indicate our feelings. These feelings we must speak. Recent occurrences show us the necessity of being frank & courageous. Satolli is determined to sustain his action toward Bp Keane, by arranging others—Card. Gibbons included, & if we lie down as cowards we shall be ruined. . . . I am afraid that Corrigan & Ryan only wish to save themselves when they ask that the Cardinal alone sign. . . . We have come upon terrible times: those telegrams have alarmed the American people—to a very high degree. We must stop such things one way or another. I have written a strong letter to Card. Rampolla—& I have two letters to Satolli, demanding from him a denial or a confirmation of those stories.

And now I give you good news, Bp Keane has recovered himself; and he is willing to be the soldier rather than the hermit. He has realized that he is disgraced, that he must fight for his honor, & for the cause which he represented. He goes to Rome—nominally as "consiliarius"—really in order to fight Satolli & Satolli's allies. I have written to Rampolla that I will go to Rome soon after McKinley's inauguration. I will wait until I can go with all the prestige of my American influence." Cf. also note 29.

[23] ACUA, MMBT, pp. 60-61.

dissension among the members, issued a statement for the press and was reported by the New York *Tribune* as saying:

The Board wishes it to be understood by the public that there are absolutely no factions nor sectional differences among the members. The election of the candidates for the rectorship was practically unanimous. To speak of the triumph of this or that party as conservatism or liberalism, Nationalism or Americanism, is to misrepresent the whole situation. All the members of the Board are equally American in spirit. They have but one thought, and that is the welfare of the University and its steady progress to the highest Catholic education.[24]

Within a few days after the close of the meeting the letter containing the *terna,* composed by Archbishop Corrigan[25] and signed by the Cardinal of Baltimore, was on its way to Rome, with a few words about the character of each of the men named. Thomas James Conaty was described as a native of Ireland who came to America at an early age, and was educated by the Jesuits at the College of the Holy Cross in Worcester. After his seminary training at Montreal with the Sulpicians, he entered upon parochial work in the Diocese of Springfield and was noted for his efforts in behalf of temperance and the Catholic Summer School.[26] Daniel J. Riordan was presented as a priest of the Archdiocese of Chicago, the brother of the Archbishop of San Francisco, like Conaty a native of Ireland who had come out to America in early life, and had already been mentioned to Rome several times as a candidate for the episcopacy. Monsignor Joseph Mooney was a native of Pennsylvania, educated by the Jesuits and in St. Joseph's Seminary at Troy, New York, where, after ordination, he taught philosophy for several years before engaging in pastoral work. At the time of his nomination for third

[24] New York *Tribune,* October 23, 1896.

[25] NYAA, G-23. J. Card. Gibbons to M. A. Corrigan, Baltimore, October 26, 1896.

[26] BCA, 94-S-5, J. Card. Gibbons to M. Card. Rampolla, Baltimore, October 25, 1896, copy. "Rev. Dmns. Thomas Jacobus Conaty, D.D., patria Hibernus, adolescens Americae littora petiit; in collegio a Sa. Cruce nuncupato, sub moderamine Patrum a Societate Jesu, intra limites dioceseos Campifontis studiis incubuit, et sacras scientias coluit in Seminaria Marianopolitano. Assumpto Sacerdotio, per nonnullos annos munere Vicarii parochi functus est, et tandem Ecclesiae parochiali S. Corde Sacrae in pago vulgo *Worcester* rector fuit praepositus, quam Ecclesiam usque adhuc felici exitu administrat. Laudatus Sacerdos totis viribus propagationi societatis Temperantiae studuit, et nunc temporis *Scholae Aestivae Catholicae* praese existit."

9

place on the *terna* he was the Vicar General of the Archdiocese of New York as well as a diocesan consultor.

While waiting for Rome to choose a rector, the University, and those connected with it, remained a constant topic of interest. The rumored animosity of Corrigan towards the University and members of the staff was sufficiently widespread for Maurice Francis Egan, professor of English at the University, to write to Archbishop Corrigan and assure him that "in spite of the insinuations of the newspapers, no man at the University here believes that you have anything but the most friendly feelings towards him." [27] Peace had by no means come to the Washington institution after the meeting of the trustees, nor had it gained any higher place in the estimation of many of the hierarchy. The Bishop of Syracuse, Patrick A. Ludden, informed the Archbishop of New York:

It appears that peace does not yet reign in ecclesiastical circles at Washington. I hope religious wars will be confined to that neighborhood. There is a rumor here that Monsignor Mooney has declined to be a candidate for the President of the University; if so I rejoice at his good sense in steering clear just now of the unfortunate institution. [28]

By November the rumors were circulating so recklessly that the press actually carried the report that Cardinal Gibbons and Archbishop Ireland, both of liberal and progressive leanings, and close friends of Keane, had been called to Rome with possibility of their removal from their high positions. [29] This report did not gain too much credence, for as the *Tribune* quoted one man, "There is not a clergyman, be he priest or bishop, regular or secular, who will not regard the statement that it is proposed to discipline Cardinal Gibbons as the veriest twaddle and as emanating from an addled brain." [30] Yet three of the University professors had cause to worry. The Baltimore *Sun* reported:

The published statement that Cardinal Satolli was to report that Rev. Dr. Bouquillon, Rev. Dr. Shahan and Rev. Dr. Pace, three leading professors at the Catholic University, should be removed has caused inquiries to pour into the city from all quarters asking if the report were true. . . . A prominent Catholic pointed out tonight that the three professors attacked

---

[27] NYAA, G-19, Maurice F. Egan to M. A. Corrigan, Eckington, Long Island, New York, October 17, 1896.

[28] NYAA, G-23, P. A. Ludden to M. A. Corrigan, Syracuse, October 30, 1896.

[29] New York *Tribune,* November 13, 14 and 20, 1896.

[30] *Ibid.,* November 14, 1896.

were all members of the famous commission which examined the doctrine of Rev. Dr. McGlynn.

"There were," said he, "originally four of them—all professors at the Catholic University. Rev. Drs. O'Gorman, Pace, Bouquillon, and Shahan. These learned men were made a commission by Cardinal Satolli to examine into the report on the soundness of the doctrine of Rev. Dr. McGlynn. As is well known, they reported that there was nothing the matter with the doctrine and that it was all right. One of them, Dr. O'Gorman, before the 'liberal' party was attacked was made Bishop of Sioux Falls. The other three remained at the University." [31]

The Apostolic Delegate, Sebastian Martinelli, Archbishop of Ephesus, was also worried by the circulation of all these rumors, but he was able, on December 3, to bring peace of mind not only to himself, but to others more personally concerned. In his Italian English he hastened to inform the Cardinal of Baltimore of what he had learned:

I beg to inform your Eminence that I have just now received a Cablegram from the Secretary of State in answer to my letter, in which I informed him about the rumor, spread in the Newspapers about the deposition of some american [sic] Prelates, and removal of some Professors from the Catholic University.

His Eminence says that the Holy Father was very sorry on hearing the agitation caused by these false news; and meantime he authorizes me to contradict the assertion as a lie and an effect of reproachble [sic] wiliness.

As it is now too late, so I will publish it to-morrow. [32]

The friends of the University were also hesitant about what the fate of the institution would be. The spirits of one who had been

[31] Baltimore *Sun,* November 18, 1896. Father Edward McGlynn was a follower of the Henry George single tax theories on land, and for his activities, especially for his disobedience to Rome and to his archbishop, Corrigan, and for his doctrine on the ownership of land, he was excommunicated. Archbishop Satolli, as ablegate, had McGlynn's doctrine reviewed by the commission of professors, and when they found in favor of McGlynn, the agitating priest was restored to good standing, thus giving a serious set-back to the prestige of Archbishop Corrigan. Thomas Bouquillon was professor of moral theology, Thomas J. Shahan and Thomas O'Gorman were both church historians, and Edward A. Pace was a professor of philosophy. For McGlynn cf. the popular work of Stephen Bell, *Rebel, Priest and Prophet* (New York, 1937). There is no definitive biography of McGlynn.

[32] BCA, 94-U-2. Sebastian Martinelli to J. Card. Gibbons, Washington, December 3, 1896. Further peace of mind came to the University through a letter from John Keane in Rome to the vice-rector, P. J. Garrigan, dated January 4, 1897, ACUA, Garrigan Papers. "I arrived here Dec. 18th. Had a long talk with Rampolla that even'g. He was evidently rejoiced to see me in Rome, & was profuse in assurances that all was well. He applied for my

most instrumental in founding the University were none too high, for John Lancaster Spalding wrote in December to Father Daniel Hudson, for years the editor of the *Ave Maria*:

The impression in Rome is that the Pope, in slapping Bp Keane in the face, has given a death blow to the University. With Bp Keane himself I have lost all patience. If the Pope had him down on all fours kicking him, each time he lifted his foot, the enthusiastic Bishop would shout;—See how the Holy Father honors me. A more disgusting state of things than our ecclesiastical situation is hardly conceivable. The only important question, it seems, is whether Abp Ireland is falling or rising in favor with Rome. If we could only hear nothing more of him, it matters little whether he fall or rise. I am sick of it all and only wish that I were away from it all. I have suffered much with rhumatism [*sic*] since my return, and doubt whether I can ever get rid of it in this climate.[33]

The faith of the vice-rector, Reverend Philip J. Garrigan, in the future of the University, however, remained firm. The cardinal chancellor had written to him after the meeting of the trustees in October, worried, perhaps, that Garrigan would follow his dismissed superior with a voluntary resignation. He thanked the acting-rector for his loyal and valuable services of the past and expressed the hope that nothing might disturb his official relation with the institution in the future.

The Vice-Rector, as you know, may serve under several Rectors, because he does not depend upon any Rector for his position; . . . . The interests of the University also demand that the Vice-Rector should remain after the incoming Rector arrives, because he is so closely connected with discipline and internal management. I may add also that if the Vice-Rector goes out after the new Rector comes, what does not happen in universities, his move may be taken as an expression of dislike for, and unwillingness to serve and work, with the new Rector.

---

audience, which I had on the 20th. The Holy Father was most loving in his welcome, said it was God who had counseled me to come, and was both emphatic & cordial in declaring that there was absolutely no charge ags't me or the Univ'y, or the Professors, or Abp. Ireland. He repudiated with indignation the imputation of his having at all changed or modified his ideas & his policy. He gave abundant assurances that my future position sh'd be honorable, useful, and satisfactory. . . . Please impress strongly on the Professors that there is no fear of an attack on them; — that they must have confidence in us here and leave all things peacefully in our hands; that they must simply redouble their energy at their work, and make it tell, and so save the reputation of the Univ'y."

[33] AUND, J. L. Spalding to Daniel Hudson, Peoria, December 6, 1896, photostat.

12

For all these reasons, my dear Doctor Garrigan, I hope that the University may long enjoy the benefit of your enlightened experience & self sacrificing devotion.[34]

Philip Garrigan remained with the University, devoted to its success during that period of trial, doing what he could to keep burning the enfeebled candle-flame of learning so nearly snuffed out by the dismissal of Bishop Keane. In December his hopes rose again when he heard from Gibbons that of the three men nominated for the rectorship, one had been chosen who was a personal friend of long standing:

I have the pleasure of informing you that I am in receipt of a letter from His Holiness, Leo XIII., announcing the appointment of the Rev. Dr. Thomas J. Conaty, of Worcester, Mass., as Rector of the Catholic University. This, I am sure, will be welcome news to yourself and to the members of the Faculties.[35]

The man designated as the new rector of the University was in several ways an admirable choice. He was not a trained educator, but there were very few among the American clergy who were. He did have a strong interest in education; he was energetic in all the works that he undertook. The point most in his favor was that he was neither an out-right liberal nor a conservative, but combined enough of each element in his character and in his life to make him acceptable to both schools of thought. At the time of his appointment Thomas J. Conaty was forty-nine years of age, having been born in Ireland in the town of Kilmallough and the parish of Crosserlough on August 1, 1847. His father, Patrick Conaty, had lived in America for several years, from 1832 to 1839, before returning to the land of his birth.

[34] BCA, 94-S-6, J. Card. Gibbons to P. J. Garrigan, Baltimore, October 31, 1896, copy. The former rector also joined in urging Garrigan to remain. "How has it been with you, dear friend? Your health was not good when I was leaving; and the strain has naturally been heavy on mind and body. But in your case, as in mine, God's Providence makes no mistake and His Grace must be sufficient for you. As His docile & faithful servant, *stand your ground firmly & bravely* until *His* voice calls you from it, if it ever does. Don't take your course in your own hands. We have no right to do that." ACUA, Garrigan Papers, John J. Keane to P. J. Garrigan, San José, California, November 1, 1896. "My cordial greetings to Dr. Conaty. I hope he rec'd me [*sic*] telegram from Paris. May his Rectorate be a splendid success. Rally round him & stick to him, all of you, and *you* especially." ACUA, Garrigan Papers, Rome, January 4, 1897.

[35] Letter, Etc. Concerning the Establishment & Development of the Catholic University of America, 1886-1905, Professor D. W. Shea's Copy. J. Card. Gibbons to P. J. Garrigan, Baltimore, December 12, 1896.

There he married Alice Lynch in May of 1846.[36] In 1850 the Conaty family came to America and settled in Taunton, Massachusetts, where Patrick Conaty had lived during his first stay in the country. Of the eight children born to the family the oldest was Thomas, who received his early education in the public and parochial schools of the town in which he lived. In 1863 Thomas Conaty entered the Petit Seminaire de Montreal (Montreal College), from which he advanced to the College of the Holy Cross in Worcester, Massachusetts. After two years in this institution, where he formed many friendships with the Jesuit professors and among the student body, he graduated in 1869. He entered the Grand Seminary in Montreal for his theological studies and after three years he was ordained on December 21, 1872, for the Diocese of Springfield, which had been established two years previously under the care of Bishop Patrick T. O'Reilly. His first assignment was to St. John's Parish in Worcester, where he interested himself not only in his parochial duties but in civic affairs as well. During the years that Father Conaty was an assistant at St. John's he had charge of the parochial school. For fourteen years, from 1873 on, he served on the Worcester School Board,[37] as well as being elected for two six-year terms to the board of the Worcester Free Public Library. When in 1880 the time came for a new church to be erected in Worcester, with a division of St. John's Parish, the one chosen as first pastor was Thomas J.

[36] ACUA, among the Conaty Papers is an undated press release covering the career of Thomas J. Conaty, most probably composed by Conaty himself. The *Dictionary of American Biography* IV, 337-338, has an article on Conaty, by William J. Kerby. When Thomas Conaty answered a letter in 1901 from a namesake in Ireland seeking a relationship, he wrote: "I have to say that I am not of the family of Nicholas Conaty, the Lord Bishop of Kilmore, although, I presume, there is remote relationship between the families. I was born in the town of Kilmallough, parish of Crosserlough, in 1847, and came to Massachusetts with my parents in 1850. My father was an only child and consequently the relatives on this side are somewhat remote. My mother was named Lynch, from Kilbride, and belongs to a very large family." ACUA, Thomas J. Conaty to Thomas Conaty, Washington, April 23, 1901.

[37] The interest that Conaty showed for his school board work is noticeable, even in later years, in the recommendation that he wrote for the man who had been the superintendent of schools. "Dr. Marble was for twenty-five years superintendent of Public Schools in this city and for fourteen years I was associated with him as one of the Commissioners. He became the "bete noire" of the A.P.A. and was driven from office almost entirely because of his fairness to Catholics. . . . Dr. Marble is not a Catholic but he is a fair man, treating all classes alike." NYAA, G-18, Thomas J. Conaty to M. A. Corrigan, Worcester, January 3, 1896.

14

Conaty. The Church of the Sacred Heart was built, and by 1884 everything was prepared for the dedication. The ceremony was well attended both at the services in the morning and in the evening, when the sermon was preached by the Reverend Philip J. Garrigan, of Fitchburg, future vice-rector of the University and "an old friend of the pastor." [38]

Father Conaty interested himself in temperance work from a very early date and was instrumental in forming the Springfield Diocesan Temperance Union, becoming its first president in 1877. From local temperance work he moved into the national scene in 1885, when for two years he was elected vice-president of the Catholic Total Abstinence Union of America, and became the president for the two following years, from 1887 to 1889. In temperance work the Worcester pastor was closely associated with Bishop John J. Keane and Archbishop John Ireland, both of whom were ardent and extremely active temperance and total abstinence advocates. It was while Conaty was president, after the 1888 convention in Boston, that the collections were begun to establish the Father Mathew Chair at the University, and the president worked hard to make sure that the effort would succeed.[39] At the Washington convention in 1891, at which Bishop Keane preached an eloquent appeal for temperance, Thomas Conaty was conspicuous, acting as sub-deacon at the opening mass at St. Patrick's, as well as expressing himself capably in the discussions at the sessions.[40] Father Conaty was the first to give the lecture on temperance for the Father Mathew Chair at the University in 1895. The chair had been given with the condition that the University would offer two lectures a year on subjects allied with Father Mathew and temperance work. In mentioning the beginning of these lectures, Father Morgan M. Sheedy in the pages of the *American Ecclesiastical Review* noted that the first lecture would be given by Father Conaty, "a former president of the Union, and one of the ablest advocates of

[38] Worcester *Telegram*, October 26, 1896.

[39] New York *Freeman's Journal*, November 3, 1888.

[40] Washington *Star*, August 5, 1891. It is to be noted, however, that all members of the hierarchy were not temperance advocates nor did they approve too strongly of what the temperance men endeavored to accomplish. John Lancaster Spalding expressed himself on the matter to his friend Father Daniel Hudson by saying, "I write to tell you how much I like what in the last number of the *Ave Maria* you have said on the temperance question. These people, if they had the power, would make us a sect of Methodists." AUND, J. L. Spalding to Daniel Hudson, Peoria, August 13, 1894, photostat.

total abstinence in the country." [41] Thomas Conaty's greatest triumph for temperance was, perhaps, the monster rally which he staged in Worcester in September, 1896. It was a rally of the Springfield Diocesan Total Abstinence Union, invitations to which had been sent to all the clergy of the city, irrespective of creed, and its purpose Conaty keynoted in his opening speech: "No matter what our creed, or nationality or politics we are all one in our belief that intemperance is a giant evil, and we are one in honoring the temperance that ennobles our mankind, enriches our labor, and strengthens our state." [42] The rally enjoyed a plethora of speeches, an oratorical contest for the Conaty Cross of Honor, and athletic competitions, all of which earned large coverage in the Worcester newspapers.

The interest of Father Conaty in temperance work persevered throughout his days at the University, although the press of other duties prevented him from taking as active a part as he would have desired. In 1901 he could look back with pleasure at his efforts to encourage temperance, as he mentioned when he had to excuse himself from attending the twenty-fifth annual convention of the Springfield Union:

The recollections of the past twenty-five years of temperance work in our Union are most pleasing. I recall the difficulties of the early years and their subsequent successes. From the beginning, there were devoted men in the work of temperance, anxious only for the welfare of the people and the glory of the Church . . . . My wish at its Twenty-Fifth Anniversary is that the spirit which created it and which permitted it great successes may lead it to greater energy in the cause which lies so near to the spiritual and temporal interests of the people. . . . We need it to safeguard the individual life, to protect the home, to give value to labor and honor and glory to God. . . . The badge of the Union as the pledge of Total Abstinence is always to me a source of greatest pride, consolation and encouragement.[43]

While Thomas Conaty was busy with his pastoral charges and his temperance and civic tasks, they by no means limited the scope of his activities. Although he had left Ireland at an early age he

[41] Morgan M. Sheedy, "The Catholic Total Abstinence Union of America. (History)," *AER*, XII (March, 1895), 190. Morgan M. Sheedy, a priest of the Diocese of Pittsburgh, was a friend of Conaty and, besides traveling through Europe with him and associating with him in educational endeavors, was vice president of the Total Abstinence Union.

[42] Worcester *Telegram*, August 31, 1896; September 7, 1896; September 9, 1896.

[43] ACUA, Thomas J. Conaty to John J. O'Malley, Washington, October 5, 1901, copy.

was not unmindful of the plight of his native land. He did not hesitate to enter into the Irish nationalist movements that were so frequently successful only in the United States. The coming of Charles Stewart Parnell to America and the formation of American branches of the Land League brought Conaty to the fore in Irish-American political agitations. At the Land League Convention in Buffalo in 1880, and again in Chicago in 1881, Conaty was made the chairman of the resolutions committee, nor did he relinquish his position of leadership at the Irish Race Convention in Philadelphia in 1883. For many years he was state treasurer of the Irish National League of Massachusetts as well as serving as the treasurer of the Parnell Fund. The Irish blood coursed warmly enough through Conaty's veins to stir him to eloquence on the question of home rule for Ireland and to share a common Irish contempt for England. In 1886 he addressed an open letter to John Boyle O'Reilly of the Boston *Pilot* defending American support of the campaign for home rule:

In view of the recent statements of an American correspondent of the *London Times,* that very few, if any, native Americans sympathise with our cause or contribute money to its support, the list which I send you is Worcester's answer to the thumping English lie. The names and business relations of these men attest to their strength in our community, and their offering of $1,350, voluntarily sent to me, prove their sincere and earnest support. I have mailed a copy of these names and drafts for the amount to Mr. Parnell directly, that this and similiar acts may furnish him with material by which to refute the calumnies so industriously circulated by a hostile English press. . . . Supplies are needed for the great battle soon to be fought for our nationality; and, thank God, our native American fellow-citizens who see the justice of our cause are ready and willing to bear a share of the burden. . . . With 225 English and Scotch members voted for Home Rule we may hope soon to win England by showing to her that intelligent public opinion, justice, and her own interests urge her to grant to Ireland what Ireland wants and without which Ireland will never be satisfied.[44]

In later years the second rector of the University would remember gratefully and conveniently this love and activity for his native land. Like all transplanted Irishmen, however, Conaty had a two-fold love of country, the land of his birth and the land in which he lived, and the love he bore Ireland served to make him love and appreciate the more the America of which he was so proud. This love of America was, undoubtedly, best shown by the frequency with which he was

[44] Boston *Pilot,* July 3, 1886. Microfilm, and unless otherwise stated, so for all other citations from the *Pilot.*

chosen as a Memorial Day speaker, and the associate membership with which he was honored by the Worcester Post Ten of the Grand Army of the Republic.

With the passage of years Conaty was justly growing in prestige, his activities were diversified but effective, and he could not easily be classified as either a conservative or a liberal. He was at least always ready to meet a challenge when good could be brought forth from it. Although not explicitly active in inter-faith movements, he did read a paper on "The Relations of the Catholic Church to Temperance," at a conference of the Unitarian Church in 1894 and another on "The Roman Catholic Church and the Educational Movement" at the Pan-American Congress held in Toronto in 1895. He had been singled out in 1889 to receive an honorary doctorate from Georgetown University during its centenary year, along with other leading churchmen and scholars. In 1892 the active Worcester pastor added to his many interests by editing and publishing the *Catholic Home and School Magazine* which he founded and kept in existence until called to the University. Nor did Conaty have to rely solely on Georgetown for a recognition of his merits, for when the *terna* to supply a new bishop for Springfield after the death of Patrick T. O'Reilly was sent to Rome, Thomas J. Conaty was second on the list. Philip J. Garrigan, vice-rector of the University, expressed his disappointment at the result when he wrote to Cardinal Gibbons:

I am well, and greatly relieved by the appointment of Rev. Dr. Beaven to the See of Springfield. "The last shall be first", it seems! While Dr. Beaven has the elements of a good bishop in him, I am sorry that Dr. Conaty, who was second on the list, and whom I know better, was not appointed. God knows better! [45]

Dr. Conaty's reputation as an educator and his prominence as a national figure was based more on another of his multiple activities, the Catholic Summer School. The Catholic Summer School was the Catholic form of the Chautauqua, inaugurated in 1874 for the purpose

[45] BCA, 90-C-6, P. J. Garrigan to J. Card. Gibbons, Washington, August 19, 1892. That Conaty was recognized by some as of episcopal calibre is shown by a letter from his ordinary written to him in 1897. "I was greatly disturbed before your settlement in Washington, that some of our Western or Southern dioceses would succeed in laying hands upon you. . . .

"Arbp Riordan intended you for Sacramento, and did all he could to get you." ACUA, Caldwell Hall Files (hereafter referred to as CHF), Thos. D. Beaven to Thomas J. Conaty, Springfield, Massachusetts, May 3, 1897.

of giving an intensive training to Sunday school teachers, but which gradually broadened out to replace, to a great extent, the lyceum as a means of extending education in a popular fashion.[46] The Catholic organization was begun in the spring of 1892 when Warren E. Mosher of Youngstown, Ohio, gathered a group of about thirty people at the Catholic Club in New York City. As a result of this meeting, the first session of the summer school was held at New London, Connecticut, in the summer of the same year.[47] One of the organizers and the president for four years, up to the time that he became rector of the University, Conaty was well able to explain the aim and purpose of the summer school, which he did in one article of a symposium for the *American Ecclesiastical Review* in 1896. He compared the summer school to the outside schools of the monasteries of the early and middle period of the Church, claiming for it the general education of the mass of the people, and calling it:

The People's University and it has as its purpose the defence and protection of truth and thus to protect the faith by giving instructions to those who are called on daily to defend the faith, and in this we have had the blessing of the Pope and of the eminent leaders of the American Hierarchy, so the school is a success. It was an experiment, but now it is only the first of the many that are to follow the example that it has set.[48]

The lectures were given in popular style, as much as possible by well known lecturers, and in such surroundings as to afford a vacation to those who attended the school. The school began its sessions in New London in 1892 where a large number of members attended. By 1893, however, a more suitable site was discovered on Lake Champlain, a few miles south of Plattsburg, New York, at Cliff Haven, where the country terrain and the lake would help the students absorb their popular education under congenial circumstances.[49] The Summer School remained a favorite project of Archbishop Corrigan, from the time of the first meeting in May, 1892, which was held under his auspices, until his death in 1902. As Conaty had predicted, the idea spread with the formation of the Columbian Summer School at Madi-

[46] Allan Nevins, *The Emergence of Modern America, 1865-1878* (New York, 1935), pp. 239-240.

[47] Worcester *Telegram,* June 29, 1896.

[48] "The University Extension Movement Among American Catholics," Thomas J. Conaty, "The Catholic Summer School and the Clergy," *AER*, XV (July, 1896), 61-87.

[49] New York *Sun,* January 29, February 14, 1893.

son, Wisconsin, in 1895, the Winter School of New Orleans founded in 1896, and the Maryland Summer School in 1900.[50]

The popularity of the Summer School was remarkable, but understandable, since it fitted in with the spirit of the times, combining the better features of the reading circle, university extension courses and the summer institutes, having a daily program of lectures, concerts, dramatic recitals and social gatherings; in all, effective in giving cohesiveness to Catholic action. In 1893 it was chartered by the Regents of the University of the State of New York and by a system of examinations it was able to offer accredited courses, becoming a forerunner of the now practically universal summer school system of university education. The appeal of the Cliff Haven school was not limited to Catholics. An early example was Rabbi Veld of Montreal who, out of curiosity, attended a few lectures and became so impressed that he remained, with his family, for the entire course. This event appealed to the news sense of the *Sun* which reported:

One of the most interesting sights in Plattsburgh during the sessions of the Catholic Summer School, was the appearance of a Jewish Gentleman, his wife and family, all wearing conspicuously the tasteful badges of the Summer School, consisting of a bow made of the Papal and American colors.[51]

The school received the support of several members of the hierarchy, especially Archbishop Corrigan of New York, who consented to offer the opening Mass in 1894. He was assisted by Bishop Henry Gabriels of Ogdensburg, who also shared with him in the ovations given at the reception tendered to the archbishop that evening under the direction of the school's president, Thomas Conaty.[52] Several of the lecturers at the school were professors from the Catholic University of America who joined with professors from other educational institutes, both American and European, most notable perhaps, St. George Mivart, to offer courses that were educationally stimulating and worthwhile.

The year 1895 saw an even larger gathering of the hierarchy at the Summer School grounds. The session opened with a pontifical Mass, offered by the Apostolic Delegate, Archbishop Satolli, at which the

[50] John T. Driscoll, "Summer Schools, Catholic," *Catholic Encyclopedia,* XIV, 334-335. A fairly comprehensive coverage was given to the Summer School by the New York *Sun* and *Tribune,* the Boston *Pilot* and the *Freeman's Journal.*

[51] New York *Sun,* August 7, 1893.

[52] *Ibid.,* July 30, 31, 1894.

Archbishop of New York preached the keynote sermon of the session, while among his auditors was his auxiliary, Bishop John Farley.[53] Archbishop Patrick J. Ryan of Philadelphia, Thomas S. Byrne, Bishop of Nashville, and Conaty's own ordinary, Thomas D. Beaven, also gave of their time and services to encourage the school; however the Bishop of Cleveland, Ignatius F. Horstmann, was unable to accept the invitation extended to him.[54]

The year of 1896 was a banner one for the Summer School with the appearance once again of the Archbishop of New York and his auxiliary, as well as Archbishop Edward Charles Fabre of Montreal and Bishops Michael Tierney of Hartford, John S. Michaud, coadjutor of Burlington, Thomas D. Beaven and Henry Gabriels. Before the opening of the session Conaty had toured the northern and central states, as well as sections of Canada, speaking for the enterprise and gathering support. As a result he was absent from Worcester when the apostolic delegate was received at Holy Cross, but he was represented at the banquet by his brother, Father Bernard Conaty, and by his curate, William E. Foley, whom the Worcester *Telegram* claimed "has a closer acquaintance with his eminence [*sic*] than any man in Worcester, having been a pupil under him while studying for holy honors [*sic*] in Rome." [55] For the first time the school was able to take up its activities by the lake, for four cottages had been built as dormitories; one twenty-room building by the Philadelphia Reading Circles, called the "Quaker Cottage," and the other and smaller three, as well as a central dining hall and an administration building, by the school corporation.[56] Two of the outstanding lecturers were Thomas J. Shahan and Edward A. Pace, both of the University. In spite of a rumor that the Bishop of Rochester was opposed to the Summer School, there were many from Rochester present, and the rumor was dispelled when it was learned that McQuaid had merely said that the institution was not fit to give the proper type of instruction to religious.[57] The summer's work had been successful and Conaty was able to report:

Between 1,200 and 1,500 people were registered, and during the three last weeks of the school the average attendance was about 400. Twenty-

[53] *Ibid.*, April 18, July 4, 1895.
[54] NYAA, G-12, Thomas J. Conaty to M. A. Corrigan, Worcester, January 24, 1895; *ibid.*, February 12, 1895.
[55] Worcester *Telegram,* May 27, 1896.
[56] Boston *Pilot,* June 13, 1896; Worcester *Telegram,* June 29, 1896.
[57] Boston *Pilot,* August 29, 1896.

two States of our Union and Canada were represented, New York leading, as a matter of course. .... All the States east of Chicago were represented, as also some of the Western and Southern States. .... The number of clergymen who have attended this session, exceeds that of any other year. Two Archbishops, five Bishops and ninety priests were registered.[58]

The Plattsburg school project did much to raise the Worcester pastor in the esteem of the hierarchy, through the contacts it afforded him with leading churchmen, and as a means of showing the zeal and ability he had for Catholic education. But it is equally true that Thomas Conaty was the able administrator who built the school into a flourishing condition, kept it true to the high aims which it claimed, and maintained his loyalty towards it even after becoming rector of the University. In 1899, when speaking of his earlier attempts to have the Knights of Columbus found a chair of history in the University, only to be deterred by a previous endeavor of the Summer School to have a Knights'-founded scholarship, he said: "I knew that the feeling was averse to that proposal, because the project was not as promising of lasting effect as the University work; but in loyalty to my old love, I said nothing for the new one." [59] The choice of Conaty for the rectorship of the University was looked on in many quarters as a vindication of the policy of the Summer School, taking away the props of those who ridiculed it as a "Sunday School," a mark of the esteem in which the institution was held by high ecclesiastics, and a sign that true conservatism should favor the work.[60]

The Summer School session of 1896 was hardly over when the news of Bishop Keane's resignation was made public, to be followed in October by the release of the names on the *terna* for his successor. With this information at their disposal, many newspapers looked upon the candidacy of Dr. Conaty as being the most likely. On October 22, the New York *World* asserted "Rev. Dr. T. J. Conaty will, it is said, be chosen. . . . Cardinal Satolli and Archbishop Corrigan are known to favor his candidacy." [61] On November 20, a premature press dispatch was received in Baltimore that Conaty had been appointed. This afforded the Baltimore *Sun* the opportunity to reassert that Conaty had the favorable eye of Cardinal Satolli and the Metro-

[58] *Ibid.,* September 12, 1896.

[59] ACUA, Thomas J. Conaty to Thomas B. Lawler, Washington, February 19, 1899, copy.

[60] "Conferences," J. McM. [Joseph McMahon], "The Clergy and the Summer School," *AER,* XVI (April, 1897), 420-423.

[61] New York *Evening World,* October 22, 1896.

politan of New York, and hence was almost certain of appointment. It evaluated the man by saying:

Dr. Conaty is identified with the conservative school of thought, although he has not taken such an active part in the discussions as to render himself obnoxious to the other party. As a man of sound learning and philosophy and schooled in the theology of St. Thomas Aquinas, he was recommended to Cardinal Satolli two years ago, and the latter visited his summer school at Plattsburgh last year. He was charmed with Dr. Conaty and said that he was the very man to be at the head of the University. . . . While Dr. Conaty represents the conservative party, he has always been a friend of Bishop Keane, and the latter has frequently lectured at his school.[62]

Congratulations were tendered to Conaty at the Catholic Alumni Association meeting held in Boston in November by fellow guests Charles W. Eliot, the president of Harvard, and J. Haven Richards, S.J., of Georgetown, as well as, a few days later, by the president of Clark, G. Stanley Hall, who also had words of praise for his old friend Bishop Keane.[63] Conaty, however, was wisely not committing himself before he received official notification. He told a reporter:

I have received as yet no official notification of my appointment, but I have been crowded with congratulations from friends from all sections of the country. . . . I am deeply moved by the kind words that have been said by the press and by individuals whose friendship any man would be proud of. While deeply sensible of the honor, coming as it does, to me, a hard working parish priest, I also realize the responsibility which the office imposes. I trust that the confidence reposed in me will find me faithful to all its obligations.[64]

The St. Louis *Church Progress* performed a service for the biographer of Conaty by collecting for its December 5 issue the words of praise that were being heaped upon him in the press from various ecclesiastical and secular sources. The Archbishop of Boston, with unwonted loquaciousness, was quoted as saying of him, "He is well known as a lecturer throughout the country, is one of the foremost scholars and ardent temperance worker, and seems the right man for the place." [65] The *Catholic Journal of the New South* spoke of the pleasure that Bishop Byrne took in the appointment of his

[62] Baltimore *Sun*, November 20, 1896.
[63] Boston *Pilot*, November 28, 1896.
[64] New York *Catholic News*, December 2, 1896.
[65] St. Louis *Church Progress*, December 5, 1896.

friend to the rectorship of the University. Philadelphia joined in the eulogizing by publishing the following:

A thorough American in his sympathy and education, it would seem that no more fitting successor to Bishop Keane could be placed at the head of the most prominent Catholic University in America. Dr. Conaty is of striking physique. He possesses a commanding presence and a musical voice of much power. As an orator, he ranks among the foremost on the American platform.[66]

As so frequently happened in the remarks of individuals and other newspapers, the *Catholic Sun* of Syracuse did not forget the former rector while congratulating the new incumbent:

Dr. Conaty has proved by his record that he is a good priest; a staunch patriot both to the nation of his birth and to the nation of his adoption; an ardent advocate of the cause of temperance, which he has nourished, fostered and developed in this country; and a brilliant projector, lecturer and president of the Catholic Summer School, which has given a great impetus to higher education. One of the most remarkable traits in the new rector is his indomitable push. Whatever he has taken hold of he has carried through to an almost certain success. . . . No doubt it will be hard for him to fill the empty chair of the gifted Bishop Keane, but we believe that, eloquent orator and well read scholar as Dr. Conaty is, he will make a noble successor to the prelate whose feet have been so wearied in going about, like the Master, scattering benedictions of learned thoughts whithersoever he went.[67]

In a similar vein the Baltimore Letter of the New York *Freeman's Journal* pointed him out as "admirably suited for the position, and, behind that, as a friend and admirer of Bishop Keane, he will largely adopt the methods of the beloved prelate in his direction of the institution." [68]

There was a possibility, however, that the newspapers might have cause to reverse their sentiments about the certainty of Conaty's becoming the University rector. If they had known what was transpiring between Rome, Washington and Baltimore in the early part of December, new rumors might have been added to those already circulating concerning the removal of certain liberal professors at the University. On December 4, Sebastian Martinelli, the delegate, hastily acquainted Gibbons with the contents of a cablegram received that day from the Cardinal Secretary of State, Rampolla, "Advise

[66] *Ibid.*, quoting the Philadelphia *Catholic Union and Times.*
[67] *Ibid.*
[68] *Ibid.*

the Cardinal Archbishop of Baltimore to suspend the communication concerning the nomination of the new Rector of the Catholic University until further notice." [69]   On the following day Martinelli was able to give added information since he had received a more illuminating cablegram, which he quoted to Gibbons:

"Continuing the subject of my telegram of yesterday, Your Excellency will make known to Cardinale [sic] Gibbons that the rumors published concerning the proposed removal of some of the Professors of the Catholic University is without a particle of foundation; informing him at the same time of the request of Msgr. Keane, you will tell him that the Holy Father authorises him to suspend the nomination of the new Rector, if in his opinion there be a grave reason for such a suspension." . . . . With regard to the second part of the message, I beg Your Eminence to let me know you [sic] determination in the matter, and whether or not you intend to suspend the appointment of the new Rector.[70]

The chancellor of the University was relieved to learn that the matter was left to his discretion, and he so informed the delegate:

As there is no reason whatever for suspending action, I shall inform the new Rector of his appointment as soon as the official papers arrive. . . . It would be very unpleasant to have in my possession the official paper appointing a Rector, and yet to suspend action because of a trivial objection. If the public found out that the papers were mailed and yet for some unknown reason not received, all kinds of surmises, suspicions and perhaps insinuations against Your Excellency and myself would be made about suppressing the Document.[71]

On December 8 the official brief of appointment arrived in Baltimore and Thomas Conaty was immediately notified by the cardinal chancellor and made aware of the contents of the letter of Pope Leo XIII, which said in part:

Yielding to your request, we have considered the names of the three candidates whom you have proposed as worthy to discharge the office of Rector. Of these We have deemed fit to choose, and by our authority we do hereby approve, the first on the list, namely, Thomas James Conaty,

---

[69] BCA, 94-U-3, Sebastian Martinelli to J. Card. Gibbons, Washington, December 4, 1896, #3791.

[70] BCA, 94-U-5, Sebastian Martinelli to J. Card. Gibbons, Washington, December 6, 1896, #3794. Keane thought that a bishop should be appointed for the prestige of the University.

[71] BCA, 94-U-6, J. Card. Gibbons to Sebastian Martinelli, Baltimore, December 6, 1896, copy.

heretofore parish priest in Worcester and president of the Summer School. Both the learning, and the zeal for the advancement of religion, which characterize this distinguished man, whom you, by your joint suffrages, recommend, inspire Us with the well-grounded hope that his efforts will not be without abundant fruits in watching over the interests of the University, as well as enhancing its lustre.

How dear to our heart is this matter cannot but be well known to you, for you are aware how untiring was our solicitude in founding this institution, that we might deservedly reckon it among the works which, in the interest of religion and science, we have, out of our loving affection, undertaken for the furtherance of the glory of your country, and which we have, with God's help, been able to bring to a happy issue.[72]

An accompanying letter from Cardinal Rampolla stated that "the Sovereign Pontiff will bestow some honor upon the new rector in order to add dignity to the office. He desires to have your opinion upon this point." [73]

The newly-appointed rector immediately came to Baltimore where he spent a few days as the guest of Cardinal Gibbons, talking over the problems of the University and planning for the future. After a brief visit to Washington, for a short interview with Martinelli, the apostolic delegate, and a trip out to the University, Conaty returned to Worcester to conclude his affairs and to receive the congratulations of his well wishers.[74] Holy Cross and the Jesuit Fathers were the first to tender to their former graduate a testimonial banquet, to which the faculty and students of the institution, as well as the clergy of the diocese and former classmates of Conaty, were invited to share in the overflow of congratulatory speeches offered to the new rector.[75] On December 21 Dr. Conaty lectured in Montreal on the "Celtic Influence on English Literature." On the following day he was honored by Laval University with two honorary degrees, that of doctor of divinity and also that of doctor of canon law.[76] Worcester again honored him on December 28 by another testimonial banquet, this time from civic groups, at which the mayor was the toastmaster and the main speaker was George F. Hoar, Massachusetts'

[72] Letters, Etc., Concerning the Establishment & Development of the Catholic University of America, 1886-1905, Professor D. W. Shea's copy, contains the official English translation, while the Latin original is in BCA, 94-T-5, Leo P. P. XIII to J. Card. Gibbons, Rome, November 23, 1896.

[73] Baltimore *Sun,* December 9, 1896.

[74] Boston *Pilot,* December 19, 1896.

[75] Worcester *Telegram,* December 15, 1896.

[76] Boston *Pilot,* January 2, 1897.

English-baiting United States senator. Perhaps the most far-fetched bit of praise came from the president of Clark University, G. Stanley Hall, who, after praising his friend, Bishop Keane, blundered on to say that papal infallibility became more plausible to him, now that the Pope had appointed Dr. Conaty as the rector of the University.[77] Not to be outdone by her upstate sister was Boston. There Conaty was feted by the John Boyle O'Reilly Reading Circle, and shared in the honors tendered to the apostolic delegate on January 4 during his visit to the Hub City.[78] On January 10 Conaty made his farewell speech to his parishioners, thanked them for their generous purse of $2,000, and parted regretfully from the parish which he had so laboriously built up, and from the members of his flock who had come to know him and to revere him as a true shepherd of their souls.[79]

The first month of the year 1897 saw Conaty on his way to Washington to take up one of the most difficult positions in the Catholic Church in the United States. The University, which had been the storm center of so many of the disputes affecting the Church in America, was waiting for its new director, a man equipped for the position by zeal, organizational ability and educational interest, but by no means a trained educator. Conscious of this defect, but willing, for the sake of the University, he entered into his task after giving thanks to Archbishop Corrigan, who had been so instrumental in having him appointed:

I wish to thank you for the kindness reposed in me by my election to the Rectorship of the Catholic University of America.

I hope to merit a continuance of that same confidence in the work which now lies before me. My only aim and object will be to do the will of Our Holy Father Leo XIII, and to those to whom the interests of the University are entrusted.[80]

[77] Worcester *Telegram,* December 30, 1896.

[78] Boston *Pilot,* January 9, 1897.

[79] *Ibid.,* January 16, 1897.

[80] NYAA, G-24, Thomas J. Conaty to M. A. Corrigan, Worcester, January 2, 1897.

Chapter II

UNIVERSITY GROWTH

From New York on January 18, 1897, in the private car of the president of the Baltimore and Ohio Railroad, the new rector departed to assume his duties at Washington. Among the group who accompanied him to participate in the inaugural ceremonies were his ordinary, Thomas D. Beaven; the Auxiliary Bishop of New York, John Farley, and Bishop Charles E. McDonnell of Brooklyn; as well as a group of influential laymen and clergy of New York and Springfield. Of the New York clergy, one was Michael J. Lavelle, who took over the presidency of the summer school upon Conaty's resignation, and another was Joseph McMahon, who had been associated with Dr. Conaty in the summer school work and in temperance activities, and who, in the future, was also to be closely associated in the development of the University.[1] On the morning of January 19, in the chapel at Caldwell Hall, Mass was celebrated by the vice-rector, Dr. Garrigan, before the assembled faculty and student body, following which Thomas Conaty read the profession of faith in preparation for the ceremonies of the afternoon.[2] The chancellor of the University, as well as the apostolic delegate, were present for the inauguration, together with the group which had accompanied the rector from New York, although his father, after making the tiring trip, was so fatigued that he was unable to be present.[3] Cardinal Gibbons and Dr. Garrigan preceded the new rector on the speaker's platform and both spoke highly of the man being installed that day. Conaty, in turn, presented his inaugural address, rendering his thanks for the honor bestowed on him, outlining the place of the University in the educational life of the day and promising to follow faithfully in the steps of his predecessor. Although roundly applauded, he did not meet with universal acceptance, basically perhaps, as one clerical student wrote to his superior, because "Most hearers, I think, are unpleasantly conscious of the fact that he does not compare well with

[1] Boston *Pilot,* January 23, 1897.
[2] New York *Evening World,* January 19, 1897.
[3] New York *Tribune,* January 20, 1897.

our late Rector, though such contrasting is hardly fair." [4]   One who was not impressed by Conaty was the Bishop of Peoria, who wrote to Father Daniel Hudson, "Father Stone wrote to my sister Mrs. Slavin that he went to Washington for the installation of Dr. Conaty and was thoroughly disgusted.   Dr. Conaty himself, it seems, was a great disappointment to him. . . . Dr. Garrigan wrote me a very urgent letter asking me to attend the installation, but I could not think of going." [5]

After the inauguration Conaty settled down to learning the administrative functions of the University.   Within the walls of the institution, troubled as the scene was by reputedly liberal and reactionary factions, Conaty was soon recognized as able to care for the responsibilities which had recently come to him.   One of the professors, in a letter to Monsignor Denis O'Connell, the former Rector of the American College in Rome, evaluated him by saying:

The new Rector is doing excellently and threatens to be a man of spirit and insight.   I do not think we shall have reason to complain, if we understand how not to expect too much from a man in his position, whose sole purpose is the welfare of this institution, and who must therefore be friendly with all who can in any way affect its growth. I *know* that he is sympathetic, that we all meet with personal good will from him, that he appreciates the *workers* here, and is thoroughly and all round an American man.

I have seen much of him in my boyhood, and I do not fear for his honesty and frankness.[6]

If Spalding had not been favorably impressed from what he had heard about Conaty's inaugural speech, the Rector of the American College in Rome, William H. O'Connell, the future Cardinal Archbishop of Boston, sent a more encouraging bit of information: "Your speech on the occasion of your inauguration has made a good impression here among the Cardinals, several of whom have spoken to me about it. . . . God has led the right man to the high post and the University will be a greater success than ever." [7]   Another and

---

[4] PFA, Joseph McSorley to A. F. Hewit, Washington, January 26, 1897.

[5] AUND, John L. Spalding to Daniel Hudson, Peoria, February 7, 1897, photostat.

[6] RDA, XXX [Thomas J. Shahan] to D. J. O'Connell, Washington, February 14, 1897.

[7] ACUA, W. H. O'Connell to Thomas J. Conaty, Rome, February 22, 1897.

more helpful letter came from Rome where Keane still maintained his interest in the University:

Dr. Conaty seems to have made an excellent first impression, & Dr. Zahm assures me that the students seem to be contented & loyal.

I hope that in this critical period of the life of the University, yourself & all its old soldiers will stand firmly by the colors & the new captain, & not give the Evil one the satisfaction of bringing harm to an institution which ought to prove such a blessing to the church of God in America.[8]

During the first month of Dr. Conaty's rectorship the new dormitory for the University was opened. This five story, red brick building was advertised as containing "forty-two suites of two rooms each, bathrooms for both shower and tub baths, and toilet-rooms on each floor, a chapel, a dining-hall and kitchen, a recreation-room, a parlor, and store-rooms for trunks, bicycles, etc." [9] The building originally was called Keane Hall, and was opened to students and members of the faculty at a cost of ten to seventeen dollars a month, depending upon the location and size of the room. The discipline of the building was in charge of a member of the faculty, aided by student proctors, following rules laid down by the rector and the senate, which covered matters such as the following:

I. All boisterous conduct is at all times prohibited in the Dormitory.
II. The loud playing of musical instruments, loud conversation and singing, and anything that might distract or disturb those inclined to study are prohibited on class days except between the hours of 12-2 and 6-8 p.m. This rule does not apply to the pool room.
III. No ladies, except immediate relatives, are allowed to visit the rooms of the students.
IV. All forms of gambling are forbidden in the Dormitory.
V. The introduction of intoxicating liquors into the Dormitory is forbidden.[10]

There were also further requirements that the students must fix whatever they break, and that those students who had their living quarters

[8] ACUA, Garrigan Papers, John J. Keane to P. J. Garrigan, Rome, March 19, 1897.

[9] Letters, Etc., circular letter printed by P. J. Garrigan, acting-rector, Washington, January 4, 1897. Originally known as Keane Hall, it is today known as Albert Hall.

[10] ACUA, Rules announced by the rector to the lay students in assembly, February 25, 1898.

outside the University grounds must have their place of residence approved by the board of governors of the Faculty of Philosophy.[11]

One of the first questions of administration with which Conaty had to deal was that of the relationship of the Sulpician president and the procurator of Divinity College to the University. The question had been hanging fire practically from the beginning of the institution, and much correspondence had been carried on between the previous rector, the chancellor, and the Sulpicians in Washington, Paris, and Baltimore.[12] The main objection was that both honor and authority were lacking to the Sulpician in charge of the divinity students.[13] Negotiations were pending for a settlement of this matter at the time of the resignation of Bishop Keane. On January 31, Conaty re-opened the negotiations by writing to M. Captier, the Sulpician superior general in Paris, who, in turn, reiterated past suggestions he had made to the cardinal chancellor.[14] Several conferences were held by the rector, vice-rector and the President of Divinity College, Francis L. Dumont, S.S., by which a final five-point agreement was reached.[15] This agreement repeated the arrangements of the constitutions as well as the previous Keane-Icard contract of 1888 and then went on, in the words of the academic senate's summary:

2. Pres. receives and assigns rooms to students of Div. College, to whom all information about students will be communicated by Rector or Vice-R.

3. Pres. makes annual reports on men to Bishops, countersigned by Rector, hence Faculty reports on men will be given him by Registrar & in turn he will report matters of general interest to Senate in writing.

---

[11] The Board of Governors of the Faculty of Philosophy at that time was composed of Edward L. Greene, Henri Hyvernat, Edward A. Pace, Maurice F. Egan, John J. Griffin and Daniel W. Shea.

[12] Cf. Ahern, *op. cit.*, 29, 115-120.

[13] SMSA, A. Orban, S.S. to A. Magnien, S.S., Washington, May 16, 1890.

[14] Passing through Paris on his way to Rome immediately after his dismissal from the University, Keane did what he could to help in the negotiations. He informed Garrigan of his activities by writing him: "I hope Fr. Captier has made satisfactory arrangements, as he promised me in Paris that he would do. I showed him that your hands were entirely too full, & urged him to authorize Fr. Dumont to make arrangements with you & the new Rector for their managing the domestic department on provisional terms of agreement, to be tested by experience, & ratified when found satisfactory. He agreed to this, & promised to write at once to that effect." ACUA, Garrigan Papers, John J. Keane to P. J. Garrigan, Rome, January 22, 1897.

[15] ACUA, RRTTS, March 16, 1897.

4. Controls everything in the community except what pertains to studies, exercises determined after consulting Rec. & Vice-R.

5. In Caldwell Hall, the Profs not acting in official capacity, takes precedence after the Rec. and Vice-R.[16]

These points met most of the wishes of the Sulpicians, one exception being the continuance of Caldwell Hall as a place of residence for the rector and members of the faculty. To this the Sulpicians had objected because of the difficulty of maintaining discipline in the house with the presence of so many who were not bound to follow the common rule, as well as the presence of a higher authority to whom appeal could readily be made for particular exemptions. It was not entirely a one-sided agreement, however, for the Sulpician procurator of the house had to assume new duties, which carried with them a practically autonomous financial control, with the University supplying whatever deficit might arise. In this way the administration was relieved of many financial and clerical responsibilities.[17] The Sulpicians were then able to impart the proper training to the priest-students and to foster the continued development of their spiritual and priestly lives.

A special matter of discipline called for the attention of the new rector, because of the custom that had risen for the students to begin their vacations a bit prematurely. Some irritation was caused when Dr. Conaty insisted on the students remaining for the last day of class before the Easter vacation of 1897, and refused permission to several when they asked to be excused earlier. When some of the professors excused men from their classes, and others changed the time of their classes to fit the wishes of the students, Conaty brought the matter to the attention of the academic senate, and insisted that there be a uniformity of discipline in the matter of classes.[18] The senate complied with this request and determined that scheduled classes should not be changed by any professor without the previous consent of the dean of the faculty. In the following meeting, the rector directed the attention of the senate to the utilization of the time of professors. Because of the lack of students some professors were being paid for teaching-hours that were not being applied. As a solution Conaty suggested that these men be used in other departments to fill out the number of teaching-

[16] ACUA, RRTTS, adopted March 16, 1897, D. W. Shea, secretary.
[17] SMSA, Procurator's agreement.
[18] ACUA, RRTTS, April 7, 1897.

32

hours for which they were receiving a salary. He further recommended that the heads of departments should arrange for public lectures to broaden the education of the student body.[19] Again the
senate agreed with the request of the rector,[20] although the men thus
affected naturally could not be expected to appreciate the efforts of
their new superior. A further change was the division of the School
of Social Sciences and the Department of Law, putting the former under the Faculty of Philosophy and leaving the latter to form the Faculty
of Law.[21] Conaty was showing that he was aware of the weak points
of the administration, and he was doing his utmost to bring about the
best results from the limited means at his disposal. Like many new
administrators, he intended to demonstrate that he was rector of the
University in fact as well as in name.

To encourage the attendance of laymen, a new method of granting
scholarships was formulated by the senate on April 7, 1897.[22] By
the terms of this offer, one baccalaureate of the graduating class of
any Catholic college was eligible for a three-year tuition-free course
at the University. The candidate had to matriculate into the department of his choice, that is, make up all the requirements before
the scholarship would take effect. The particular aspirant would be
determined, in the case of a conflict, by the rank in the graduating
class. The offer was to be valid for five years and countermanded all
other scholarships previously offered to colleges.[23] Besides the question of increasing the student body, that of securing professors from
among the religious troubled Conaty, and he asked various members
of his faculty for their opinions. The report of Thomas Bouquillon,
professor of moral theology, was rather complete and seems to have
been influential in determining the future policy of the rector. In his
report Bouquillon showed by the constitutions and the presence of
George M. Searle, a Paulist, and professor of mathematics and
astronomy, that the use of such men on the teaching staff could be
allowed. He substantiated this by citing the attempts of Bishop
Keane to secure the services of both a Jesuit and a Benedictine.
Although this would be helpful in securing many good men, he

[19] ACUA, RRTTS, May 11, 1897.
[20] ACUA, RSS, May 11, 1897.
[21] ACUA, RRTTS, May 11, 1897.
[22] ACUA, RSS, April 7, 1897.
[23] *Year Book of the Catholic University of America, 1897-'98* (Washington,
1897), p. 41.

thought, nonetheless, that the disadvantages would far outweigh the advantages. In the first place he claimed that it would be impossible for the religious to have the proper *esprit de corps* for the University, being naturally interested, in the first place, in their own religious congregations and only secondarily in the University. They would also be too independent of the authority of the University. There were two other dangers that seemed evident to him. First, the religious order would think that the chair which it held should always be retained by one of its members. Secondly, the possession of a chair would merely whet its appetite for the control of the entire University.[24] Whatever the effect of this report might have been on the rector's mind, no members of communities or orders became attached to the teaching body of the University during Conaty's administration.

One other innovation in the first year was the inviting of an alumnus to give a baccalaureate sermon to the graduating class. The man honored with inaugurating this custom was the former president of the Alumni Association, Father J. P. Fitzgerald, of Baltimore. The rector asked for support "to make this last Sunday of the year an event in the University life, and hence every member of the University should help us in giving as much éclat as possible to the day." [25] The concluding semester of the 1896-1897 school year had given Conaty an opportunity to orientate himself to the University surroundings, to weigh and to determine the abilities of the men on the staff, to see some of the weak spots and to lay plans for further development. He stressed the practical side of the courses, emphasizing the graduate character of the work.[26] After the summer vacation, part of which was spent on collection tours for the University, he returned to Washington and the 151 students of the institute prepared for an eventful year.

The first event of importance in the scholastic year of 1897-1898 was the meeting of the Board of Trustees scheduled for October 20. The rector had his report prepared for that meeting. In one section he presented the general condition of the institution:

As this is the first regular meeting since April, 1896, it is my duty to present to you the condition of the University during that time.

---

[24] ACUA, undated confidential report to the rector, in French, covering four legal size pages, and entitled, "Sur le Recrutement du corps Professoral dans le clerge Régulier."

[25] ACUA, RRTTS, June 3, 1897.

[26] NYAA, G-24, Thomas J. Conaty to M. A. Corrigan, Washington, February 27, 1897.

There is reason for thankfulness to Almighty God that, despite the sudden and unforseen changes that were made at the beginning of the last session, there has been no interruption in the work of the University and no embarrassment in its administration. The severe shock which came to the friends of the University in the change of its popular and much beloved Rector has been followed by a spirit of loyalty to his successor. It has been my purpose to take up the work of the University where he laid it down and to carry it on according to my best lights in the hope of realizing the ideals which had been set before the University from its inception.[27]

Following a mention of the stress that had been laid on the graduate character of the work in the University, the rector announced the resignation of Dr. George M. Searle, the Paulist, because of his desire to return to missionary work. Simon J. Carr also resigned from his fellowship in the Department of Oriental Languages, because of the press of diocesan labors. Shortly before the meeting, Frank K. Cameron, associate professor of chemistry, had likewise tendered his resignation to take a better position at Cornell University. To balance these losses, the new associate professor of sociology, the Reverend Doctor William J. Kerby, was welcomed to the teaching staff in the fall of 1897, after completing his education at the University of Louvain.[28] Acting on the suggestion of Joseph Banigan, widely known as the "Rubber King", and a member of the Board of Trustees,[29] Conaty recommended the formation of an executive committee of the Board of Trustees to handle the affairs which required prompt action. With this the board agreed[30] and appointed the cardinal chancellor, the Archbishop of New York, and the rector of the University to form the committee. Following the regular report of the rector, there was a special report on the internal condition of the institution, in which the rector asked the Board of Trustees to remove the professor of dogmatic theology, the Very Reverend Joseph Schroeder, from the faculty of the University.[31] Claiming that the peace of the house demanded such a move, the rector was able to

[27] *Eighth Annual Report of the Rector of the Catholic University of America, October, 1897* (Washington, 1897).

[28] ACUA, Report of the Dean of the Faculty of Philosophy to the Senate, October 12, 1897.

[29] ACUA, Joseph Banigan to Thomas J. Conaty, Providence, October 18, 1897. Banigan was unable due to the press of business to attend the meeting personally.

[30] ACUA, MMBT, October 20, 1897.

[31] *Ibid.* The question of Schroeder's removal is more fully treated in Chapter V, 148-157.

have his point carried only after a long struggle and with much more publicity than had been anticipated. Aside from the Schroeder incident, the trustees expressed themselves as well pleased with the manner in which the University was being conducted. A further loss to the staff came in that same month with the resignation of the professor of Hellenic literature, the Reverend Daniel Quinn,[32] which required a shifting of courses and of men to meet the new situation. As a result, the Reverend Doctor Edmund T. Shanahan, associate professor of philosophy, took over the classes vacated by Monsignor Schroeder, and the instructor in comparative philology, George M. Bolling, carried on the instruction that had been given previously by Professor Quinn.[33]

One of the solutions for the many difficulties that arose within the institution was thought by Conaty to be found in a consideration of the constitutionality of the regulations governing the academic senate. In one of the senate meetings he suggested:

There is a very well defined feeling that these regulations conflict with the Constitutions, and that they are the source of much trouble in the University—interfering as they do, in the minds of many, with the well-defined privileges of the Administration, as marked out in the Apostolic Constitutions. The Rector would also suggest that some action be taken towards a translation into English of the Constitutions, as also of the documents. In order that a better understanding may be had of these Constitutions, it would be well for us to have a recognized commentary upon them; for much trouble seems to arise leading to differences of opinion and entanglements, because of mistaken ideas with regard to the rights and privileges guaranteed by the Constitutions.[34]

The Reverend John T. Creagh, assistant professor of canon law, was appointed to make the English translations of the constitutions and documents, aided by Edmund Shanahan.[35] For the other matters requested, however, the rector was due for a long wait. There were many starts, but the commentary and the evaluation of the senate records were completed only at the closing of his career as rector.

Conaty was more successful with another measure which demanded immediate attention. The Spanish-American War came suddenly upon the country during 1898 and it was only natural that the University students would be among the many volunteers. Rather than

[32] NYAA, G-24, Thomas J. Conaty to M. A. Corrigan, Washington, November 30, 1897. The case of Quinn will be treated in Chapter IV, 104-107.
[33] ACUA, RRTTS, January 11, February 7, 1898.
[34] ACUA, RRTTS, April 28, 1898.
[35] ACUA, RRTTS, May 10, 1898.

see the educational life of these men suffer for their patriotic zeal, Dr. Conaty lent his support to a resolution covering such cases when it appeared before the University senate in May, 1898.[36] The resolution, as passed by the senate, provided that if any student should be prevented from taking the examinations for his degree, or from completing his dissertation, by reason of military or naval service, an extension of one year after the expiration of such service would be granted to fulfill whatever requirements were lacking. If the requirements were made up within the specified time, the degree that was being sought would be granted as of the date it would have been originally received if military service had not intervened.[37] Towards the war of 1898, the University had made its gesture; towards the peace that would follow it was to make a greater contribution.

As the first full year of rectorship was drawing to a close, two things impressed Dr. Conaty. He felt very strongly that the time of the students was being wasted, in the first place because they were unfamiliar with the practical procedures of graduate work. To prevent them from being "several months floundering about ignorant of the real practical ways of University study," he recommended "the preparation of a little manual which might serve as hints for study, research, theses work and such like." [38] It was on the second point that his ire really arose. Complaints of the insufficient work of some of the instructors had reached him through students, who, for this reason, were indisposed to return. Further investigation led to the discovery that this situation was known to the heads of the departments, but that they had not conveyed the information to the administration. Such a wasting of the students' time and the University's limited funds could not be tolerated, to say nothing of the damage that was being done to the University's reputation in the learned world. What had been accomplished, however, far outweighed what had been neglected, and the rector found himself forced to say:

I have to congratulate the Senate and the Faculties upon the satisfactory work of this year. Opening in storm, it has closed in sunshine. Peace and harmony have characterized the year. A spirit and earnestness for good work have actuated the members of the different teaching bodies. We have to congratulate the University, and to thank Almighty God.[39]

---

[36] ACUA, RRTTS, May 10, 1898.
[37] ACUA, RSS, Resolution adopted by senate, May 10, 1898.
[38] ACUA, RRTTS, June 2, 1898.
[39] Ibid.

According to the New York *Freeman's Journal*, the school session of 1898-1899 opened "under very flattering conditions and there is every prospect for a prosperous year." [40] Two new professors were introduced to the student body on the opening day. One was James A. McDonald, formerly a student of law at Harvard, who joined the Faculty of Law. The Reverend Richard Henebry, the second addition, assumed his duties as associate professor of Celtic languages and literature after receiving his doctorate of philosophy from the University of Greifswald in 1898, while a fellow of the University under the Gaelic chair foundation. The *Freeman's Journal* was also interested in the coming meeting of the Board of Trustees, for a new member of the board was to be chosen to fill the place vacated by the death of Joseph Banigan. [41] The editors were not correct in their predictions. The man chosen by the executive committee of the Board of Trustees was another of the kings of the day, "Packing King" Michael Cudahy of Chicago. [42] The *Journal* was without forewarning of what was the most newsworthy event of the trustees' meeting. The financial condition of the University was a source of worry to the trustees. From the fifteen endowed chairs, not all of them as yet completely funded, from the thirteen scholarships, [43] as well as from collections and donations, the University had realized only $133,906. The expenditures for the year of 1897-1898 had been $130,851, leaving only a working balance of $3,055, hardly sufficient to keep the University in existence, let alone have it flourish and increase its activities. [44] To meet this financial crisis, as well as to re-

[40] New York *Freeman's Journal*, October 8, 1898.

[41] Joseph Banigan had emigrated from Ireland as a boy, and after being apprenticed in the jewelry trade had become interested in the growing rubber business and eventually worked himself up to the head of the Rubber Trust, which earned for him the title of "Rubber King". He was noted for his generosity and had already established the Banigan chair of political economy at the University, as well as giving $4,000 annually for library improvements. *CUB*, IV (October, 1898), 524-526.

[42] NYAA, G-28, Thomas J. Conaty to M. A. Corrigan, Washington, October 23, 1898.

[43] *Year Book, 1898-'99*, pp. 9-10.

[44] "University Chronicle," *CUB*, IV (October, 1898), 527. In January Conaty had been hopeful for a good year, for in his report to the Divinity Fund Association, which had given $1,200 in 1896, to the University Fund Association, which had contributed $1,600, and to the Chapel Fund Association, which had sent in $930, he mentioned: "The long-continued depression in business for the past few years has interfered with the success of our Associations, and the

lease John J. Keane from his Roman exile, the trustees voted to ask the return of Keane, so that he might devote at least a year to the collecting of funds. They empowered the cardinal chancellor to write the Holy Father in the name of the trustees seeking this privilege.[45] On November 1 the Archbishop of Baltimore mailed the letter which gave a summary of the University's financial standing and the request for the return of Keane. He said:

They [the University trustees] were happy to see that large institution in a satisfactory condition; they valued especially the Rector's skill and prudence, the professors' zeal and the perfect harmony between them, the discipline and work of the students, both lay and religious, the truly Catholic spirit of all, and their devotedness to the Holy See.

The proper maintenance and the necessary progress of the institution naturally drew the Board's attention to the problem of resources. Unfortunately during the past few years these resources have not increased as much as was hoped. The long economic crisis the country has gone through, followed by political agitation, as well as the alterations which in his wisdom, the Holy Father saw fit to bring on in the government of the University, and still other circumstances, all, put together, are the cause of the lack of that increase. Today, thanks to successive endowments, the University has a steady income of 65,000 dollars. . . . But, to meet the ever-increasing needs one would have to have each year at least 30,000 dollars more. Evidently, it is necessary to reduce expenses. That is impossible not only because such a move would hinder the advancement of the University, and destroy its efficiency, but also because the University is already governed according to the principles of the strictest economy. Two alternatives are left: have recourse to a system of loans which would lead to disaster or make a special effort to increase subscriptions and especially bequests and endowment funds. The Directors considered the second.

They suggest, Your Eminence, that one person, acting in the name of the American Episcopate, and supported by it, travel through the United States in order to inspire rich Catholics with interest in the University and to entreat them to be generous. Naturally, such a delegate must be duly authorized and must have qualities which will recommend him to the public. Now, the Bishops think that the former Rector, the Archbishop of Damascus, with his talents, the esteem in which he is held, the affection and popularity he enjoys could perform that difficult but important task

---

University has suffered in common with all educational institutions. Now as prosperity comes we may expect a revival of interest in the aims and purposes of the University." ACUA, Report to the Associations, January 15, 1898.

[45] ACUA, MMBT, October 11, 1898.

successfully. On his part, Monsignor Keane, full of zeal and self-sacrifice, is ready to accept the work, provided, of course, it will be the will of the Holy See.

Therefore, unanimously, the Archbishops and Bishops, directors of the University, entreat His Holiness to permit Monsignor Keane, while still maintaining his position at Rome, to be released from the obligation of residence and allowed to remain in the United States in order to devote himself to the work of recruiting the necessary funds for the development and completion of the Catholic University.

Your Eminence, when presenting this petition, the Archbishops and Bishops do not intend in the least (need it be affirmed), indirectly to force the Holy See to change the decisions it made two years ago; on the contrary they are quite satisfied with the present situation and put all their trust in the actual Rector. The Rector himself will not consider this a lessening of his authority, or competition, but only a precious help in the work he cannot accomplish alone.[46]

The Roman reply to this letter took a reversal of emphasis, stressing the first paragraph quoted above, and devoting only two sentences, most prudently phrased, to the question of the return of Keane:

His Holiness expressed himself as well pleased with your report, and rejoiced at the praise Your Eminence gave to the prudence of the Rector, at the zeal of the professors and the application of the students attending the University. All this is a source of comfort to His Holiness and it is his hope that this important Institute will grow and develop with the coming years. It also gives His Holiness great joy to see the interest the aforementioned Prelates take in the material side of the University. As to the matter mentioned in your letter, I am pleased to notify Your Eminence that the Holy Father is not adverse to approve the request expressed in your letter. However, he considers it best to await a more opportune time to put this into practice.[47]

While waiting for the return of Archbishop Keane, Spalding showed his continued interest in the University, an interest that was active enough for him to put his services at the disposal of the institution.

[46] BCA, 96-S-1, J. Card. Gibbons to M. Card. Rampolla, [Baltimore], November 1, 1898, which is the original French version from which this translation has been made. In the report made to Cardinal Ledochowski of the Propaganda, under whose jurisdiction the University fell, sent on November 25, 1898 by the Cardinal of Baltimore, mention was again made of the need for the services of Keane (BCA, 96-T-6).

[47] BCA, 96-T-3, M. Card. Rampolla to J. Card. Gibbons, Rome, November 16, 1898, which is in Italian from which the above was translated. Since the matter of Americanism was beginning to be acute in France and Rome, that might explain why Leo XIII thought the time was not opportune.

Following the meeting, he expressed his opinion on the future of the school to his friend, Daniel Hudson, in a letter of October 28:

You have heard no doubt that Abp Keane has consented to return to America and give his time to collecting for the University. This is generous and I think he may meet with success. The future of the University is more promising, and the heads I think begin at last to see that there is need of great economy. In fact what I would like to see is retrenchment.[48]

The desire to see John Keane enter into the work of collecting remained strong in Spalding's mind. It expressed itself in the correspondence with the rector on the matter of a lecture that the Bishop of Peoria was going to deliver in Washington for the benefit of the University. He wrote:

It is extremely difficult for me to go to Washington this winter, but as you seem to think I can do some real good and as the Marquise [de Merinville, *née* Mary Gwendoline Caldwell] urges me so strongly to accept the invitation I shall do my best to be with you about the middle of Jan. . . . It would be well to get Abp. Keane to go to work as soon as possible. The Rich have plenty of money, and if Leo were to die things might change. I would urge him to come as soon as possible.[49]

Again when final arrangements had been made for the Spalding lecture to be given on January 13, 1899, the final line of the letter read, "I hope Abp. Keane will soon enter into the work of getting money." [50] The Bishop of Peoria was able to infect the frequently cautious Gibbons with his desire. The Cardinal Archbishop of Baltimore, with a view to the fact that it might reach other eyes after Keane's, wrote:

After careful consideration of the question and in view of all the circumstances, I am strongly led to believe that the sooner you begin the better for the work. Business is booming, stocks are rising, the market gives splendid indications and careful business men agree that this is a good time for you. Therefore I would request you to ask the Holy Father to permit you to come at the close of Lent so as to begin, at the latest, in the month of May. Bishop Spalding has spent some time at the University and gave some lectures which created great interest and had some success. He told the Rector and told me that he was anxious to have you

---

[48] AUND, J. L. Spalding to Daniel Hudson, Peoria, October 28, 1898, photostat.

[49] ACUA, J. L. Spalding to Thomas J. Conaty, Peoria, November 15, 1898.

[50] ACUA, J. L. Spalding to Thomas J. Conaty, Peoria, December 4, 1898.

begin and that he stands ready to go with you and help you as far as his duties will permit. There can be no doubt of success and thus our hearts will be cheered by the feeling that our University will enter into the New Century fully endowed, at least in the work in which it is now engaged. This I am sure will be cheering news to our Holy Father.[51]

By May the return of Archbishop Keane was assured, and the newspapers made up for what they had missed at the time of the trustees' meeting by giving the matter wide circulation as well as wide interpretation. The Washington *Times* gave an account of what was intended and helped to dispel some of the more lurid stories.

It was rumored that he [Keane] was to be reinstated as rector of the Catholic University, and that Monsignor Conaty, the present rector, was to be made Bishop of Columbus. This report was unfounded, according to an official of the university. If Rome were to reinstate Archbishop Keane, this official said, it would be an acknowledgement that it had erred in displacing him so summarily, and Rome never acknowledges that it makes an error.[52]

The report then went on to give the statement of Dr. Conaty that Keane had been called back to fill out the endowments of the institution and to help in the enlargement of the work. It further praised Archbishop Keane for what he had done while rector, claiming that "the university is practically his monument." [53] Keane remained in Rome doing what he could to defend the Church in the United States during the Americanism troubles. Finally, on June 22, 1899, he received permission to enter upon his new work in a letter from Cardinal Rampolla which stated:

The Holy Father has always regarded the Catholic University at Washington with particular affection: he earnestly desires that it prosper, and that it fully realize the ends for which it was established. Hence His Holiness highly approves the intention of the Episcopate of the United States to appeal to the generosity of their faithful people in order to supply the financial needs of the University. And as your Grace has been asked to undertake this work, the Sovereign Pontiff bespeaks happy results for your zealous endeavors, and bestows upon yourself and upon the work the Apostolic Benediction.[54]

---

[51] BCA, 97-C-1, J. Card. Gibbons to John J. Keane, Washington, January 26, 1899, copy. Cf. Chapter V.

[52] Washington *Times,* May 29, 1899.

[53] *Ibid.*

[54] NYAA, G-36, J. Card. Gibbons to M. A. Corrigan, Washington, November 20, 1899, extract from Gibbon's letter on the work for the University.

A few days before the meeting of the trustees on October 11, 1899, Archbishop Keane arrived in Washington and took up his residence at Caldwell Hall, which was to be his headquarters during his collection tours.[55] Even the eloquence of Keane, together with the appeal that his sufferings for the University must have engendered, was not enough to bring the desired co-operation. His first tour covered Washington, Baltimore, Philadelphia, Springfield, Providence, and New York.[56] The former rector of the University could not send a very encouraging report from Boston, as he rather despondently informed Conaty:

I found from the start that prospects in Boston were very poor for me. So I asked the Archbishop to let me use his name, and work for the endowment of an Archbp. Williams Chair, as the only hope of success. He himself consented; but at the same time he cut the ground from under most of my calculations by saying that no appeal must be made to the clergy for it, as he must appeal to them very shortly for the Seminary chapel just completed. I have received, however, subscriptions amounting to $20,000, and assurances for some ten thousand more; so the work is well started. . . . I bring home $6300; more will be paid in a few mos.; a good deal will be on the basis of paying the interest annually & securing the principal in will, or paying it in a few years. To secure the endowment of the Chair even in this way will be an achievement. Bps. Beaven & Harkins are cooperating in it.

I shall get to the Univ'y, please God, Friday forenoon. Maybe you will be all away.[57]

In spite of the readily offered co-operation of Archbishop Corrigan in New York, the work was no more encouraging in that section, and Keane was by this time having his troubles with millionaires;

Things are quite as slow here as I expected. One of my millionaires ill in bed for weeks, another worried by attacks on his syndicates, &c. Next

---

[55] "University Chronicle," *CUB*, V (October, 1899), 523.

[56] *CUB*, VI (January, 1900), 130-131.

[57] ACUA, John J. Keane to Thomas J. Conaty, Philadelphia, December 20, 1899. The financial arrangement for securing the interest and then obtaining the principal later was one that Keane had successfully used previously. In this way the donor remained in possession of the principal, usually a block of stocks, while all the interest accruing went to the University, and upon the death of the donor the University would receive possession of the stocks themselves. In this way the person giving the stocks could retain control of the company, as far as the stocks would allow, while the University would receive all the profit from the stocks themselves. Matthew Harkins (1845-1921) was Bishop of Providence, and Thomas D. Beaven (1851-1920), Bishop of Springfield.

Sunday at St. Stephen's. I will spend the week at Fr. Colton's.—Bp. McDonnell not ready to admit the work just yet—as I rather feared.[58]

All things being considered, the collecting trips of Keane were not very profitable to the University, not that he lacked the zeal, but the field in which he worked was too limited. What good he might have been able to accomplish, if he had remained longer at the task will never be known, for on July 24, 1900, he was returned once more to diocesan duties by being named second Archbishop of Dubuque.

Two further attempts were made during the administration of Conaty to have the financial worries of the University solved by the employment of special collectors. Immediately following Archbishop Keane there was Dr. Henry Austin Adam, a lecturer of national reputation, who had as his special field, in distinction to Keane's, the small donations that people would ordinarily hesitate to send. The other, and later, collector was the previously mentioned New York priest, Joseph McMahon, who intended to appeal especially to the priests of the country. Both of these shared a common fate with Archbishop Keane, that is, success of the most modest type. The financial worries, of which these collectors were but symptoms, continued to plague Thomas Conaty until the end of his rectorship, and they were to become even more crucial under his successor.

The Board of Trustees in their October, 1898, meeting had done more than ask for the return of Keane; they also elected the first general secretary of the University.[59] The man chosen had been secretary of the senate for many years, along with his duties as professor of physics—Daniel W. Shea, Director of the School of Technological Sciences. While the officer was known, the exact duties of the office were not, and the rector tried fruitlessly in the next two meetings of the senate to arrive at some definition of the general secretary's duties.[60] One of the first official communications of Shea, as general secretary, was a notification that emphasized the need for

[58] ACUA, J. J. Keane to Thomas J. Conaty, New York, January 17, 1900. Charles E. McDonnell (1854-1921) was Bishop of Brooklyn.

[59] "University Chronicle," *CUB,* IV (October, 1898), 528.

[60] ACUA, RRTTS, December 13, 1898 and January 10, 1899. *The Constitutions of the Catholic University of America,* English translation, Chapter V, #6 defines the duty of the general secretary thus: "The General Secretary shall accurately enter in the records everything pertaining to the admission and examination of students and to the conferring of degrees, and whatever may be worthy of notice in the daily administration of the University." p. 3.

economy and the leakage of confidential information from the University. He stated:

There are no funds at our disposal this year, for making additions to the Library and Laboratory equipments of the various Departments; and further, that all to whom this notice is sent be reminded that this information, as well as all other that may be sent to them in a similar way is intended for their private information only.[61]

A rather caustic commentary on the board meeting of 1898, as well as on University life in general, was given by the professor of sacred scripture, Charles P. Grannan, in one of his very informative letters to his friend in Rome, the former Rector of the American College, Denis J. O'Connell. After treating on the question of Americanism, he went on to report:

The last meeting of the Board was the first for many years at which some harmony reigned. The directors have agreed to put their hands into their pockets and meet some of the expenses. This is a good sign,—for the first time. They are acquiring some sense of their responsibilities towards the institution over which they preside. . . . Big John [Ireland] was not present at the last meeting of the board. In other ways also he has been going back on us for the last year. He refused us Shields, after his course at Johns Hopkins, and since. . . .[62] We have a slight decrease in

---

[61] ACUA, D. W. Shea to the members of the Faculties, Washington, November 28, 1898.

[62] Ireland explained his refusal to permit Shields to teach in the University in this manner: "Pray consider well my position in regard to Fr. Shields. I am under deep obligations to Mr. Hill: I must show him results in our Seminary. Theology he does not understand: what he can see & value is science. I must then, give at once a large place in our programme to Science. Delay in doing so would be disastrous. I am certain that he would not forgive me if I were to part with Fr. Shields. Professors and Priests think as I do on the matter. I cannot do otherwise, however great my desire to please you. . . . So please forgive me. The University is a big Institution; one man out of it, little harm is done. St. Paul is a small thing, & one man ruins or makes it." ACUA, CHF, John Ireland to John J. Keane, St. Paul, July 23, 1895. The Reverend Thomas E. Shields later became one of the outstanding professors at the University, receiving his appointment as instructor in physiological psychology in the fall of 1902. Cf. *Thomas Edward Shields* by Justine Ward (New York, 1947). The affections of Ireland for the University varied and after the dismissal of Bishop Keane they hit a low ebb. After Conaty's inauguration he wrote to Philip J. Garrigan: "I received some weeks ago a letter from Father Carey, telling me that he is losing his time at the University, and not at all fitting himself out for the duties which await him in St. Paul.
"I hope you and my other friends in the University will understand my position in this matter. Fr. Carey I depend on to be my first teacher in Latin and

the number of our matriculate students of Theology. The Paulists have this year thirty instead of twenty of last year. The Marists also have quite an increase. We may get the usual number. As to the number of lay students, there is no great increase. Some conjecture that the number is smaller than last year. I have forty eight regular attendants in my class of S.S.,—the largest class in the establishment. The next largest counts about twenty. Some have only five, and one Professor has but one student, & one has none. All is very quiet.[63]

Although the financial situation of the University would long be in a poor condition, in 1899 there was made a connection that has proven itself of great value, not only to the institution but also to the Catholic lay students of the United States. Conaty, after earlier attempts, was successful in gaining the attention of the Knights of Columbus in their convention held in Hartford in March, 1899. Through the efforts of the vice-rector, Philip J. Garrigan, who presented the matter to his brother-knights on the convention floor, and to whom the rector gave full credit,[64] the Knights of Columbus voted to establish a chair at the University which was but a harbinger of their future generosity. The rector took great pleasure in reporting the event to the Archbishop of New York:

For some time there has been an effort made to interest this large body of Catholic gentlemen in the University work, and this year by a unanimous and enthusiastic vote it was decided that the Organization would take measures towards establishing a Chair of American History in the University, as an object worthy of the labors of the Knights of Columbus.[65]

One of the students of the University, Father Maurice J. O'Connor, perhaps used this as a basis when, during the ensuing summer, he wrote to the rector:

Since I came North I have been very much pleased at what I consider a feeling of greater interest in the University, its work, Professors, etc., at the tone of friendliness now comparatively marked. It is a change which

---

Greek. St. Francis College is at stake. I am then obliged under every consideration to give him the opportunity to become a first class teacher.

"I am writing to him to see you about his going to John Hopkin's [sic] University. He can board either at St. Mary's or at St. Joseph's Seminary." ACUA, John Ireland to P. J. Garrigan, St. Paul, January 24, 1897.

[63] RDA, 'Grapes' to 'Doctor' [Charles P. Grannan to D. J. O'Connell], postmarked Washington, October 26, 1898.

[64] ACUA, RRTTS, March 14, 1899.

[65] NYAA, G-28, Thomas J. Conaty to M. A. Corrigan, Washington, March 11, 1899.

has to a considerable extent taken place within the last year, as I could easily observe by conversations with people, priests & laymen, whom I met last summer and who then spoke quite differently. I can't help regarding it as a happy augury.[66]

The school year of 1898-1899 had a further importance besides the attempts to grasp at the solution of financial difficulties. It was the year in which the first administrative and scholastic organization under the rectorship was completed, although it was by no means final.[67] The major governing body of the University was the Board of Trustees. It was composed of seventeen ordinary members of whom eight were archbishops, five were bishops, one a priest and the other three were laymen.[68] With these, *ex officio,* were associated all the archbishops of the United States as an advisory board. The officers of the University were four in number, the chancellor, rector, vice-rector and general secretary.[69] The governing body of the University itself, which treated of the academic problems of the University and whose actions could be reviewed by the trustees, was composed of the *ex officio* members, the rector, vice-rector, the general secretary, the deans of the faculties and the presidents of the University Colleges, as well as two professors delegated from each of the University faculties.[70] This group, called the academic senate, was scheduled to have monthly meetings, but could be called for special sessions. For the student body of 168 members, there was a teaching

[66] ACUA, Maurice J. O'Connor to Thomas J. Conaty, East Weymouth, Massachusetts, July 11, 1899.

[67] When Conaty forwarded the proofs of the *Year Book* for 1899-1900 to the Archbishop of New York, he characterized it by saying, "This schedule is the first expression since the complete organization of the University Departments." NYAA, G-28, Thomas J. Conaty to M. A. Corrigan, Washington, March 11, 1899.

[68] For 1898-1899 the members were: Archbishops Gibbons, Williams, Corrigan, Ryan, Ireland, Chapelle, Riordan and Keane; Bishops Spalding, Maes, Foley, Horstmann and Farley; Monsignor Conaty; Messrs. Michael Jenkins of Baltimore, Thomas E. Waggaman of Washington, treasurer, and Michael Cudahy of Chicago. *Year Book, 1899-1900*, p. 8.

[69] These officers were, respectively, James Cardinal Gibbons, Thomas J. Conaty, Philip J. Garrigan and Daniel W. Shea. *Year Book, 1899-1900*, p. 10.

[70] Beside the three previously named men, the senate was composed of Thomas J. Shahan, Dean of the Faculty of Theology, Edward A. Pace, Dean of the Faculty of Philosophy, William C. Robinson, Dean of the Faculty of Law, Francis L. M. Dumont, S.S., President of Divinity College, the only existing University college, Thomas Bouquillon and Edmund Shanahan from the

staff of thirty-four.[71] Among the students of the University there was a further four-fold classification, depending upon the type of work that was being done. In the first classification came the matriculates, or those whose past credits had been sufficient to have them accepted as candidates for degrees. Since the educational standards of the day were extremely variable and not all colleges graduated their men with adequate training or the proper courses to meet the entrance requirements of the University, there was a second classification of candidates for matriculation. This group included all those who were making up preparatory or ancillary courses before being accepted as matriculates. Those students who were not working for a degree but were taking certain courses were called special students. Upon the completion of their course work, together with the passing of an examination, there was given to this class a certificate attesting to the amount and character of work that had been accomplished. The final group were the auditors, or those who merely attended the lectures but no other exercises without special permission.[72]

The organic structure of the academic field of university work was split up into three faculties and the Board of Instruction of Tech-

---

faculty of theology, Maurice F. Egan and Edward L. Green, from the faculty of philosophy. *Year Book, 1899-1900,* p. 9.

[71] The *Year Book, 1899-1900* gives a break-down of the figures on page 20.

PROFESSORS AND INSTRUCTORS

Professors	15
Associate Professors	7
Assistant Professors	2
Instructors	6
Lecturers	1
Fellows	3
	34

STUDENTS

School of Sacred Sciences	74
School of Philosophy	20
School of Letters	11
School of Physical Sciences	4
School of Biological Sciences	1
School of Social Sciences	3
Schools of Law	45
School of Technological Sciences	10
	168

[72] *Year Book, 1899-1900,* p. 34.

nology. The first faculty had been that of theology. In 1898 it offered three degrees, the baccalaureate, licentiate and the doctorate of sacred theology. The baccalaureate was conferred on those who, after completing their seminary course in philosophy and theology, passed a four-hour written and a one-hour oral examination in the matter required for admission to matriculation in the divinity school. A written dissertation, approved by the faculty, together with the defense of fifty theses, after the successful completion of two years of study in the University, entitled the student to the licentiate degree. For the doctorate two more years of study after the licentiate, together with a dissertation of scientific merit, approved by the faculty and printed, and the defense of seventy-five theses, were required. The faculty was composed of the Department of Biblical Sciences; the Department of Dogmatic Sciences, composed of apologetics and dogmatic theology; the Department of Moral Theology, including moral theology and canon law; the final department was that of historical sciences, comprising church history and patrology.[73]

A more diversified faculty was that of philosophy, which seemed to gather within its limits all that could not be classified elsewhere. Admission to any of the schools within the faculty was granted to those students who either possessed a baccalaureate degree from some college in good standing or could pass an equivalent examination. The first degree granted by this faculty was that of master of philosophy. It was bestowed on those who, after at least two years of resident study, fulfilled the requirements in a major and a subordinate subject, as well as submitted an approved dissertation and came successfully through the oral and written examinations in their two subjects. For the doctorate of philosophy, besides the dissertation and the examinations, three years of resident study covering a major subject and two subordinate subjects were demanded. The School of Philosophy proper comprised the Department of Philosophy; the School of Letters numbered among its departments that of comparative philology, Sanskrit, Semitic and Egyptian languages and literature, Latin, Greek, Celtic as well as English language and literature. The School of Physical Sciences included the departments of chemistry, physics, mechanics, astronomy and mathematics. While the School of the Biological Sciences was content with the department of botany, the school of the Social Sciences was divided into sociology, economics and politics.

[73] *Year Book, 1899-1900,* this material, as well as the subsequent data on the other faculties will all be from this same source unless otherwise noted.

The two remaining academic sections were the Faculty of Law and the Board of Instruction of Technology. The Faculty of Law was composed of two sections. The professional school of law was the part which treated the elementary work of the legal practice. It covered a three year period and awarded the bachelor of laws degree. The second school, or University School of Law for graduates of professional law schools, offered a galaxy of degrees ranging through the bachelor, master and doctor of laws, the same three degrees in civil law, as well as doctor *utriusque juris* and the doctor of law.[74] The Board of Instruction of Technology, while not in a very thriving condition, offered work that would lead to the degree of civil engineer, electrical engineer, mechanical engineer as well as the degrees of master and doctor of science.

At the disposal of the students of the University was the chapel in Caldwell Hall, with thirteen altars for the use of the priest members of the faculty and the student body. There were also libraries of over 17,000 volumes in Caldwell and McMahon Halls, the psychological, physical and chemical laboratories and the ethnological and chemical museums. For those interested in biology, the University possessed a herbarium, containing the collections of Dr. Edward Greene and the Langlois and Wibbe collections. Completing the pretentiously named and rather poorly equipped facilities was the astronomical observatory.

The condition of the last two mentioned sections, law and technology, was by no means stable or pleasing to the rector, or to the faculties themselves. Before the school year of 1899-1900 began, two of the staff of the School of Law resigned because they were not satisfied. In April, 1900, Monsignor Conaty reported to the senate on the affairs of the school, especially concerning the re-appointment of two men, Edmund B. Briggs and Charles H. Goddard, as instructors in law:

As to the conditions in the Law School, the Rector has carefully examined into them, and is satisfied that the appointments of Dr. Briggs and Mr. Goddard are the best that can be done in the circumstances. As to Dr. Briggs, there is no question of his usefulness and success as a teacher in the Departments placed under his care. Mr. Goddard's appointment is necessary, in order that the work scheduled may be done.[75]

---

[74] The initials for these degrees were, respectively: LL.B., LL.M., LL.D., B.C.L., M.C.L., D.C.L., J.U.D., and J.D.

[75] ACUA, RRTTS, April 3, 1900.

That Conaty was not very satisfied with his professors is evident from the words of advice he was able to give another man in a like predicament:

It is a very difficult matter to obtain candidates such as you desire for the Law School of the University. We are at our wits end every year to find material sufficient for the work at the meagre salary we are able to pay.[76]

The anxiety over professors, aggravated by the absence of Charles Warren Stoddard of the English department because of sickness, was further complicated by other worries. One of these was the attempt to force the City and Suburban Railway to move its tracks from the University grounds to the middle of Bunker Hill Road, or some place on the proposed extension of Michigan Avenue.[77] In all, the worries of the year were lightened somewhat only by the fact that the vice-rector aided in the financial affairs, having been made the assistant treasurer of the University by the Board of Trustees.[78] More directly, however, the rector was cheered by the honor brought to the University through the visit of the President of the United States. Toward the close of the school year on June 1, President William McKinley accompanied by his private secretary, George B. Cortelyou, and the Secretary of the Navy, John Davis Long, an old friend of the rector, visited the young institution. In the assembly room of McMahon Hall, Monsignor Conaty, before the assembled professors and students, expressed his welcome to the President in words that showed the spirit in which the visit was received, as well as the character of the University:

The aim and purpose of the University are fixed by the aims and purposes of the Catholic Church in education, and like the Catholic Church, with its message of knowledge to the world, it knows no race line and no color line, while its doors are open to non-Catholics who may desire to receive instruction at its hands. . . . We recognize no aristocracy here but the aristocracy of education, and we strive to build that as the source of strength in our national life.

Mr. President, the cross which surmounts our building is indicative of our religious faith, and the flag which floats to the breeze beside

---

[76] ACUA, Thomas J. Conaty to Father Edward D. Keely of Ann Arbor, Michigan, Washington, April 7, 1900.

[77] ACUA, Thomas J. Conaty to Senator James McMillan, Washington, February 26, 1900, copy.

[78] "University Chronicle," CUB, VI (January, 1900), 132.

it is indicative of our national spirit. . . . Under this roof minds are taught to love the cross and reverence the flag. Catholic Americans, we are taught and we teach loyalty to God as the source of loyalty to the Republic. We honor you as the Chief Executive of our Republic, chosen by the suffrages of the people to the office you so nobly fill, and our American hearts are filled with pride as we welcome you under our university roof.[79]

The reply of the President was brief, and while flattering in tone, it was indefinite and concerned education alone. Because, no doubt, of the thriving A.P.A. movement, and its political influence, there was no reference to Catholicity.[80] Monsignor Conaty conducted the party through the buildings and then entertained them for some time before the Chief Executive returned to the White House.

In the following scholastic year the Board of Instruction of Technology came under consideration, in great part because of the report submitted in 1899 to the trustees by the director, Daniel W. Shea, who mentioned:

During the past year there has been correspondence with about thirty young men who wished to come here to study Engineering. Fully two-thirds of these did not have more than a high school education, and they were not encouraged to come. Most of the remaining third had sufficient preparation, but our small corps of teachers of Engineering, meager equipment, and very limited curriculum,[81] deterred them from coming,

---

[79] *Ibid.*, Visit of President McKinley, pp. 449-451.

[80] In one of the A.P.A. broadsides put out for the 1900 presidential election, the University had received mention. One paragraph in this diatribe against Catholicism is worth mentioning. "Intrenching herself in Rome under the guise of religion with her legions of Concubines and Libertines, she hypnotized, hoodooed, debased, enslaved, robbed, murdered and drenched all nations in blood, and at the present time she is intrenching herself in Washington, D.C., under the mask of a University, which if allowed to be consummated, will cost America her civilization and with America all civilization on earth will disappear and mankind reduced to the darkest barbarism and bandits that ever lived on the earth since Adam." ACUA, CHF.

[81] The four courses offered were: applied mathematics, covering analytic mechanics, mathematical physics, and drafting; civil engineering, including topographical engineering, bridge engineering, road engineering, and railroad engineering; electrical engineering, offering one course in direct and one in alternating current appliances and machines; mechanical engineering, with prime movers and machine design being its component parts. Shea was the director of the school and the staff consisted of Albert F. Zahm, associate professor of mechanics, Josiah Pierce, assistant professor of civil engineering, and René de Saussure, associate professor of pure and applied mathematics. Of the last two, the first departed from the University in 1899 when his contract was not

though they very much desired to be here. This correspondence, and many other facts that have come to me during the past four years, indicate pretty clearly that this division of the University would quickly become one of its strongest parts, and one of very great aid to the Catholic young men of this country, if it were fittingly endowed.[82]

In their meeting of October 10, 1900, following another discouraging report on the school by the rector, the trustees appointed a committee on technology composed of Archbishop Corrigan, Bishop Maes and the rector, to determine in the first place whether the school should be continued and, if it were, what the nature of the work and maintenance should be. To aid them in their investigation, at the suggestion of Conaty, the senate appointed their own committee on technology, naming Dr. Shea, the Reverend John J. Griffin, professor of chemistry, and the rector.[83] The financial situation did not augur much success; in fact Corrigan wrote to the rector at the end of November:

Can nothing be done to diminish expenses by dispensing with unnecessary luxuries in the way of teachers without pupils, or with so few pupils as not to justify the burden?
Unless something can be done in this direction, the future is very dark—For my part, however reluctantly, I would feel constrained to resign.[84]

The situation was somewhat improved, however, when, in the following month, Michael Cudahy, the latest addition to the trustees, presented $50,000 to the University. This gift was to be used in paying off its current indebtedness and the funded debt, for Cudahy considered that the most important means of stabilizing the University's economy.[85] Perhaps this donation, and the hope that it might be followed by others from the same source, encouraged the senate committee to report on January 8, 1901, that the work

---

renewed and the second in 1900 when a death in the family necessitated his return to Switzerland.

[82] *Tenth Annual Report of the Rector of the Catholic University of America* (Washington, 1899), Appendix F. Report of the Director of the School of the Technological Sciences, p. 39.

[83] ACUA, RRTTS, November 13, 1900.

[84] This note was unsigned or undated, but it was on Corrigan's stationery and filed with a letter discouraging new expenditures, ACUA, M. A. Corrigan to Thomas J. Conaty, New York, November 28, 1900.

[85] ACUA, Thomas J. Conaty to John J. Keane, Washington, December 11, 1900, copy; NYAA, G-28, Addenda, Thomas J. Conaty to M. A. Corrigan, December 21, 1900.

in technology should either be properly developed or discontinued. To offer the full list of courses, there would have to be additions to the faculty, two men in the first year and one a year for the next two years. If the work was to be continued, then there would be required a $5,000 appropriation for salaries and a like amount for equipment in 1901-1902. As an alternative, if the board could not see its way clear to provide at least $10,000 a year for the next few years, all that remained was to discontinue the work at the end of the school year in 1901.[86] How optimistic this report was is best demonstrated by the remarks in its first appendix:

The School of the Technological Sciences has, at present, five resident students and two non-resident students. . . . The school has but one teacher employed especially for technology, namely, the assistant professor of Civil Engineer [sic]. It has equipment in instruments and books which cost about $45.00.[87]

There can be no doubt that Shea was discouraged, as the offering of his resignation on March 11, 1901, demonstrated, but he still maintained enough hope to be able a year later to give a general summary of what had been accomplished:

The Board Committee met at the University in April 1901, and decided that an effort should be made to raise the money needed. The Archbishop of New York consented to have the work of raising the money begun in his archdiocese, and the Committee appointed Rev. Dr. Griffin and Dr. Shea, delegates, to proceed to New York with letters from the Rt. Rev. Rector, and instructed them to endeavor to interest business men there, in our School of Technology, after having received a letter of commendation from the Archbishop of New York.

The delegates went to New York Jan. 1, 1902, with a letter from the Rt. Rev. Rector, and secured from Archbishop Corrigan the letter he had promised. Several business men, interested in Engineering enterprises, were visited, who very kindly listened to the statement of the needs of the School, and helped devise plans of operation. Partial arrangements were made for future consultations. While the encouragement was not all that the delegates could desire, and while they feel certain that the raising of any considerable sum means long, hard, and persistent efforts, yet they think that the efforts already begun should be continued.[88]

---

[86] ACUA, Report of the Senate Committee on Technology, received by the Senate, January 8, 1901.

[87] Ibid., Appendix I.

[88] ACUA, Report from the Director of the School of Technological Sciences Submitted to the Rector and the Academic Senate, March 11, 1902.

By October, however, hope had again dimmed, for in the *Thirteenth Annual Report* Daniel Shea noted:

With the consent of Archbishop Corrigan and Archbishop Ryan, efforts were made in January and in May of this year, to interest in the School of Technology men engaged in engineering enterprises in New York and Philadelphia, but it was deemed inopportune to continue the effort for the present.[89]

The Board of Instruction of Technology had to wait until 1904 and the new rectorship before its reorganization and development would take place to any notable extent.

The lack of support received by the technological branches was somewhat symptomatic of the general lack of interest that was being manifested in the University throughout the country. The cardinal chancellor thought that a solution to this difficulty could be found in a papal letter urging support of the University. In his report on the institution to the Congregation of the Propaganda, Gibbons suggested this by saying:

A letter of sympathy and encouragement from the Holy Father would awaken our Catholic people to a greater sense of their duty to the University, and would bring the Catholic collegiate system in closer touch with the University, as not only the crowning of our educational system, and the helpful guide of our educational work, but also it would place the cherished work of our Illustrious Pontiff beyond all possibility of failure.[90]

It was, however, during the visit of Gibbons to Rome in the spring of 1901 that his object was achieved,[91] and on June 13, Leo XIII signed the following:

The great interest with which, from the very beginning of Our Pontificate, We have regarded the Church in the United States of America

---

[89] *Thirteenth Annual Report* . . . (1902), Appendix F. Philadelphia had been visited because of the interest of Archbishop Patrick J. Ryan in the School of Technology; he had even become an unofficial member of the trustees' committee, NYAA, G-28, Addenda, Thomas J. Conaty to M. A. Corrigan, Washington, February 8, 1901; *Ibid.*, February 18, 1901; *Ibid.*, April 25, 1901.

[90] ACUA, English translation of the French report to the Congregation of the Propaganda by J. Card. Gibbons, May, 1901.

[91] Cf. BCA, M. Card. Rampolla to J. Card. Gibbons, Rome, June 14, 1901. "In one of the visits Your Eminence graciously paid me, you expressed the wish that I would interest myself in favor of the Catholic University in Washington. As I felt it my duty, I did not fail to speak of the matter to our Holy Father. His Holiness has deigned to write to Your Eminence a letter which he

caused Us, among other things, to urge the speedy founding of a great University at Washington, and once founded to strengthen it with Our authority and every evidence of good will. For the needs of this age have been especially dear to Our own heart, namely, that the young men who are the future hope of the clergy should be most thoroughly imbued, first, indeed, with virtue, but at the same time with divine and human learning also. What We have learned from time to time concerning the Washington University has shown Us that Our confidence has not been misplaced; and now the report which you have just made to Us testifies that it is taking on a still more gratifying growth, both through the generosity of Catholics and through the skill and influence of its teachers. One thing still remains to be desired, and that is that this noble institution should increase in the number of its students, and this is to be effected by the interest and zeal of the Bishops. If, perhaps, by sending students to Washington, they seem for the time to be depriving themselves of useful workers in their dioceses, they will, in the end, reap a far greater gain both for themselves and for the whole American Church, since the clergy shall be educated under one and the same teaching, and animated by one and the same spirit.

Hoping for the accomplishment of these good things, with the same desire which you are striving for the good and honor of your Churches, We most lovingly impart to you, Our Beloved Son, to the Rector, to the professors, and the students of the Washington University the Apostolic Blessing, as a pledge of Our Love.[92]

Words of praise, unfortunately, are sometimes spoken too soon. The University year that opened on October 1, 1901, was destined to be a very important one for many members of the faculty, for the rector and for the University itself. It was a year of administrative nightmares and personal heartaches. The need for new contracts with the professors was learned through the sad experience endured with the man in possession of the chair of Gaelic.[93] The same scholastic year saw the loss of several other members of the staff, either through resignations or the unwillingness of the authorities to renew contracts.[94]

---

honored me to send to you and which as you will see is at the same time a eulogy of the said University and is intended to bring about a greater attendance of students." This is a translation of the Italian original noted above.

[92] ACUA, Leo XIII, PP to J. Card. Gibbons, Rome, June 13, 1901, English translation. The Latin version may be found in *CUB*, VII (October, 1901), 509.

[93] The failure to reappoint the Reverend Doctor Richard Henebry will be discussed in Chapter IV, 115-124.

[94] Among those who tendered their resignations that year were Edmund B. Briggs; Alfred Doolittle, the director of the Astronomical Observatory; Charles Warren Stoddard of the English department; and the secretary of the

At the trustees' meeting in the fall of that year the Reverend Joseph McMahon was appointed to travel throughout the country seeking to complete the endowment fund, the need of which was emphasized by Cardinal Gibbons:

Your plan, as explained in your letter, of raising money for the purpose of founding scholarships at the University, & thereby to encourage students to devote their time to the higher studies with greater earnestness, meets with my hearty approval. . . . For the present however, as the University is in great need of funds for current expenses, which it is not able to meet with its present income, I consider it more pressing to raise money for this purpose.[95]

Perhaps the most important action that the trustees took at this meeting was the formation of an investigating committee. This committee would hold meetings at the University and make a complete report of their findings at a special meeting of the board to be held in April, 1902. Conaty reported to the senate on February 11, that the committee had completed its investigation. While the full report would be given after the special meeting of the trustees, "One of the most anxious enquiries is that concerning the expenditures of the University Funds, and it is the desire of that Committee to find if there be any Department in the University which may not be considered necessary for our present needs." [96] The special meeting took place on April 9, and by April 15 the rector was ready to make known the results of the meeting. He gave a twelve-point report that covered most of the objections that had been brought against the administration by the staff, as well as taking care of questions of discipline and, at the same time, providing both for retrenchment and development. [97] To complete the losses for the year there came the appointment on March 21, 1902, of Dr. Garrigan, who had been a faithful and able

---

Apostolic Delegation, as well as lecturer on ethics, the Reverend Frederick Zadock Rooker. The Contracts of Charles H. Goddard, instructor in law, and Josiah Pierce, the assistant professor of civil engineering, were allowed to expire, as happened in the case of Henebry. After a long dispute the registrar, Philip Robinson, the son of the dean of the School of Law, was dropped. The more important of these will be mentioned again in Chapter IV.

[95] BCA, 99-Q-3, J. Card. Gibbons to Joseph McMahon, Baltimore, April 23, 1902, copy.

[96] ACUA, RRTTS, February 11, 1902.

[97] ACUA, RRTTS, April 15, 1902. The investigation and its results will be treated in Chapter IV.

support to the rector during the previous years, as first Bishop of Sioux City, Iowa.

The discouragements of 1901-1902 were not entirely without mitigation, even though they were to reach their climax at the November, 1902, meeting of the trustees. The term for the first rectorship of Conaty was drawing to a close and thus, a *terna* had to be prepared for Rome. The names of the rector, of Monsignor Denis J. O'Connell, and of Thomas J. Shahan, professor of church history, were submitted to the Holy See for consideration for the next rectorship. The Institute of Pedagogy, the plans for which had been approved in the special April meeting of the Board of Trustees, was put into operation in New York on October 1, establishing a branch of the University that was soon to flourish and to expand with success. On October 9 the rector was able to report to the senate:

Rev. Dr. Pace was appointed Dean and given charge of the work. . . . Dr. Pace and Dr. Shahan from the University are assisted by others who form the corps of instructors. By the last report 118 teachers had registered in the institute. The new Archbishop of New York is thoroughly in sympathy with the work.[98]

John M. Farley, the new Archbishop of New York, an original trustee and a faithful friend to the University from the beginning and through all its vicissitudes, was told of even more ambitious plans for the institution by the rector:

I am informed that there is a movement on foot among some of the most eminent Catholic physicians to establish a Catholic faculty of medicine to be associated with hospital work. It has often occurred to me, and perhaps more particularly at this time, that it might be possible for us to establish a University faculty of medicine in New York, and in this way bring the University in touch with a new element of interest and strength. I understand that there is in New York, as in all our cities, a certain dissatisfaction among our physicians at their inability to enter to any extent, or to control hospital work. The non-Catholic physician, even though of lesser ability, seems to have the entree, especially to positions of honor and distinction on hospital staffs, while our Catholic physicians have either to stay outside, or be satisfied with the crumbs that drop from the table.

It seems to me that the time is ripe for a development along absolutely Catholic lines in hospital and medical work, in which sound ethical

---

98 ACUA, RRTTS, October 9, 1902. The Very Reverend Edward Aloysius Pace was the professor of philosophy. Archbishop Corrigan of New York had died on May 5, 1902, and had been succeeded by John M. Farley on September 25 of the same year.

principals may be instilled into the young physician under Church influence. . . .

I write you to ask to turn this matter over in your mind, and I will call on you during the meeting of the Association of Universities, when we will be able to discuss the matter more fully. The thought of establishing faculties of law and medicine in large centers has been in my mind for a couple of years. At present I am discussing the question of a Law School in Chicago. We desire to reach out, as the Chicago University is doing, and establish ourselves in large centers, and in this way make the Catholic University the great center of the higher professional school development. It is certainly worth thinking over seriously.[99]

Unfortunately, with the financial situation as acute as it was, these plans of Conaty could not be realized at the time, and as yet, they have been accomplished only in the broadest outline by the various branch summer sessions of the University.

The question of funds played a prominent part in the meeting of the Board of Trustees in November, 1902. The *Catholic University Bulletin* optimistically reported that the board found the finances in a most satisfactory condition, but then the report went on to give a break-down of the finances that would prompt one to question the validity of its assertion:

During the year the receipts amounted to $158,917.29 and the disbursements to $155,268.73, leaving a balance of $3,648.56. Of the amount received $66,517.25 came from the earnings of the trust funds and other ordinary sources of revenue. There have been received in bequests during the year $26,370.95; from sales of property, $33,222.19; by endowments this year, $18,465.41, and from the Bishops' Guarantee Fund, $10,400. Eleven thousand seven hundred dollars were paid this year on the general indebtedness of the University. The gross indebtedness of the University is $193,500; the assets on hand amount to $59,493.10, making the net indebtedness $134,006.90, or $11,700 less than last year.[100]

One financial worry at least was settled in that year, and one of the many lawsuits that arose over matters of contested wills and property settlement came to a conclusion. Among the properties that had come

---

[99] NYAA, I-6, Thomas J. Conaty to John M. Farley, Washington, December 22, 1902. The point of having a University medical faculty had been broached before, once by Satolli while he was apostolic delegate in 1894, cf. Ahern *op. cit.*, and again in 1900 by Dr. Edward F. Crane of London, cf. ACUA, Thomas J. Conaty to Edward F. Crane, Washington, March 15, 1900, copy.

[100] "University Chronicle," *CUB*, IX (January, 1903), 170. At the same meeting Bishop Matthew Harkins of Providence, Rhode Island, was chosen to fill the place on the Board of Trustees vacated by the death of M. A. Corrigan.

to the University through the donation of Monsignor James Mc-Mahon [101] had been a tract of land on Riverside Drive in New York City. In 1897 this land had been sold for $100,000 by an executory contract to be followed by a deed when certain payments had been made. After making a small payment and erecting a building costing around $10,000, the entire project was abandoned, leaving the building unpaid for, and with no further payments on the purchase money. After the University took the land back and again put it up for sale, the contractors made claims on the University. The first trial resulted in a judgment against the University for $10,419.88 in favor of the contractors which the University appealed only to have the first decision reaffirmed by a divided court. On the second appeal the decision of the two lower courts was reversed by a unanimous judgment of the six judges present for the hearing and the threat of having to pay for the unwanted building was removed.[102]

Financial considerations by no means limited the elegance of the reception that was tendered on December 8, 1902 to Diomede Falconio, the new Apostolic Delegate to the United States.[103] At the banquet following the solemn Mass in the morning, Conaty gave expression to what had motivated him during his years as rector and to what his university idea was:

This country needs a university center of Catholic thought, where religion and science in their highest forms may combine to make known the marvelous truth of God; where scholarship aims to make known and defend religion, and give glory to our common manhood. Its mission should be to wield a vivifying influence on the whole educational system, to

---

[101] It was the donation of Monsignor McMahon that financed the building of the hall named after him, cf. Ahern, *op. cit.*, 80, 98.

[102] "University Chronicle," *CUB*, IX (January, 1903), 174-176. Correspondence on this case may be found in ACUA, letters of Abram I. Elkus, of James, Schell and Elkus to Thomas J. Conaty.

[103] Of this event Conaty reported to the senate, (ACUA, RRTTS,) December, 1902, "I also felt it important to omit nothing that would tend to the success of the reception, even though it demanded a little larger expense than is customarily incurred for such an occasion." Falconio, as a member of the Franciscans, had been sent to America as a missionary in 1865 and had been ordained by Bishop John Timon of Buffalo on January 3, 1866. Monsignor Falconio had been the first Apostolic Delegate to Canada, and had been appointed to succeed Sebastian Martinelli on September 30, 1902, taking possession on November 21, 1902. Bonaventure Cerretti, "Legate," *Catholic Encyclopedia*, IX, 120. Cf. also Noel Conlon, O.F.M., "Falconio—A Franciscan Portrait," *Provincial Annals*, IV (January, 1943), 17-30.

unify and elevate it, as also to give tone to all Catholic institutions; to set a definite standard of scholarship that will arouse in clergy and laity a love for the highest intellectual attainments; to advance the interests of science and widen out the horizon of human knowledge, by producing men prepared to do the work of science under the inspiration and guidance of revealed truth; to show the world that the Catholic Church is not afraid of truth wherever found, but on the contrary is eager for the largest possible measure of truth. Thank God, this has been done by the Catholic University. The University is, and will be, in one sense, an object lesson, showing the attitude of the Catholic Church to the highest development of the mind.[104]

Within a few weeks after the reception of the new apostolic delegate, the chancellor, Baltimore's cardinal archbishop, received the official notification that jurisdiction over the University had been changed from the Congregation of the Propaganda to that of the Congregation of Studies[105] and the appointment of a new man as rector. At the meeting of the Board of Trustees on April 22, 1903, the resignation of Thomas J. Conaty as second Rector of the Catholic University of America was accepted, and the new rector was inaugurated in the office.[106] Conaty, by now a bishop and soon to take up the administration of the Diocese of Monterey-Los Angeles, left behind him an institution that had grown under his rectorship, if not in financial security or to any striking degree internally, at least in its scope in the Catholic educational life of America. His words at the reception of

[104] "The University and the Apostolic Delegate," *CUB*, IX (January, 1903), 147.

[105] BCA, 100-G-2, F. Card. Satolli to J. Card. Gibbons, Rome, January 14, 1903. Such a change had been contemplated previously, as M. A. Corrigan had been informed by Salvatore M. Brandi, S.J., in a letter of November 21, 1897, (PFA-A, photostat), at the time of the Schroeder affair: "I have delayed answering Your Grace's letter of October last in the hope of being able to give the information you wanted concerning the University. But things remaining *in statuo quo,* I can only say for the moment that the University has been and *perhaps* is still under the exclusive jurisdiction of the Propaganda. Card. Mazzella told me that when he was Prefect of the Congregation of Studies the proposal was made to him to transfer the University from the Congregation of Propaganda to that of the Studies, but he objected, unwilling, as he was, to take, as a Jesuit, the odium of the measures that were then contemplated [Keane's dismissal]. Now that Card. Mazzella has been promoted to the Congregation of Rites and that Card. Satolli has succeeded him in the Studies, the question of the transfer has come up again and very likely has been decided by the Holy Father. But up to yesterday I was unable to ascertain the final decision."

[106] ACUA, MMBT, Washington, April 23, 1903.

Diomede Falconio were more than a defining of the abstract meaning of a Catholic university. They were a recounting of his own endeavors during his rectorship, the expression of what he had attempted to do, and what he had been able to a great extent to accomplish. If his project had not been completely and permanently established, at least the foundations had been laid upon which others could rear and perfect the superstructure.

Chapter III

EDUCATIONAL FOUNDATIONS

The work before the second rector, the Rt. Rev. Mgr. Thomas J. Conaty, D.D. was first of all conciliation. He found the friends of the University discouraged; its enemies exultant. Gradually, he restored harmony, appeased passions, minimized antagonisms. In establishing the conferences of seminaries and colleges he united the Catholic educational system, under the University's leadership. The Catholic Institute of Pedagogy in New York resulted from these conferences. The existence of Trinity College is largely the work of Dr. Conaty.[1]

This editorial of the Boston *Pilot,* at the time when the second rector was completing his term of office, offered a brief summary of what Thomas Conaty had attempted to do during his rectorship. His efforts were well founded, both on the apostolic letter of Pope Leo XIII approving the Constitutions of the University, (March 7, 1889), and the Constitutions themselves. The Holy Father had emphasized in his letter, "We exhort you all that you should take care to affiliate with your University, your seminaries, colleges, and other Catholic institutions according to the plan suggested in the Constitutions, in such a manner, however, as not to destroy their autonomy." [2] The chapter of the constitutions on "Studies and Students" contained two sections which were referred to by Leo XIII:

3. The authorities of the University should take care to confer with the directors of Catholic colleges and seminaries in our country so that all may labor unitedly to advance the education of our Catholic youth.
4. Colleges and seminaries, without prejudice to their autonomy, may by authority of the Board of Directors be affiliated to the University. When this has been done the diplomas conferred by such colleges as evidence of the acquirements of their students shall be accepted in lieu of an examination for admission to the University.[3]

---

[1] Boston *Pilot,* April 4, 1903. The *Pilot* spoke too glowingly of the harmony that Conaty brought to the institution. Although he tried to accomplish this end, he was not always successful, and his entire rectorship was a struggle to bring that peace so needed for true development.

[2] *Constitutions of the Catholic University of America,* English translation, 1889, p. 2, Leo XIII to J. Card. Gibbons and American Hierarchy, Rome, March 7, 1889, p. 2, Leo XIII to J. Card. Gibbons and American Hierarchy, Rome, March 7, 1889.

[3] *Ibid.,* Chapter V, Studies and Students, 3, 4, p. 10.

With this regulation to guide him the rector was able, within six months of his inauguration, to diagnose and to suggest a remedy for one of the more pressing difficulties of the University:

It is found that in some of the departments the requirements are placed so high, that it is impossible for us to expect our men to be fitted for them. It will be a matter for consideration for the University to enter into a closer adaptation, that the work of the University may begin where the college work leaves off. In order that we may have some information upon which to base our work, I have requested from eight of the prominent Catholic colleges a copy of questions used in the examinations of their graduates. By comparison we can strike a fair average, and thus be able to find where our work should practically begin; for if between the work of our best colleges and the departmental work of the University to which we invite those graduates, there be a chasm, it is necessary for us to consider how we shall bridge it over.[4]

It was not enough that the University should adapt itself to the standards of the colleges, for leadership and the elevating of education could not be accomplished in such a manner. Conaty continued his report to the senate by informing that body:

I have also had the Dean of Philosophy cause to be prepared by the heads of departments a Materia Examinis, which might serve as a basis in the first place for entrance examinations to the School of Philosophy, and secondly as a standard for the work which colleges should do to fit their graduates for University work. This will also be acceptable to many of the Bishops for the examination of students wishing to enter the seminaries, and will serve to force the colleges to do better work.[5]

His request for copies of examinations resulted in an enthusiastic, if somewhat defensive, letter from J. Haven Richards, S.J., the president of Georgetown University:

Allow me to express my sincere gratification at your taking this step. There is nothing more necessary it seems to me, than to have the differences between the various Catholic Colleges in method and standard brought to light and fully understood. At present, as you probably well know, the state of Catholic Collegiate education in the United States is almost chaotic. We here in Georgetown, together with a number of other Jesuit Colleges and Mt. St. Mary's, have long been engaged in strenuous efforts to maintain and advance our standards. We have carried out our examinations with the greatest rigidity; we keep down and even put down

---

4 ACUA, RRTTS, June 3, 1897.
5 *Ibid.*

64

to a lower class those who fail, and in case of continued and incorrigible laziness or stupidity we request the parents to remove the student from the College. This naturally keeps our number down to somewhat restricted limits, but we very much prefer this to such a "turba" as would result, and does in many Catholic Colleges result, from another plan. At present our authors are so arranged that the students finishing at the best classical High Schools of New England enter in Freshman and are obliged to spend four years in College.

In a recent article in the American Catholic Quarterly Review,[6] Father Murphy, President of the Holy Ghost College at Pittsburgh, makes some severe strictures upon the standard and methods of Catholic Colleges. He enunciates his propositions universally, and says that they apply even to the oldest and best of Catholic Colleges in the country. I can say with entire truth that, so far as Georgetown is concerned, they are utterly mistaken and false.[7]

With the Catholic educational system as unorganized and as weak as that suggested by the words of Conaty and Richards, and the need for integration coming more clearly to the mind of the rector, it was to be expected that Conaty would have some suggestion to make to the Board of Trustees when it assembled in the fall of 1897. Treating the clergy and the laity separately, he mentioned regretfully that so many had to spend several months reviewing matter that should have been treated in the various seminaries, before they were able to take the examination for the baccalaureate in theology and to become matriculates in the University. The solution to this would be to have more seminaries follow the example of St. Paul and become affiliated with the University.[8] As far as the lay students were concerned, they too were losing time by the amount of work they had to make up before they could become matriculates. Further, "it has been a serious question to know how to bring the Colleges into closer touch with the University, and there is at present an effort being made in that direction." [9]

The Board of Trustees gave the rector approval to go ahead with the contemplated meeting of seminary presidents, to which he soon gave his close attention. The question of affiliation of seminaries

[6] John T. Murphy, C.S.Sp., "Catholic Secondary Education in the United States," *ACQR,* XXII (July, 1897), 449-464.

[7] ACUA, J. Haven Richards, S.J., to Thomas J. Conaty, Washington, August 5, 1897.

[8] *Eighth Annual Report of the Rector of the Catholic University of America, October 1897* (Washington, 1897), pp. 8-9.

[9] *Ibid.*

was not, by any means, a new one. The St. Paul Seminary had become affiliated to the University in the fall of 1894. In the same year Boston's St. John's Seminary had also opened negotiations with the institution in Washington for a like purpose. The Boston negotiations ended without definite results, but they did succeed in having conditions for affiliation drawn up. For the baccalaureate there was to be a written examination, given by the seminary professors. The examination papers were to be sent to the University and kept in the archives of the School of Theology.[10] The examination was to be on the matter covered in the third and fourth year course of theology, after the candidate had taken at least three years of theology, including courses in dogma, moral, scripture, church history, and canon law. The marks earned in the previous year were to be considered, and at the oral examination, a member of the University faculty would preside.[11] With the refusal of the request of Abbé John B. Hogan, S.S., rector of St. John's at Brighton, that the examinations in Hebrew and canon law be dispensed with, the negotiations reached an impasse.[12] In spite of the knowledge of this past failure and after consultation with many seminary presidents, invitations were issued for a meeting to be held at St. Joseph's Seminary in New York on May 25, 1898.[13]

The presidents of ten seminaries gathered at St. Joseph's on the ap-

[10] ACUA, Report prepared for the April 21, 1903, senate meeting, here quoting from the Senate Records, I, 119, April 20, 1894.

[11] *Ibid.,* p. 133, June 8, 1894.

[12] *Ibid.,* p. 140, February 10, 1895.

[13] Three points were outlined by the theological faculty to aid the rector in preparing for the conference. "It was deemed that the Rt. Rev. Rector should emphasize the following points: 1) The relation of the University to the Seminaries which is set forth in the Apostolic letters establishing the University. Each institution, whether Seminary or University, retains its own identity and its own life, while at the same time all with the University form, or are intended to form but one organization. 2) The University is not in competition with any Seminary or any other educational institution in the country; since the University begins where they all leave off. 3) The object of the University is not to perfect, is not to do well, what the Seminaries have done ill or well. It is to do another kind of work and to do it in another manner. Our object is to specialize, whereas the Seminaries generalize. Hence, we depend on the Seminaries, for it is clearly impossible to specialize, when there has been no preceding general training. . . . There would also be more advantage all around if Presidents of Seminaries made a good choice of young men for the University and if they chose from such young men, once they have made a University course, their future Seminary Professors." ACUA, CHF, Faculty Records, November 15, 1888-May 31, 1901, 142nd session, May 6, 1898, pp. 206-208.

pointed day, while letters of approval came from five others who were unable to be present.[14] In his introductory speech Dr. Conaty mentioned that from his experience in Catholic education, he believed that there was lacking a spirit of organization, and he gave as the purpose of the meeting the establishing of an educational conference which would bear fruit in the years to come. The first thing to be determined was the relationship between the seminaries and the University, and the setting of some standards, so that both could work together to achieve the proper ends of each.

The University and the seminary are closely bound to one another; one is built upon the other, and both are built upon the college. The University is not something far away and standing by itself, with pretensions which ignore the existence of other educational agencies. It is an integral part of the system, closely bound up with and depending upon the other parts. The same blood courses through its veins, the same interests actuate its life, the same aims and purposes bind it to success. . . . Our young cleric must be prepared to meet the issues of the hour—issues no longer between the true Church of Christ and the sects, but between revealed religion and all forms of agnosticism and false individualism. . . . He must also be prepared to enter into the field of social and economic reform. . . . The battle of the future is to be a philosophical battle, as well as scientific and historical. It will be a defence of the very foundations of belief. . . .

The University is the highest expression of the Church in education, and to us Americans, our University should be the pride and idol of our hearts. It was a bold step on the part of the bishops to inaugurate the University; but the educational system was not complete until the University was established. Like all institutions, the University is of slow growth; that which springs into being in a night oftentimes fades and withers before the morning sun. It has taken many years to develop our seminaries and place them upon the splendid footing of to-day. Like them, the University is not merely for our day and generation, it has been built for the centuries. It is as yet in its youth, and must experience all the difficulties that come with youth. . . .

The time has come now, and the University is better prepared than ever, to take a step forward to still better work for the clergy and laity

---

14 "Educational Conference of Seminary Presidents," *CUB,* IV (July, 1898), 397-405. The seminaries represented were St. Mary's, Baltimore; St. John's, Boston; St. John's, Brooklyn; Mt. St. Mary's Seminary of the West, Cincinnati; Mt. St. Mary's, Emmitsburg; St. Joseph's, New York; Niagara University; St. Charles, Philadelphia; St. Patrick's, San Francisco; Seton Hall, New Jersey, while letters were received from St. Bonaventure's, Alleghany, New York; St. Meinrad's, Indiana; Kenrick, St. Louis; and St. Paul Seminary, Minnesota.

of the United States; but it needs the continued co-operation of the seminaries and colleges; it needs the touch that gives ambition for work as well as direction; it needs the friendliness that comes with the kindly word of direction and the conscientious co-operation in the preparation for the work.[15]

The speech must have had its effect, for it was voted to form a permanent organization. Since professors were to be included in the following meetings, the name chosen for the organization was the Educational Conference of Seminary Faculties.[16] The next meeting was scheduled to be held at St. Charles Borromeo Seminary in Philadelphia on September 1, 1899. The support of Abbé Hogan, who had been on the original University faculty, was secured through the New York meeting at which he had represented St. John's Seminary. He wrote a very favorable article for the *American Ecclesiastical Review* of October, supporting the proposals of the University rector who, he claimed, had a right to expect this co-operation which could be so easily given.[17] Conaty himself was able to report to the senate:

The spirit manifested was excellent, the relations towards the University were kindly but strongly considered, and in the judgment of all present the conference was productive of good results. A meeting of college presidents upon somewhat the same lines will be held about the beginning of October, and we may anticipate from it equally good results.[18]

Although the work had started out so auspiciously, after the subsequent meeting in Philadelphia the organization became dormant until

15 *Ibid.,* pp. 399-405.

16 *Ibid.,* p. 398.

17 J. Hogan, "Seminary and University Studies," *AER,* XIX (October, 1898), 361-370. That members of the University still looked with some suspicion on the efforts of Abbé Hogan was shown in the following month: "The Dean presented a communication received by the Rector from Dr. Hogan, acting presumably as a representative of the Seminaries, asking that the materia examinis in Moral and Dogma be divided in the same way as in the other studies, so that the students may choose one part on which to stand examination. Dr. Shahan said that we are entering on a contest with the Seminary presidents and that Fr. Hogan is evidently the head of the opposition. It is certain that we are going to receive suggestion after suggestion, and we must be on our guard lest we become gradually entangled more and more: but that it is a question whether perhaps by yielding this point we cannot gain in other respects." ACUA, CHF, Faculty Records, November 15, 1888-May 31, 1901, Session 148, November 9, 1898, pp. 221-222.

18 ACUA, RRTTS, June 2, 1898.

1904.[19] New life was then breathed into it by Conaty's successor at the University in order to incorporate it with two other Catholic educational organizations into the Catholic Education Association on July 14, 1904.[20]

One of the organizations to which the Educational Conference of Seminary Faculties joined itself in 1904 was the Association of Catholic Colleges, another group inaugurated by Conaty, and to whose beginning he had made reference when reporting to the academic senate on the first meeting of the seminary presidents. At the October, 1898, meeting he broached the subject to the Board of Trustees and received a favorable reply, so that what had been begun with the seminaries could now be extended to the colleges. During the Christmas vacation circulars were sent to ninety-five colleges. By January 10, 1899, thirty-one replies had been received, all of them favorable.[21] Originally Conaty had planned to hold the first meeting in New York in February, but due to the enthusiasm shown by some of the western and mid-western colleges he determined to hold the meeting in Chicago during the month of April. Realizing his inability to care for all the details in Chicago and still carry on his duties at the University, the rector formed a committee of Chicago priests and

[19] Results were obtained in the University since conditions were laid down for affiliation. "The recommendations contained in the Report of the Committee on Affiliation which were adopted by the Academic Senate Feb. 5, 1901, were read. They were: 1) 'That at the end of the second year of the seminary course, the names of those students who desire and who are adjudged fit by the faculties of the respective seminaries to present themselves as candidates for the Baccalaureate in Sacred Theology, the year following the second year aforesaid, be furnished the Rector of the Catholic University of America, and upon approval by him, be entered on the list of non-resident students of said University; 2) That students then enrolled shall be eligible for the degree of S.T.B. from the Catholic University of America upon passing an examination satisfactory to the Faculty of Theology of said University; 3) That towards the end of the third Seminary year, a written and an oral examination of such students be held at the respective seminaries, under the direction of the Faculty of Theology of the C.U.A. and in the presence of a proper number of the members of said Faculty; 4) That students passing their examinations shall receive the degree of S.T.B. from the C.U.A., which degree shall be conferred formally at the University by its Chancellor or Rector. The diploma may be presented by an officer of the respective seminary at the time and place that the University and seminary may agree upon.'" ACUA, CHF, Faculty Records, November 15, 1888-May 31, 1901, Session 188, May 10, 1901, pp. 277-278.

[20] Francis W. Howard, "Catholic Educational Association," *Catholic Encyclopedia*, V, 305-306.

[21] ACUA, RRTTS, January 10, 1899.

educators to manage the more detailed local preparations for the proposed conference. The committee was under the chairmanship of Father Hugh McGuire of St. James' Church, who generously offered the use of his church hall for the sessions.[22] By March the preliminaries had been taken care of and Conaty was able to send out the formal announcement calling the conference for April 12-13. He suggested that two representatives come from each college, one in behalf of the administration, the other for the faculty. The work of the gathering was outlined, offering general topics that were applicable to all concerned and setting a pattern of two or three speakers followed by an open discussion.[23]

The conference was opened by a solemn high Mass at which the sermon was delivered by Morgan M. Sheedy of Altoona, Pennsylvania. The Archbishop of Chicago, Patrick A. Feehan, extended a few words of welcome at the conclusion of the Mass. The speech of Dr. Conaty at the first session supplied the general purpose of the convention, stressing the need of unity in Catholic education for the achieving of its ends; a speech revealing the educational ideals of the man himself. Although there are different ways of achieving unity, there is only one reason for education: "The very soul of a body of educators like this is the spirit of God, one aim and one purpose actuating all, the very aim and purpose which direct the efforts of God's Church in the establishment of the Kingdom of God in the hearts of men." [24] Education was based on the oneness of Christian life and to it belonged the same type of unity. Since every person could not or would not continue on to the highest level of education, each school should complete its own scope of training. No phase of education, on the other hand, should try to do the work of a higher or lower section; the University should not attempt to do the work

[22] ACUA, Thomas J. Conaty to J. Zahm, C.S.C., Washington, February 27, 1899, copy.

[23] NYAA, G-28, a general bulletin dated March 14, 1899, from the Catholic University of America, and signed by Thomas J. Conaty. The seven topics, assigned to various educators and college professors were: "The Typical Catholic College: What Should It Teach and How;" "Problems of Catholic Education in Our Present Social Needs;" "The Catholic College as a Preparation for a Business Career;" "What the College May Do for Preparatory Schools;" "College Entrance Conditions;" "Requirements for College Degrees;" "Drift Towards non-Catholic Colleges and Universities—Causes and Remedies."

[24] *Report of the First Annual Conference of the Association of Catholic Colleges of the United States, held in St. James' Hall, Chicago, April 12 and 13, 1899* (Washington, 1899), p. 22.

belonging to the colleges, the colleges should not expect to enter into university work. Conaty went on to show that education should not prepare men to live in the past, but should be the living, directing force of the present and the future:

We have witnessed the scientific phase which education has taken; we notice now the sociological. It is our duty to take note of these tendencies, and with truth, the knowledge of God, the supernatural to guide us, we should lead youth into all fields of scholarship, placing their education in touch with the scientific and social tendencies, and control both by the great truth of God under the guidance of the Church of Christ. . . . College must put man in touch with science illumined by faith and with humanity ennobled and redeemed by Christ.[25]

The very foundation of the University system showed the unity that was intended:

Universities sprang from the mighty movement of the human mind, which arose about the eleventh century, and continued until 1300. The intellect of the young nations needed the touch of the living Word. The purpose of the university was to bring all arts and philosophies under the sway of Christ, to establish the kingdom in which all men are one. From the rise of the universities until the Reformation, the system of study was linked with Christian unity, for one life pervaded Christendom. With heresy came the shattering of unity and the divorce of the university from Christian unity.[26]

Colleges, too, came in for the analysis of the University rector, an analysis that could at times be caustic:

Indeed, we have reached the time when the college is to be tested, not by the general name of college, but by the interior construction of its system, through which the results demanded by our conditions are obtained. The time has come when the name over the door is not a sufficient attraction to the student world. . . . College, as has been well said, is the time and place for accumulations, by which the mind is stored with facts, but it is also the time and place for teaching man how to use these facts in the varied demands of life. The important question is not what one studies, but how one studies. The college should develop sound intellectual habits,

---

[25] *Ibid.,* p. 24. Conaty was not in favor of accepting everything proposed by scientists, and in a speech made at the conclusion of the conference, he drew an important distinction: "Science and religion: how beautiful the combination! Nothing in science is to be dreaded! Much to be dreaded from scientists. For let us not forget that there is a difference between science and the dicta of scientists. For science is unerring and true, the scientists weak and fallible." *Ibid.,* p. 181.
[26] *Ibid.,* p. 26.

fostered by live teachers who lead one to be alive, to take advantage of opportunities, to unfold, and thus to develop himself. The teacher makes the school. He is more important than text-books or apparatus. "Have a university in shanties," says Cardinal Newman, "nay in tents, but have great teachers in it." [27]

Coming to a conclusion, the purpose of education and of the conference was once more emphasized and the keynote given to the work:

The ultimate purpose of education is to form citizens for the city of God; while doing this, it also fits them for the duties of life. It establishes and develops the supernatural virtues, intellectual and moral, which are essential in fitting them for the world. . . . It becomes us to study our educational system, to tie together their frayed strands, to unify it and make it harmonious, to link part with part, and all the parts into a whole that all may contribute to the moral and intellectual development of our Catholic youth. Criticism is not a mark of ingratitude—it is oftentimes the indication of true affection, for it tends not to destruction, but to perfection. . . . This conference is not called to discuss defects so much as to re-establish foundations. The results of the discussion of the conference will be to accentuate topics for future conferences. The thought to-day is the thought of ideals. If we reach that result, we shall have succeeded in the work proposed for us.[28]

In the four sessions that were held during the two days much was done to realize this aim. A permanent organization was formed, to be known as the Association of Catholic Colleges of the United States, and its first president was the man who founded it, the rector of the University. With a final speech by the Bishop of Peoria, the delegates dispersed to implement their ideas and to plan for the gathering of the following year.

It was but natural that Conaty should be pleased at the results of the conference, and he was quick to inform the Rector of the American College in Rome about it, although more for the sake of the University than for himself:

I know that you will be pleased to hear that the Conference was marked in every particular. The greatest of confidence, and the utmost of harmony prevailed. It was a decided step in advance, and under the direction of the University, it was an indication of confidence on the part of the entire Collegiate body of the United States.[29]

---

[27] *Ibid.,* pp. 28-30.

[28] *Ibid.,* pp. 34-38.

[29] ACUA, Thomas J. Conaty to William H. O'Connell, Washington, April 25, 1899, copy.

From Rome Conaty received congratulations that must have pleased him, perhaps more for the man who sent them than for the words themselves. Archbishop Keane wrote him: "I congratulate you heartily on the satisfactory issue of this very important step. God grant that it may inaugurate an era of universal good will toward the University on the part of the Colleges." [30]

During the first week of December, 1899, the rector was active once again preparing the schedule to be followed at the second annual meeting. One topic included had a definite bearing on a problem of the day. To the man chosen to handle this point, Timothy Brosnahan, S.J., Conaty wrote:

The second topic selected was "Relative Merits of Courses in Catholic and Non-Catholic Colleges for A.B. Degrees." It seemed to me, and the Committee agreed with me, that you would be the best man to prepare this paper, as you have given considerable attention to the question. . . . A comparison of the different courses may be made, from which it will be seen whether or not our courses are better, equal or poorer. This will give an opportunity to bring up, indirectly at least, the question in which we are so much interested concerning the blacklisting of our Colleges by Harvard.[31]

The subject upon which Conaty addressed the Association was also one that had been for some time demanding attention, and upon which

[30] ACUA, John J. Keane to Thomas J. Conaty, Rome, May 6, 1899. In the same vein, Keane wrote to Garrigan, "It is an excellent move, and, if he meets with *honest* cooperation, it must do great good." ACUA, Garrigan Papers, John J. Keane to P. J. Garrigan, Rome, May 5, 1899.

[31] ACUA, Thomas J. Conaty to Timothy Brosnahan, S.J., Washington, December 20, 1899, copy. An article in the section entitled "Conferences," under the heading of "The Case of Boston College and Harvard University," *AER*, XXIII (August, 1900), 173-175, gives a review of this so-called blacklisting. Harvard at first had accepted merely the diplomas from Georgetown, from among all the Jesuit colleges, for admission to its Law School. Boston College and Holy Cross, after they protested that their standards were as high as Georgetown's, were placed on the list. Other Jesuit institutions in turn protested that their standards were also as high. Harvard settled the matter by dropping all but Georgetown from the list of recognized schools for admission to its School of Law. All men would be accepted in the Law School, but, if an average of 75% was not maintained, they would be dropped. If the diploma was acceptable, all that was required was an average of 55%. The reasons given by Harvard were that the Boston College and Holy Cross men had poor records and that in the academic section of Harvard the graduates of these schools would only get into the sophomore class. The *AER* claimed that these assertions were baseless. Cf. *Sacred Heart Review,* January 13, 1900.

the University would soon turn its eye. To the fifty-two delegates, representing seventy-two colleges, assembled in Chicago on April 18-19,[32] the rector of the University delivered his "Plea for Teachers." [33] This address was an eloquent picture of what the perfect Catholic teacher should be. He urged:

But while we consider the improvement of our school methods, and a more careful grouping of studies, it is proper that we should not lose sight of the most important element in our educational work—the teacher. . . . The best dispositions in the world, even that high symbol, the religious habit, are not guarantees of success in teaching. . . . The ideal teacher is the one who has a vocation to teach, and this implies aptitude. . . . He must be on fire himself, if he would stir up a consuming fire in the lives of others. Then, too, the teacher himself should be forever a scholar, for the sake of his youthful disciples, as well as for his own enjoyment.

The first requisite for a college teacher should be a thorough modern and critical knowledge of the subjects to be taught. . . . But to-day any scholarship worthy of the name implies some acquaintance with the science of education, readiness to learn from the experience of others, to profit by their success or failures. . . .

A second requisite is ability to impart knowledge—otherwise the accurate scholarship is like a mine of precious metal, hidden in the bowels of the earth.

. . . Ability, willingness are not enough. The successful teacher must have enthusiasm. There must be, in himself, a love for his work, a passion, as it were, to have all who come in contact with him love his work as well as he loves it himself. . . .

We cannot insist sufficiently upon the importance of the spirit of religion in our teacher, that he may be a fitting instrument in the work of Christian education.

. . . Right here, however, it may be well to say that often enough the blame laid upon teachers as incompetent should be visited upon the

---

32 The subjects chosen for this meeting were: "Uniformity of Entrance into Freshman Class;" "The Relative Merits of Courses in Catholic and Non-Catholic Colleges for the Baccalaureate;" "The Elective System of Studies;" "Religious Instruction in College;" "The Teaching of Modern Languages in College;" "Development of Character in College Students."

33 The example of the English hierarchy in setting up a system by which Catholic teachers could receive certificates, recognized by the government, when sisters were refused admission to Cambridge Teaching College, had influence on the choice of this topic, as well as in the establishment of the Institute of Pedagogy. Cf. *AER,* XXII (April, 1900), the article by M.S.R. on "A Catholic Normal School for High School Teachers," 394-397, and also "Conferences," "The Need of Catholic Normal Schools for Women," 409-412.

student who frequently pursues in an aimless, half-hearted way, courses for which he has no taste, when he is sent to college for social reasons or kept there against his will.

. . . The noble office of teacher is ever open to the layman, who may justly wear in society the magisterial pallium, and take his place as a defender and illustrator of Catholic truths.[34]

Success attended this second meeting, success for Conaty, for the University and for the Association. The support received from the University rector in the Boston College-Harvard controversy seemed to gain the friendship of the Jesuits, for a Notre Dame sister wrote:

I had a visit from Rev. Father Quirk, S.J., after the meeting in Chicago. I think you have made a conquest of all the S.J.'s, he was more than enthusiastic of your whole work, said you stood shoulder to shoulder with the Society, defended their teaching etc. I hope after this they will be loyal to the Society or rather to the University.[35]

A Canadian educator was also impressed by the words of Conaty, and was in hearty agreement with him:

. . . I hope that I am not doing Catholic Colleges an injustice in saying that, generally, it is in this matter—the equipment of the man who is to teach—that they have made the least efforts. . . . Now without saying anything about it to the world at large, we all know, that not uncommonly a young man having finished the sophomore class in a Catholic College, has a cassock put on him next September and is given a class to teach. . . . As I told you, I attach immense importance to your advocacy of a better training for teachers in Catholic Colleges, and I may tell you now, that Fr. Roche and myself have since put a scheme on foot which promises very soon to have young Basilians looking to a completion of their training as teachers at Washington University.[36]

The matter of proper training for teachers, as brought out by the meeting of the Association, was serious enough to have the rector report to the Board of Trustees in 1900: "The most important demand

[34] *Report of the Second Annual Conference of the Association of Catholic Colleges . . . 1900* (Washington, 1900), pp. 67-84.

[35] ACUA, Sr. Julia, S.N.D., to Thomas J. Conaty, Cincinnati, May 9, 1900. Along these same lines, Edward A. Pace wrote to Conaty from Florida, on May 1, 1900 (ACUA): "It would be a great step in advance if we could just get one of the S. J. younger men to take a course at the University—in any branch. This would have to be arranged quietly with the Superiors, rather than in open conference."

[36] ACUA, M. V. Kelly, C.S.B., to Thomas J. Conaty, Assumption College, Sandwich, Ontario, Canada, May 14, 1900.

which I judge is made upon the University by the Conference, and which is the outcome of the present collegiate conditions, is the establishment of a Chair of Pedagogy at the University." [37]

An extra day was added to the conference of 1901, which was again held in Chicago on April 10-12.[38] To the forty-two delegates, representing fifty-two colleges, the president stressed three important points: the encroachment of state legislation on education, the place of the high school, and the unity of the Catholic educational system with its capstone in the University. While speaking in the earlier sessions of the conference Conaty lashed out at the encroachment of the state on education, pointing out that there was a well defined trend toward educational legislation directed by the universities. In this way the universities endeavored to make the high schools the feeders for these institutions, while cutting off the Catholic and other private schools from the educational system.[39] Conaty's answer to this was: "We are citizens as well as Christians, and we refuse to bend the knee to the fetich of State paternalism, and claim by virtue of our citizenship the right to educate our people in schools which our conscience approves." [40] In his main speech, "The Catholic College of the Twentieth Century," he explained this point more in detail. Here he supplied the only possible Catholic answer:

Against our system, as against the systems of all private schools, and especially religious ones, is the well-equipped and thoroughly unified organization of state instruction, sustained by public funds. Starting with

---

[37] *Eleventh Annual Report of the Rector . . . 1900* (Washington, 1900), p. 5.

[38] The topics treated in this conference were: "The Catholic High School Movement;" "The Teaching of Science;" "Teaching of History in Colleges;" "The Teaching of English in College;" "Educational Legislation in the United States;" "The Study of Greek."

[39] This question had been broached in the *American Ecclesiastical Review,* XXII (January, 1900), 4-31, in an article, "Trend of Modern Educational Legislation," signed P.R., and with this the development of Conaty's ideas were very similar. It was occasioned by the controversy over the White Bill in New York. The writer attacked the educational set-up in New York, with the Board of Regents and the state school superintendent, and he inferred that the state was attempting to control education through legislation rather than by directly taking the schools into its hands. From the individual state, it went to the federal government and the writer foresaw a threat in the formation of a federal department of education and the idea of a national university.

[40] *Report of the Third Annual Conference of the Association of Catholic Colleges . . . 1901* (Washington, 1901), p. 135.

the primary grades, reaching as a desired result to the completion of intermediate work, the state system at public expense has developed into the high schools, and in many states maintains the university, in which, at public expense, even professional schools are found. . . . The danger from state legislation interfering in every possible way with private enterprise in education, the disposition of every experimentalist in the name of education, to still further enlarge the sphere of state paternalism, the ever-increasing encroachment of state universities upon all forms of public instruction, even in private schools, the disposition to centralize education, to the extent of national control, and last but not least, the political machine which threatens to lay hands upon educational forces for its own ends—all these are reasons which urge us in self protection to safeguard the principles upon which our education depends and bind together all parts of our system for the purpose of successful defense. . . . All for each and each for all, that there may be no weak strand in the chain which binds us together; for the test of the system is the weakest and not the strongest part. . . . No allowance will be made for our poverty or our weakness. We must compete with the best and in the ways in which the best equipped colleges work or we lose the field. Hence more system is demanded.

. . . We may find a third fact in the effort very clearly defined during the past few years by which universities with rich endowments are striving for the control of the State schools, the dictation of the schedule of work, the papers for the examination of teachers, the definition of the scope and purpose of all public instruction, the desire to have all teachers receive the university degree or certificate of university approval. The trend of educational legislation is the result in many quarters of the Universities' desire for control of all schools—private as well as public.[41]

The greatest threat, and the least noticed, was that of the high school in which the Catholic system was sadly deficient:

The danger from the high school movement to the collegiate and university parts of our system, to my mind, is greater than even that which threatens the parochial school. Hence I assert that this is one of the most important problems for the college. Take the high school from our system, or neglect to develop it according to the demands of the people, and you are practically forcing the graduates of your parochial schools into the State high schools, which even more in the future than in the past, are to be the feeders upon which the university depend. . . . Our parochial school without its high school is apt to become a feeder to the non-Catholic college and university.[42]

---

[41] *CUB*, VII (July, 1901), 306-310.
[42] *Ibid.*, pp. 311-312.

The solution to these difficulties lay in determining the part to be handled by colleges, and the part by the university, but mainly by concentrating on the development of one Catholic university:

Graduate work today is the accepted function of the university, in the proper sense of the term. . . . It requires laboratories and libraries, thoroughly equipped with the best and latest scientific apparatus. Competition is so keen that if we would enter into it we must be prepared to do the work as it is done by the universities liberally endowed. It costs millions to properly endow a modern university. . . . Just as the Catholic college has to compete with the non-Catholic college, so the Catholic graduate school must compete with the non-Catholic university, or else withdraw altogether from the higher education. . . .

What seems to me the practical solution, as also a practical conclusion, is, that we recognize the fact that we cannot, with our present means, maintain several schools equipped to do graduate work capable of competing with non-Catholic institutions. It is the duty of the colleges, out of loyalty to the system and with desire for the best results, to do their best to build up the University, which our Holy Father, in accordance with the wishes of our Hierarchy, has constituted as the head of our educational structure and to which he wishes all schools and colleges to be affiliated. . . . Every college should feel that it exists, not merely for the students, few or many that pass through its halls, but for the schools below it as also for the University above it, the university existing for it as well as for the whole system.[43]

Conaty was not unsupported in his assertions concerning the place of the University, as has been mentioned previously, and he was further able to read a letter from the apostolic delegate which urged practically the same stand.[44] The Association whole-heartedly offered its support and in ten resolutions accepted all the proposals of its president, as well as delegated him to present the work of the Association to the meeting of the archbishops in November. Especially was he to speak for the Catholic high school.[45]

Wide publicity was received by this conference, particularly on the point of state legislation hindering schools, as was to be expected after all the past school conflicts. In explanation Conaty reported to the academic senate: "There was no criticism of national education, nor was there any attempt whatever to build up an antagonism to the

[43] *Ibid.,* pp. 314-317.

[44] *CUB,* VII (July, 1901), 386-387, Sebastian Martinelli to Thomas J. Conaty, Washington, April 23, 1901.

[45] *Ibid.,* "The Third Annual Conference of Catholic Colleges," p. 385.

national educational idea. The headlines in the newspapers were entirely misleading and untrue to the action taken or considered." [46]
The real object being attacked was the arbitrary policy of State Superintendent Charles Rufus Skinner of New York:

In many states, notably in New York, an applicant to the Normal Training School may be a graduate of the best Catholic college in the State; his degree will count for nothing unless State Superintendent Skinner, or those under his direction, shall be satisfied that the preparatory college training contained the schedule of work required of the State high schools. So that it is not so much a question of a man's education, as it is having a man pass through an arbitrarily fixed schedule, which must be accepted by the State Superintendent.[47]

Faithful to the request of the conference, and aided by a committee of University professors,[48] the rector called the attention of the archbishops to the establishing and developing of Catholic high schools.[49] The archbishops promised to give all possible aid to the movement. It remained a question of interest throughout the year,[50] and a problem that has not even yet been entirely solved.

The last conference of the Association of Catholic Colleges that Conaty was to attend as the Rector of the University took place in Chicago on July 9-10, 1902, with sixty delegates representing forty-one colleges and parochial schools in seven dioceses.[51] The final link

[46] ACUA, RRTTS, April 25, 1901.

[47] ACUA, Thomas J. Conaty to John J. Shea of the Philadelphia *Catholic Standard and Times,* Washington, April 30, 1901, copy. Conaty also mentioned unsuccessful laws attempted in New York, Illinois, Missouri, Alabama, Massachusetts and Pennsylvania. He ended by saying, "I give you these items for your information in the direction of editorial thought in this matter, but do not wish at present to be quoted."

[48] ACUA, RRTTS, April 25, 1901, together with a letter to the committee composed of Edward A. Pace, John J. Griffin, Charles P. Neill and George M. Bolling.

[49] BCA, 99-F-8, Minutes of the Annual Meeting of the Archbishops of the United States, 1901.

[50] Cf. *ACQR,* XXVI (July, 1901), 485-499, James A. Burns, C.S.C., "Catholic Secondary Schools." *Ibid.,* XXVII (October, 1902), 782-812, Lorenzo J. Markoe, "Education by the State; or, The Evolution of a State Religion." *AER,* XXV (December, 1901), 509-516, Conferences, "The Work of Our Parochial School Superintendents." *Ibid.,* Louis S. Walsh, "Unity, Efficiency, and Public Recognition of Catholic Elementary Schools," 481-489.

[51] The topics for this conference were: "Intellectual and Moral Education in Catholic and Non-Sectarian Systems;" "Principles of Pedagogy in Collegiate

was created by the addition of the parochial school, whose represent-atives made up the Parish School Conference. In all, then, the three groups which formed the Catholic Educational Association could properly be said to have been the result of the educational guidance of Conaty.

Although the unification took place under his successor, the groundwork for that unification was laid at the 1903 meeting of the Association by Conaty himself, then Bishop of Monterey-Los Angeles. He gave an account of this meeting to the third Rector of the University:

I came East as I agreed to attend the Conferences and you will pleased [sic] to know that they were very successful especially the one on Parochial schools at which twenty-five dioceses were represented. As I could not consult with you, I was at sea as to future management but I accepted the Presidency on condition that I would be free to arrange with you as to the future. I worked from the beginning for the headship of the University in the Educational unification and I am anxious only to cooperate with the University Rector along those lines. I am ready to do my share of work at any time for the good of the cause. It has the elements of great strength and we cannot afford to let it get away from us. A Committee from each Conference was appointed to consult with you as to the feasibility and plan for a National organization. Some time after Christmas they will no doubt meet you and be advised by you.[52]

A month later he again wrote expressing satisfaction that the new rector had stepped into control of the organization:

I was delighted to hear from Father Conway by letter this morning, that you see your way towards taking charge of the Conference of Colleges and Schools. This place belongs to the Rector, as I have always asserted. I was sorry that you were not at home in time to consult with you about the last meeting, but as you requested, I made it a point to go East and attend the Conference and hold them in line. I am sure you will find the Conference in good condition and ready for the leadership which you will bring to them. . . . I have written Father Conway resigning my position in your favor, and I have advised him to have this supplemented by the vote of the other standing committee. There may be some little question

---

Work;" "The Training of Teachers" (presented by Bishop Conaty); "Methods of Teaching History in College;" "Teaching of Social and Political Sciences in Colleges."

[52] ACUA, O'Connell Papers, Thomas J. Conaty to D. J. O'Connell, New York, November 10, 1903.

as to the formality of the action, but I have advised Father Conway to pay no attention, but to go right ahead.[53]

In spite of the fact that the Association of Catholic Colleges called for the greater part of Monsignor Conaty's attention in educational movements of a national scale, the formation of another organization had him among its members, although not in so active a way. Because of the practice of certain German universities in granting the degree of doctor of philosophy to Americans on easier conditions than to their native students, the University of California, with the support of Harvard, Columbia, Johns Hopkins and Chicago, issued an invitation in 1900 to several other universities to meet in Chicago to protect the dignity of the degree. Together with this, there was a desire to bring about some uniformity of conditions for the granting of degrees in the United States.[54] The Catholic University of America received its invitation somewhat tardily, most probably through the interest of the well-known educator, G. Stanley Hall.[55] This tardiness might explain why the rector did not give the movement his whole-hearted support at the outset. When the invitation was received, the matter was presented to the senate which determined that it should be accepted. The Reverend Edward A. Pace of the Department of Philosophy, and the General Secretary, Daniel W. Shea, were delegated to attend the conference with the rector.

At the first conference, held in Chicago on February 26, 1900, eleven universities were represented. Besides those who had issued the circular calling the meeting, and the Catholic University of America, there were present delegates from Clark, Leland Stanford, Michigan, Pennsylvania and Princeton. Cornell, Wisconsin and Yale sent letters showing their sympathy with the movement. Although nothing definite was determined concerning the activities of the Ger-

53 ACUA, O'Connell Papers, Thomas J. Conaty to D. J. O'Connell, Los Angeles, December 21, 1903.

54 ACUA, Convocation Notes, March 7, 1900.

55 Cf. ACUA, Thomas J. Conaty to G. Stanley Hall, Washington, February 6, 1900, copy. "You are certainly very kind to give your time to the matter of the representation of this University at the Chicago Conference. I have not as yet heard anything from it, except through your letters. Should an invitation come, I will take pleasure in informing you." Although Hall was a friend from Worcester contacts of Conaty, he was also a friend of John J. Keane and Edward A. Pace, and it has been asserted that it was through Pace and Hall that the University received the invitation. Dr. Hall was the president of Clark University of Worcester, one of the original members of the Association.

man universities, a permanent organization was formed, and the Association of American Universities came into being. One of the members of the committee to draft the articles of association was the Rector of the Catholic University of America, who by this time had become much more enthusiastic for the movement. The officials for the Association came from the universities issuing the invitation, under the presidency of Charles W. Eliot of Harvard. Those to whom invitations to the first meeting had been sent became charter members of the Association. Other universities might be admitted on the vote of the members. The rector was pleased with the standards that his University held, and he felt proud to report upon his return:

The views of the different delegates were freely expressed with regard to the home universities in the matter of the Ph. D. degrees, and your Rector feels safe in saying that the delegates from the Catholic University presented a very strong position held by us in this matter, and it was pleasant for us to note that in some respects we were in advance of all other universities in some of our requirements for the degrees, while we were on a level with them in everything else.[56]

Membership in the Association, which was formally accepted in a letter of Conaty to the President of the University of Chicago, William Rainey Harper, on June 12, 1900,[57] brought a much needed increase to the prestige of the University. Conaty looked on this as "the cachet of approval to the Catholic University, as being one of the great universities engaged in graduate work," [58] but he also considered it a challenge to maintain that standing in the face of the competition coming from the other American universities. The rector, again with Pace and Shea, attended the second meeting in Chicago in February, 1901, but he was not very much impressed by what was accomplished.[59] The third meeting took place in New York on December 29-30-31, 1902, and this time the rector and Daniel W. Shea were

[56] ACUA, Convocation Notes, March 7, 1900.

[57] ACUA, copy: "I have the honor to inform you that at the June meeting of the University Senate, the invitation to membership in the Association of Universities was presented, and the Senate voted unanimously to accept membership."

[58] ACUA, Convocation Notes, March 7, 1900. Cf. *Eleventh Annual Report of the Rector . . . 1900* (Washington, 1900), p. 4.

[59] ACUA, RRTTS, March 12, 1901: "Many questions were discussed of great interest to graduate work; but the University delegates failed to find much that was practical in what was done."

the Catholic University of America delegates. At that meeting the University was appointed to the executive committee for the following year. Of more lasting import was the decision of the group to maintain and increase its membership on very conservative lines, accepting only the most carefully selected institutions of higher learning.[60]

As Conaty had so frequently emphasized, the school depends to a great extent upon its teachers; and in all his educational activity, the rector of the University manifested this interest in a practical way. All the credit, of course, must not be given to him, for there were others on his staff who frequently supplied him with information and aided him with suggestions. Perhaps his three closest advisers, after the vice-rector, were Thomas Bouquillon, Thomas Shahan and Edward Pace, all men of ability.[61] It was Pace who was, in the main, responsible for the development of the Institute of Pedagogy. The rector was instrumental in putting Pace's suggestions into operation from the point of general university administration. The earliest beginnings along these lines came in February and March, 1898, with the lectures of Pace on psychology at the Cathedral Library University Extension Centre, directed by Father Joseph McMahon in New York. These lectures were primarily intended for teachers who were preparing for the New York State Regents' examinations.[62] In the fall of that same year, Pace, as the Dean of the Faculty of Philosophy, urged the establishment of a Department of Pedagogy on the trustees, saying: "The training of teachers is an important function of the University and the most valuable service that it can render to the colleges."[63] In the following year he again reported the need for such a department in the University, basing it upon the necessity demonstrated by the Association of Catholic Colleges,[64] but his plea was still without avail. In 1900 the rector also asked for the establishment of such a department, as has been previously mentioned,[65] but once again no definite action was taken. By 1901

[60] ACUA, RRTTS, January 13, 1903.

[61] Cf. Ahern, *op. cit.*, for the activities of these men in the University.

[62] "University Chronicle," *CUB*, IV (April, 1898), 292.

[63] *Ninth Annual Report of the Rector . . . 1898* (Washington, 1898), Appendix D, p. 25.

[64] *Tenth Annual Report of the Rector . . . 1899* (Washington, 1899), Appendix D, p. 31.

[65] Cf. Note 37, Chapter III, 176.

the committee on organization did have a resolution adopted by the trustees, but it was not encouraging:

In view of the necessity of economy in the administration we suggest that the establishment of a Pedagogical Department be postponed, but that the Professors of all the Departments be reminded that, as many of their pupils will be professors in the future, they teach them how to impart to others the knowledge they acquire, especially by their own example of lucid instruction.[66]

The conditions in New York were such that the principal's license was given only to those possessing a collegiate degree or who had pursued studies for sixty hours in an approved college or university course. Catholic men, who were teachers, were able to comply with this requirement by attending the College of St. Francis Xavier in New York for university extension work. Catholic women were not so fortunate. For them there were only non-Catholic institutions, where there was a danger of their faith being weakened by anti-Catholic philosophies.[67] The investigating committee of the Board of Trustees, which was at the University in the early months of 1902, or more properly, Bishop Spalding of Peoria under the suggestion of Joseph McMahon of New York, took the first definite steps toward the formation of an Institute of Pedagogy. As a part of the investigating committee's activity, they recommended the establishment of such an institute in New York City, as a five or six week summer school. Spalding and Bishop Maes of the committee, together with Joseph McMahon and Edward Pace, called on the aging Archbishop of New York on February 12, and secured his approval for such a move. A meeting of those interested in such an institute was held in that same month. Over 200 were present, and all were enthusiastic. Further details were worked out at a meeting of school superintendents and principals. It was agreed that if the University would take care of psychology, logic and history, the remaining subjects could be handled by Jesuits, Christian Brothers and certain of the school principals who possessed the Ph.D. degree. Moreover, all expenses would be assumed locally.[68] Within the University, on the other hand, agreement on the establishment of the institute was

[66] ACUA, MMBT, November 20, 1901, p. 93.

[67] ACUA, Undated memorandum on the establishment of an institute of pedagogy.

[68] ACUA, Rector's report to the Executive Committee on the Institute of Pedagogy, undated.

lacking. When the matter was submitted to the approval of the senate, they thought that the lack of a department of pedagogy in the institution itself, the scarcity of professors, and the inability adequately to control the institute, were obstacles too insuperable to anticipate success. As a result they voted that "the University is not prepared to take charge of an Institute of Pedagogy in New York City." [69] Their decision, because of the determination of John Lancaster Spalding and others interested in the project, was overridden by the April meeting of the Board of Trustees:

The proposed action of Rev. Dr. McMahon with regard to the School of Pedagogy, or rather a course of Lectures for the teachers of New York City, was endorsed heartily and considered a very efficient way to bring the work of the Catholic University and of its financial needs to the notice of the public.[70]

In April the foundation was laid and McMahon was able to write the rector:

Dr. Pace is to be the man prominently before the public in connection with this new work, and I should like to have some official announcement made so as to obviate any unpleasantness or misunderstanding. I have received a very nice letter from Dr. Shahan, who is quite sympathetic with the work. I regret to learn that Dr. Shanahan has been talking quite freely in an adverse sense up in New England, but I am sure it arises from some misconception. The success of the work is the only thing I can see that will arouse any enthusiasm for the University here in New York. . . . It is imperative also that official announcement be made in the press to the effect that the department is to be inaugurated in the Fall, as our friends of the Summer School here are industriously exploiting the action of the Senate of the University, apparently being unaware of the reversal of the action by the Trustees. The Jesuits have renewed their offer as to the use of St. Francis Xavier's College for the school, so that that heavy item of expense is removed.[71]

On May 13th the rector was able to report to the senate that authorization to proceed with the institute had been received, and that the super-

---

[69] ACUA, Report of the Senate, March 12, 1902. A further reason for refusing was offered by Charles Grannan in one of his letters to Denis O'Connell, when he mentioned that McMahon was not well liked by many in the senate and the fear of conflict with the Catholic Summer School, under the direction of another New York priest, Michael Lavelle. RDA, unsigned and undated.

[70] ACUA, MMBT, April 9, 1902, p. 97.

[71] ACUA, Jos. H. McMahon to Thomas J. Conaty, New York, April 24, 1902.

vision of the work would be in his hands.[72] By October the work had begun and the first report was encouraging:

The Institute of Pedagogy, in New York, established by the Board of Trustees, began its work on the first of October. According to the instructions received by the Committee of the Board, the Rector made arrangements for the corps of teachers necessary to comply with the law. Rev. Dr. Pace was appointed Dean and given charge of the work. . . . Dr. Pace and Dr. Shanahan from the University are assisted by the others who form the corps of instructors. By the last report 118 teachers had registered in the Institute. The new Archbishop of New York is thoroughly in sympathy with the work.[73]

At the insistence of Pace,[74] Conaty used the work in New York to request again the consideration of the establishment of a department of pedagogy in the University.[75] The trustees were not to be hurried, and their discussion was written down in the minutes as follows:

The Pedagogical work of the School of New York was now thoroughly discussed. The danger of scattered activity, of absence of Professors from the University was pointed out; the enlarged action of the Faculties, University extension, the fact that the work of the University was better known and was more thoroughly appreciated by the country at large, were dilated upon. On the whole, the sentiment of the Board seemed to favor progress on the lines of outside pedagogical work.[76]

Although Thomas Conaty and his staff had endeavored to have a department of pedagogy established in the University without avail, they were successful in giving the impetus to two important phases of the University's academic life. They had shown the practicality of University extension work and they had laid the foundation for the department of education in the University.

The attention of the rector was not taken up entirely outside the University, for he was aware of the developments that were going on in the neighborhood of the institution. As he was interested in the affiliation of more remote colleges and seminaries, so was he likewise interested in those institutes which had sprung up on and

---

[72] ACUA, RRTTS, May 13, 1902.

[73] ACUA, RRTTS, October 9, 1902.

[74] ACUA, Edw. A. Pace to Thomas J. Conaty, [n. p.] November 8, 1902.

[75] *Twelfth Annual Report of the Rector . . . 1901* (Washington, 1901), p. 11.

[76] ACUA, MMBT, November 12, 1902, p. 100.

around the University grounds. Under the rectorship of Bishop Keane there had been drawn up terms of agreement for these institutions which invited the religious orders and congregations to establish houses of study in connection with the University.[77] Each religious house was free to give whatever superior courses were required by their constitutions, but to avoid rivalry, these courses were to be for their own students only, no one else being admitted without the express permission of the University senate. For the relations in scholastic matters between the houses and the University and between the houses themselves, the supervisory authority of the Board of Trustees was to be recognized.[78] The first to establish such a house were the Paulists, and during Conaty's administration they made two additions to their St. Thomas College.[79] The Paulists were to be responsible for another development of the University, the Apostolic Mission House, which would have as its purpose the preparing of secular priests for the home and colonial missions.[80] By May, 1902, the work had progressed enough for Walter Elliott, C.S.P., to write to the rector:

Our project for the new Mission House is now pretty well ready for making the collections, and I have already several thousands of dollars promised. I write to you to know the prospects of our locating at the University.

The institution is to be owned by the Catholic Missionary Union, a corperation [sic] as you know, made up of the Archps of N. York, & Philadelphia, two secular priests (now Father Taylor & Dr. Dyer) and our Superior General, Father Doyle & myself. That corperation [sic] will also have immediate charge, raising the funds to build & support the institution, appointing the Rector & his assistant. But all this will be under the supervision of the Archbishops of this country, or of the University board.[81]

For the first year, since the proposed building was not ready, the Apostolic Mission College was located on the upper floor of Keane

[77] Cf. Ahern, op. cit., 87-88.

[78] ACUA, Terms of Agreement between the Catholic University of America and Religious Bodies establishing Houses of Study in connection therewith. Undated, but around 1892.

[79] 1897 and 1898.

[80] "Conferences," "The Proposed Seminary for the Home and Colonial Missions," AER, XXVI (January, 1902), 75-78.

[81] ACUA, Walter Elliott to Thomas J. Conaty, Chattanooga, May 10, 1902.

Hall.[82] On November 13, before a large group of the hierarchy who had assembled for the archbishops' annual meeting, the ground was broken by Cardinal Gibbons,[83] who was also on hand to lay the cornerstone on April 23, 1903. The Mission House, as projected, was to cost $50,000 and to occupy a plot of ground 200 feet square near the eastern gate of the campus.[84]

An earlier foundation than the Mission House and, perhaps, the most famous of the University group, was the Franciscan Holy Land College, popularly known as the Monastery. In November, 1897, Father Godfrey Schilling, O.F.M., wrote to Cardinal Gibbons for permission to erect a house of studies for the Franciscans. He gave as its purpose: "The College therefore will serve as a study house for the various Franciscan provinces of the United States, where their graduates can have the benefit of a postgraduate course at the Catholic University." [85] Permission was granted to Schilling, but he did not want publicity at that early date. He wrote to the rector: "Kindly withhold any statements regarding the college, especially in its connection with the Holy Land—at least for the present—as they would only result in causing me great inconvenience." [86] The solemn dedication of the college and chapel of the Franciscans took place on September 17, 1899. The ceremony of dedication was performed by Cardinal Gibbons and the Mass offered by the Apostolic Delegate, Sebastian Martinelli. "The College of the Commissariat of the Holy Land" was the official title of the institution; however, it was also known as "Mount Saint Sepulchre." [87] Although the foundation seemed to prosper from the start, it was not without the difficulties that so often attend an enduring work. By November, 1901, Godfrey Schilling was on his way to Rome, at the command of his superiors. The secretary of the apostolic delegation, Frederick Zadock Rooker, gave one version of the story when he tried to pave the way for

[82] ACUA, Thomas J. Conaty to Walter Elliott, Washington, September 29, 1902.

[83] "University Chronicle," *CUB,* IX (January, 1903), 172.

[84] "University Chronicle," *CUB,* IX (July, 1903), 444. The original Mission House is at present the Administration building.

[85] BCA, 95-V-5, Godfrey Schilling to J. Card. Gibbons, New York, November 12, 1897.

[86] ACUA, Godfrey Schilling to Thomas J. Conaty, New York, December 6, 1897.

[87] "Dedication of the Franciscan College," *CUB,* V (October, 1899), 515. Cf. *Ninth Annual Report of the Rector . . . 1898* (Washington, 1898), pp. 7-8.

Schilling in Rome through the good offices of Monsignor Denis O'Connell:

I want you to do me a favor. Father Godfrey Schilling, the Franciscan who has been for some years the Commissary for the Holy Land here and who has built the monumental church and monastery out by the Cath. University, has, through the machinations of envious brethren in his order been relieved of his charge and called to Rome by his general. Some friend has suggested that by a little manifestation he might obtain a place in St. John Lateran as one of the penetenzieri of confessors there and such an appointment would be very satisfactory to him. . . . Schilling is a very decent fellow and has always been very kind to me and I should like very much to see him get what he wants. . . . Schilling is a very talented man, speaking six or seven languages well, and is a very square, honest fellow.[88]

The matter was not settled by the removal of Schilling, and in the uncertainty over the matter the vicar-general of the Franciscans presented a strong request for a settlement to the cardinal chancellor of the University:

The Definitorium General of the Order here in Rome had often discussed the position of the Washington College & Commissariate of the Holy Land. Nothing very definite was known about it. There were scarcely any documents. In point of fact, the whole thing seems to have been settled during a period of transition in the year 1897 when the General for the time being had already resigned, (Father Luigi la Parma, now Archbishop) & before the appointment by brief of his successor, Father Luigi Lauer, who died last August. By degrees it began to come out that Fr. Godfrey Schilling had built a very large college, instead of a place to house only some *ten* or *twelve* students. . . . Notwithstanding the warnings of the late General, Fr. Godfrey doggedly stuck to his idea. The climax came last September, the Definitorium General thought it well to remove him from the position & from the country & to appoint another to take his place. . . .

Very well: I discovered some time since that he himself, *without any reference to the authorities of the Order,* had entered into a kind of contract or agreement with Your Eminence, that the College at Washington should be annexed to the University with the obligation of sending *all* the students to the University!

This I am sorry to say I cannot accept, as it is in direct contradiction to our Constitutions. I am quite willing to make [the] Washington monastery a House of Study having its own Professors & sending *some* students to the University for special subjects, as we do in Louvain & elsewhere, but I cannot go further. If this does not suit, I am quite

---

[88] RDA, F. Z. Rooker to D. J. O'Connell, Washington, November 8, 1901.

willing to sell the Monastery & Church, with the permission of the H. See, & to withdraw all the Religious who are there.[89]

The reply of the Archbishop of Baltimore, equally as strong and equally as judicious, served to clear up the misunderstandings that had arisen:

As Ordinary of the Archdiocese of Baltimore I had been asked for permission to establish the College, & I granted it. The letter of the Secretary of Propaganda, certified to the permission granted by the Holy See for such an establishment, was placed in my hands. I send you a copy of this letter.

Into the merit of the question arising between Father Schilling & any other authority in the Order, it is not proper for me to enter.

The University in making arrangements of an academic character with Institutions or Houses of Study in its neighborhood, has always respected the autonomy, and, where it was necessary, has so modified those arrangements as to keep intact the obligations imposed upon any Religious Community by its Constitutions.

While the University does not insist on having the students from such Houses of Study to attend its courses, it is always willing & prepared to give instructions & assistance to such students as may, with the permission of their Superiors, apply for admission & be fitted to take up its work.[90]

The reply of the vicar-general of the Franciscans showed that the matter had now been clarified by the presentation of the full facts in the matter:

Owing to the absence of certain documents, when I entered into office here, I could not ascertain how matters stood. . . . The only way out of the many difficulties, created in all good faith by Fr. Godfrey, was his removal from the States, & his transfer to the Holy Land.

I have now arranged to have the course of Theology transferred to Washington, & in due time some of the best students of the various American Provinces will be sent thither to attend the University. The Rules regulating the relations between the University & the surrounding Religious establishments are all that can be desired & entirely different from what a communication, made by Fr. Godfrey to the late General, led me to believe. I fully and frankly accept the situation now so clearly stated.[91]

The monastery has continued as a monument to the Franciscans, a show-place in the nation's capital, with a life-size statue of the

[89] BCA, 99-N-1, David Fleming to J. Card. Gibbons, Rome, March 21, 1902.

[90] BCA, 99-P-7, J. Card. Gibbons to David Fleming, Baltimore, April 15, 1902, copy.

[91] BCA, 99-R-1, David Fleming to J. Card. Gibbons, Rome, May 3, 1902.

founder placed in the church in the site where he spent so many hours after his return to the work of his heart, Mount Saint Sepulchre.

There was also a period of uncertainty for another of the foundations at the University, Holy Cross College. From Rome in 1898 Archbishop Keane wrote to Baltimore's cardinal to inform him:

When Father Zahm was leaving Rome he begged of me that a strong pressure should be brought to bear, by Your Eminence, and a few of the Archbishops, upon the Father General of the Holy Cross and upon himself as Provincial, to prevent the removal of the College of the Holy Cross from connection with the Catholic University. Father Corby declared, not long before his death, that he intended to accomplish this in their next Chapter. Father Zahm is determined to hinder this, but can only be sure of doing so through the cooperation of the Bishops, which he asks.

I beg Your Eminence to write a letter to the Father General, and another to Father Zahm, the newly-appointed Provincial, both of whom are now at Notre Dame, Indiana:—offering congratulations upon the appointment of Dr. Zahm, and impressing upon both of them that the removal of the Holy Cross College from the University would at any time—and especially in view of the recent trials of the University—be an injurious act which the Hierarchy could not regard as friendly; that it would moreover be prejudicial to the Congregation of the Holy Cross itself; and that it would not be in accordance with the recently expressed views of the Holy See. . . .

Dr. Zahm is a devoted friend of the University, and so is the Father General, but there are many in the Chapter who are not enlightened enough to have such views, and who nevertheless have votes; — hence the importance of the letter now requested.[92]

The cardinal followed the request made by Keane, for which he received the thanks of Dr. Zahm.[93] Not only was Zahm successful in having the house of studies retained at the University, but he further was able to develop the institute and to build a new Holy Cross. The cornerstone of the new building was laid on March 19, 1899, by the Bishop of Sioux Falls, Thomas O'Gorman, professor-emeritus of church history at the University, who could truthfully say in his address that day: "The days of doubt and hesitation are over; the future

[92] BCA, 96-A-10, John J. Keane to J. Card. Gibbons, Rome, January 24, 1898. John A. Zahm was a close friend of Keane and O'Connell in Rome before becoming the Provincial of the Holy Cross Fathers in the United States.

[93] BCA, 96-C-3, J. A. Zahm to J. Card. Gibbons, Notre Dame, February 18, 1898.

is secure; we hail the blessing of the cornerstone of this building as the augury of a second decade more successful, even if less stormy, than the first decade of the University." [94] The formal dedication came on October 13, with a stirring speech by the Bishop of Peoria on "The University: the Nursery of the Higher Life," before a large gathering of the hierarchy then present in Washington for the meeting of the archbishops.[95]

The Marists also were among the early religious communities at the University. They, too, began their new house of studies under the rectorship of Thomas J. Conaty. The work progressed slowly, for although the beginnings were made in August, 1899,[96] the cornerstone was not blessed until November 1, 1902.[97] The Benedictines were represented in the University in 1899 by Father Placidus Fuerst, O.S.B., through the permission of his superior, Adelheim Odermatt of Mount Angel, Oregon, to whom Conaty wrote, "I am very glad that you make the great effort to send your young professors to be trained at the University." [98] A further variation came to the University by the enrollment of Cuban priest-students, through the action of the Bishop of Havana, Donatus Sbarretti, who had been friendly with the men of the University during the time he served in Washington as auditor of the Apostolic Delegation before his appointment to Havana.[99] The Sulpicians joined the little group around the University in 1901, by taking over the house formerly occupied by the Holy Cross Fathers. The new preparatory college of the Fathers of St. Sulpice was named St. Austin's and was placed under the direction of Very Reverend James F. Driscoll, S.S., and Reverend Francis E. Gigot, S.S.[100]

Negotiations for the final house of studies of a religious congregation founded at the University during Conaty's rectorship were initiated in January, 1902, with the visit of the Dominican provincial

[94] "The New Holy Cross College," *CUB*, V (April, 1899), 287-288.

[95] "Dedication of Holy Cross College," *CUB*, V (October, 1899), 518.

[96] "University Chronicle," *CUB*, V (October, 1899), 524-525.

[97] "University Chronicle," *CUB*, IX (January, 1903), 171-172.

[98] ACUA, Thomas J. Conaty to A. Odermatt, O.S.B., Washington, April 30, 1900, copy and *ibid.*, October 18, 1899, copy.

[99] BCA, 98-D-5, Donatus Sbarretti to J. Card. Gibbons, Havana, April 10, 1900; BCA, 98-D-9, Donatus Sbarretti to J. Card. Gibbons, Havana, April 19, 1900; ACUA, Thomas J. Conaty to Donatus Sbarretti, Washington, May 1, 1900, copy.

[100] ACUA, RRTTS, October 8, 1901.

to the rector. Although the Dominicans had intended to build near the University before, in 1892,[101] the matter of affiliation with the University had prevented such a move. From the beginning of the negotiation in 1902 it seemed as though that point could be adjusted safely, for in the statement prepared by the provincial the matter was explicitly brought out in a manner favorable both to the University and to the constitutions of the Dominicans:

IV. We do not seek affiliation with the University. We respect it and entertain the most friendly feeling toward it. We pay our homage to it by asking His Eminence to permit us to place our House of Studies beside it. We would, however, be entirely independent of it, not only in the administration of our House, but in everything connected with the course of studies to be pursued in that House by our students. To be more precise, we would ask, in all matters except one, specified below (V), the same complete independence of the University which we would enjoy if located in another diocese one hundred miles distant from that institution. This independence we would ask, not because we underestimate the University or consider ourselves in any way superior to its personnel, but because we are obliged to do so by our Constitutions, which have been repeatedly sanctioned by the Holy See.
V. We would enter into no rivalry with the University. We would educate the students of our Order exclusively, and I hereby promise and agree that no student not of our Order shall be permitted to attend our scholastic exercises without the consent of the Senate of the University. And I give full assurance that this agreement will be considered binding by my successors in the office of Provincial. Our own laws forbid outside students to *reside* in our convents.
VI. Our students attending the University courses would be obliged to comply with the requirements of that institution in the matter of obtaining degrees.[102]

When reporting these negotiations to the senate, Conaty showed that the matter could be agreeably handled and he stated: "From this it will appear that all the interests of the University have been safeguarded." [103] Matters proceeded peacefully enough until it came to the publication of the establishment of the new Dominican house. Lawrence F. Kearney, the Dominican provincial, submitted a news release to the rector, who changed the wording slightly and sent the

[101] Cf. Ahern, *op. cit.,* 84-88.
[102] ACUA, L. F. Kearney, O. P. to Thomas J. Conaty, Washington, January 27, 1902.
[103] ACUA, RRTTS, February 11, 1902.

new version back to Kearney with the explanation: "I thought that perhaps it is just as well not to emphasize the non-aggregate or non-affiliation with the University. That is a matter between the University and the Dominicans, and if brought too much to notice, might lead to enquiry or comparison with others." [104] The Conaty revision, however, touched off a forthright statement from the provincial:

I deeply regret that we are at variance on what I consider a most important point regarding the announcement to be made to the public. The conditions laid down by Bishop Keane when rector of the University caused us ten years ago to abandon a cherished design. That design had been made known to the public. Ten thousand times since then we have given to Bishops and priests of the country the reason why we gave up the project of transferring our House of Studies to Washington. More than once we have been upon the very point of publishing a statement on the entire transaction in the press. . . .
Now the statement which you submit would make it appear that we are coming to Washington on precisely the same terms which have been accepted by the religious congregations already established there—terms which we are known to have rejected ten years ago. I should regret very much that by carrying out the views of my council and my own views I should give offence to you or to any connected with the University. It seems to me that our confidence in the University is sufficiently manifested by our efforts to locate our house of studies near it. . . .
I must therefore decline to publish the statement which you kindly sent me this afternoon. And if His Eminence, the Cardinal, should require of us that we make such a public announcement, I would take steps at once to locate our House of Studies in another diocese. I would not "emphasize" the non-affiliation with the University, but would ask the right to declare it in simple terms. Could I assert it with less emphasis than it is asserted in the paper which I sent you today, I would gladly do so.[105]

Conaty was quick to realize his mistake in deleting the cherished phrases. He readily gave his approval to the Dominicans to publish their own statement on the opening of the house of studies. He wrote to Kearney:

I need not assure you that the feeling that "All is well that ends well" gave me great satisfaction in this particular action. I am sure that the relations between us will continue pleasant, and that if ever there should

---

[104] ACUA, Thomas J. Conaty to L. F. Kearney, O. P., Washington, February 13, 1902, copy.

[105] ACUA, L. F. Kearney to Thomas J. Conaty, Washington, February 13, 1902.

come a difference of opinion, we will both be frank enough to discuss the matter as friends, in the true interests of your great Order and of our noble University.[106]

By the time of the trustees' meeting in November, everything seemed well settled for they noted in their minutes: "The Provincial of the Dominicans in the U.S. has notified the Rector, that his Order intends putting up next spring a building for 12 Fathers and 75 Novices, to be their Mother House of this Country." [107]   On April 23, 1903, the ground was broken by Cardinal Gibbons for the projected quadrangle on Bunker Hill Road, opposite the University, on the day that the Bishop-elect of Monterey-Los Angeles was resigning from the rectorship of the University.

There was one other educational institution that played an interesting part in the University life during the years of Conaty's rectorship, and in its foundation he was very instrumental. This was Trinity College. Sister M. Euphrasia of the Sisters of Notre Dame de Namur, stationed in Washington, was surprised one March day in 1897 to receive a call from the vice-rector of the University. When he departed, she wrote to the Cardinal Archbishop of Baltimore:

This afternoon good Doctor Garrigan called to tell me that quite unexpectedly he had seen you, and, in conjunction with the Very Rev. Rector of the University, had talked over the project of our founding a school near them. He told me that you desired me to send you a statement as to what we desired to do, the probable scope of our classes, in fact, our intentions, upon receipt of which you would lay the matter before your council. Now, Your Eminence, of course this requires thought, consideration and consultation, which, in turn, necessitates *time;* therefore, I beg you to have patience with me if I seem to delay longer than you would expect, as I will do all in my power to expedite the matter, as well as to insure its ultimate success.[108]

Following a trip to New England to confer with the superior, Sister Julia, she was able to speak more definitely.[109] She informed Gibbons,

[106] ACUA, Thomas J. Conaty to L. F. Kearney, O.P., Washington, February 27, 1902, copy.

[107] ACUA, MMBBT, November 12, 1902, p. 100.

[108] BCA, 95-K-8, Sr. M. Euphrasia to J. Card. Gibbons, Washington, March 15, 1897.

[109] BCA, 95-L-4, Sr. M. Euphrasia to J. Card. Gibbons, Washington, March 22, 1897.

"I have just seen the Very Reverend Rector of the University, and also our good Dr. Garrigan, acquainted them with our plans etc. They will now be quite prepared to speak in our name at the Council on Monday." [110] The Baltimore archdiocesan consultors met on April 5 and took a favorable view of the project. The archbishop was able to send the required approval, as well as his own opinion: "As for myself, I am persuaded that such an institution, working in union with, though entirely independent of, the Catholic University will do incalculable good in the cause of higher education, and I am happy to give the project my hearty approval." [111] At a later date, when the purpose of Trinity College had become more specific he gave a further commendation:

I am pleased to know that the institution which you propose to establish, is intended *exclusively* for Post-Graduate work, and, therefore, will not come in conflict with the existing academies for Catholic young ladies, but will be to them what the University is to our Catholic Colleges. . . .

Such an institution under your able and experienced direction, and in the shadow of our great University, will, I am convinced, offer educational advantages to our young women, which cannot be found elsewhere in our country. It will relieve the University authorities from the embarrassment of refusing women admission, many of whom have already applied for the privilege of following our courses, and will be a light and a protection in faith and morals to that class of students, while pursuing the highest branches of knowledge.[112]

Trinity College was not without opposition in its beginning, as the pages of the Baltimore *Sun* for August 30, 1897, show:

The project to establish in Washington an institution to be known as Trinity College, for the higher education of women, under the auspices of the Sisters of Notre Dame, has aroused the opposition of German Catholic papers. It has also been reported that Monsignor Schroeder, professor of dogmatic theology in the Catholic University, has been the leader of the opposition. Inquiry among the friends of Monsignor Schroeder shows nothing to connect him with the opposition, and it is not believed by them that he has any intention of antagonizing it. On the other hand, it is pointed out by those who believe Monsignor is at the head of the op-

---

[110] BCA, 95-M-2, Sr. M. Euphrasia to J. Card. Gibbons, Washington, April 3, 1897.

[111] Sr. M. P., "Trinity College," "Miscellany," *CHR,* XI (January, 1926), 662.

[112] BCA, 95-Q-6, J. Card. Gibbons to Sr. Julia, Baltimore, June 21, 1897, copy.

PHILIP J. GARRIGAN

position that the antagonism to the scheme is manifested principally in German Catholic papers, to which Monsignor Schroeder is a contributor, and which usually reflect his views. . . .

Trinity College is not and was never intended to be a branch of the Catholic University, although its mission is to offer to women what the university offers to men.[113]

More than American eyes were viewing the projected establishment with doubt. Among them were those of the former Apostolic Delegate to the United States, Francesco Cardinal Satolli, as he made known to Gibbons:

I have learned also of the project of a University for the weaker sex (*per il debele sesso*) (as we are accustomed to say in Italian); this affair, as mentioned in the newspapers, has made a disagreeable impression here, particularly so because it was described that it would be a dangerous addition and amalgamation of Institutions, for the teaching of students of both sexes. . . . Still, well aware of your wisdom and that of the other interested parties, I am assured that after considerable and mature thought in this matter all will be guided as prudence and the exigencies may dictate.[114]

Although Satolli said that he was willing to leave the matter to the discretion of the interested parties, the then Apostolic Delegate, Archbishop Martinelli, had some suggestions to make:

The ground purchased lies, as I am told, so close to the present Catholic University, that to avoid all adverse commentary in the future, this particular site ought also to have the approbation of the Holy See before any building would be erected thereon.

I make these suggestions because some news of this matter has already reached the ears of the Holy Father from sources unknown to me, and it seems not to have met with his entire approbation.[115]

Gibbons gave a speedy reply to these criticisms. To Martinelli he responded:

Trinity College will have no official or organic connection whatever with the Catholic University. The teachers will be supplied by the Community of Notre Dame; probably from time to time the Sisters might

---

113 Baltimore *Sun,* August 30, 1897.

114 BCA, 95-S-4, F. Card. Satolli to J. Card. Gibbons, Rome, August 15, 1897, which is the original in Italian from which this translation was made.

115 BCA, 95-S-6, Sebastian Martinelli to J. Card. Gibbons, Atlantic City, August 23, 1897.

invite Professors of the University and of Georgetown College to give lectures to the young ladies on some particular branch.

With regard to the site chosen by the Sisters for their College, I made no suggestion to them, nor did I know the place they had chosen till the selection had been made. On inquiry I now learn that the College is about one third of a mile from the University. As your Excellency is aware, Geot. [sic] College & the Visitation Convent are much nearer each other than will be the proposed institution to the University—yet no inconvenience has resulted though they have been in existence there for a hundred years.[116]

In a more indignant tone he informed Satolli: "I am happy to inform Y. E. that the reports which have reached Rome with regard to a new female school of higher studies are utterly false or greatly exaggerated, and are the offspring of ignorance and malice." [117] By November Rome gave its approval to the plans for establishing Trinity: "His Holiness, after having considered the matter well, thinks that there should be nothing more said concerning the difficulties in the way of the project of the erection of an Institute for females in the vicinity of the Catholic University." [118] In an article that was generally inaccurate, the New York *Tribune* told the story of Trinity College, but it was only useful in supplying one phase of the tale with any truthfulness and that dealt with the non-acceptance of women at the University:

Ever since the Papal University of America was founded, applications from women students who held college degrees, but wished to go still higher, have poured in without ceasing, but were constantly refused solely because of their sex. The young women were much aggrieved at this, particularly when it became known that contrary to the inflexible rules of all schools south of Mason's and Dixon's line, the Catholic University intended to admit negroes. At the inauguration of the philosophy department the chancellor, Cardinal Gibbons, announced this policy by saying that intellect had no color, and that black, white, red and yellow

---

116 BCA, 95-S-7, J. Card. Gibbons to Sebastian Martinelli, Baltimore, August 25, 1897, copy.

117 BCA, 95-S-9, J. Card. Gibbons to F. Card. Satolli, Baltimore, September 5, 1897, copy.

118 BCA, 95-V-7, Translation of letter No. 40670 from His Eminence, Card. Rampolla, received at Apostolic Delegation and registered November 27, 1897, No. 5425-5416. Conaty's advice to the sisters at this time was, "Do not exult too loud, but proceed joyfully in secret, grateful that the difficulty has been overcome." Sr. M.P. *op. cit.,* p. 664.

men would be welcome had they the brains to follow the courses.[119] One progressive young woman wrote to the Cardinal and asked if intellect had a sex. But the Baltimore prelate refused to see the matter in this light, and women were debarred.[120]

At a later date the *Intermountain Catholic* had its prophecy for the proposed college:

If the Catholic University opens its doors to the students of Trinity College and they are given equal opportunities with the students of the former, then little fear need be entertained for the success of the latter. But if this new institution is to be a sort of left-handed appendage to the Catholic University, nominally in connection with it, but really not fully enjoying its privileges, it seems to us fatuous to hope that Trinity College can draw to it Catholic young women who are now at such places as Chicago, Ann Arbor, Cornell, etc., where they know they enjoy opportunities not inferior to their non-Catholic sisters. . . . The day is gone when you can deprive our brainy, ambitious young women from the highest and the best in education. She insists in having all the advantages of her brother, and she is right. The world "do move." [121]

The premature release of the news of Trinity's foundation was a blow to the plans of Sister Julia, who had not wanted any advance publicity until substantial funds had been collected. It almost put an end to the project in its inception. With the adroit encouragement of Sister Euphrasia, together with the support she received from the University's rector and chancellor, the work was continued.[122] On December 8, 1900, the cornerstone of the college was laid by Dr.

[119] Cf. Boston *Pilot,* December 12, 1896: "In the afternoon the degree of Bachelor of Social Science will be conferred on Mr. William T. S. Jackson. This is the first instance in which a degree in Social Science has been conferred; and, strange as it may seem, it will be conferred on one of our colored students, who is a professor on half time in the Colored High School of Washington, formerly a student for many years of Amherst College, and who made a very brilliant examination for this degree, which is given in course, by the University."

[120] New York *Tribune,* June 6, 1898.

[121] *Intermountain Catholic* (Salt Lake City), December 2, 1899.

[122] ACUA, Sr. M. Euphrasia to Thomas J. Conaty, Washington, November 9, 1898. In this very long and rather hurried letter, the good sister supplies countless arguments to Conaty to use on the sister superior. Cf. BCA, 95-S-8, Sr. Julia to J. Card. Gibbons, [n.p.], September 2, 1897: "You will find Sister M. Euphrasia most deeply interested in all that regards our great work. She will be rather inclined to be too ardent, and will require some restraint instead of a spur." Evidently Sister Euphrasia believed that a spur could be used on Sister Julia to better purpose than a restraining hand.

Philip Garrigan.[123] Almost a year later, the solemn dedication took place on November 22, 1901, before a group of distinguished leaders, both religious and secular, as well as the twenty-three deeply impressed students.[124] The Rector of the University preached at the ceremonies, during which he eloquently set forth the place of women in Catholic education, saying in part:

In an age when intellectualism is being unjustly and rudely divorced from the supernatural, when religion is asserted to be a vague, indeterminate, unessential quality in advanced knowledge, it is important that Christian schools of higher study should open their doors to the training of women along the lines of intellectual development, side by side with the piety and simplicity of intelligent Christian faith. . . .

It is, indeed, refreshing to see Trinity College for women arise side by side with our great University in the very Capital of the Nation, to assert before the whole world that true education, true learning, true development is that which leads to a better knowledge of God, and that Christian womanliness and Christian scholarship may go hand in hand to make the cultured Christian woman the glory of the Church and the salvation of the State. . . .

To Trinity the University gives greetings as to a younger sister. It bids her enter upon the work, trusting in God for the blessing that will bring success. *Vivat, floreat, crescat.*" [125]

---

[123] "University Chronicle," *CUB,* VI (January, 1900), 132.

[124] "Solemn Opening of Trinity College," *CUB,* VII (January, 1901), 120-123.

[125] *Ibid.,* nor did the University ignore Trinity in its early days. The vice rector served as chaplain until his appointment to Sioux City, Iowa, while the first class taught in the new college was one in church history by Thomas Shahan of the University faculty. Cf. Sr. M. P., *op. cit.,* p. 674.

Chapter IV

PERSONALITIES

The mere recounting of events will often afford good chronology. The true significance of those events can be understood only when they are portrayed against the background of the personalities who participated in them. The events will demonstrate the greatness, or the pettiness, of the characters that produced them. The remaining chapters endeavor to paint the background of conflicting personalities that makes the accomplishments of the second rector, mediocre as they might appear to some, stand out in their proper light. The slightest advancement that is made in an atmosphere of contentions seems remarkable, and of contentions there seemed to be no end during the entire rectorship of Thomas J. Conaty. An excellent sample of the University life at the outset of Conaty's term was given in a letter of one of the clerical students to his superior on the occasion of the patronal feast of the Paulist Fathers:

At the High Mass yesterday — Dr. Conaty celebrant — Fr. Aiken preached. You remember him doubtless as here in '92 and now preparing for the Chair of Apologetics. He spoke on the boldness & fairness & progressive character of S. Paul, commended this as a model for the University, & spoke a bit of the need of welcoming advances in science, & being careful of scientific men as well as of less harried children. Conservatism, Liberalism, Progress, Antiquated Notions, were mentioned somewhat freely in the sermon. Drs. Grannan & Bouq. beamed with pleasure, the former especially, exhibiting his smiles of approval. Mgr. McMahon wriggled uncomfortably & curled up in scorn—his critique as given out afterwards was that the sermon should be made into a bonfire, & I am not sure he would not have placed the preacher in a like position.[1]

---

[1] PFA, Joseph McSorley, C.S.P., to Augustine F. Hewit, C.S.P., Washington, January 26, 1897. The Reverend Charles F. Aiken later became the professor of apologetics. Charles P. Grannan was professor of sacred scripture, Thomas Bouquillon of moral theology, and both of them were favorable towards the liberal school of thought of the day. Monsignor James McMahon was the benefactor whose generosity had been responsible for the building that bears his name; he spent the later years of his life at the University. The conflicts in the University were but a shadow of the general world conditions but, perhaps, were made more acute there through the dismissal of Bishop Keane.

It was while surrounded by such ever shifting and opposing groups that the former Worcester pastor would spend his years at the University. They were not to be without their reward, neither were they to be without their suffering.

The first reward after his inauguration was not to be long delayed; in fact it had been suggested together with the brief appointing Conaty to the rectorship.[2] The suggestion from Cardinal Gibbons as to what form this honor would take was sent by the Baltimore prelate to the Cardinal Secretary of the Propaganda in April, 1897:

When Your Eminence made known to me that Our Holy Father the Pope had appointed Dr. Conaty Rector of our Catholic University, Your Eminence also expressed the desire to know what I thought of Our Holy Father's intention of bestowing upon the new rector the dignity of the episcopacy. . . .

I wanted to see for myself what would be the attitude of the new Rector, the impression he would make on the University and upon outsiders, the skill and the prudence he would show in the performance of his duties which, in the circumstances, were quite delicate and difficult.

I am happy to announce to Your Eminence that everything happened as I wished. Dr. Conaty has lived up to the expectations of the American episcopate and of the Holy See. He has not yet accomplished much outside work because he wanted to become perfectly acquainted with the interior state of affairs, and take an exact account of all that needs to be done for the proper management of the University. In that, he has acted prudently and I am happy to add that he is a director worthy of his task.

I also wanted to take the advice of my colleagues, of the Board of the University, and having done so immediately with some of them, since the meeting would not take place until October, I found that they all felt as I did.

Therefore, it is with the utmost confidence that through the intervention of Your Eminence, I ask His Holiness to please elevate Dr. Conaty to the dignity of bishop and grant him a titular bishopric.

For the position of the University and for the Catholic Church in the United States it would require that he be given no less a dignity.[3]

This suggestion of a mitre for Conaty seemed at first to meet the approval of Rome, for Rampolla informed Cardinal Gibbons:

I hastened to make known to the Holy Father your sentiments of esteem.

---

[2] Cf. note 73, Chapter I, 26.

[3] BCA, 95-M-1, J. Card. Gibbons to M. Card. Rampolla, Baltimore, April 1, 1897, copy. The original of this letter is in French from which this translation has been made.

His Holiness in expressing to me his pleasure, deigned at the same time to receive with good will your proposal in regard to Dr. Conaty, new Rector of the Catholic University. Now although His Holiness had not first thought of elevating him to the episcopal dignity, there is no difficulty in honoring him with this character and to insure at the same time the honor of the Institute and render more fruitful the labors of the same Rector.[4]

However, the dignity and honor of the episcopal office were not to come so quickly and easily to the new rector. After further consideration of the matter, and some consultation, a second letter was received from Cardinal Rampolla, bearing the information:

Now, however, owing to the opinion of some persons of authority, amongst whom is a Bishop, it has been made to appear that it would be too soon to elevate the Rev. Conaty to the episcopal dignity at the present time. Hence, the Holy Father, to keep his given promise has thought that this could be deferred for the time being, and thus prepare Dr. Conaty for the episcopal dignity by naming him His Domestic Prelate. His Holiness, holding in high esteem the Archbishop of Baltimore, wishes to know if the plan of the Holy Father is acceptable to the Archbishop of Baltimore and on his part will at an opportune time carry it out.[5]

It was some weeks before Conaty was informed of his new office, and then only in a very informal way. At a dinner given by Brother Justin, the president of Manhattan College, for the Apostolic Delegate, Sebastian Martinelli, a surprise announcement was made, as the New York *Tribune* recounted it:

The guests were at dessert when Dr. Conaty entered, accompanied by Brother Bernard. He was cordially welcomed, and Brother Bernard introduced him to the assembled guests, using the words, "Permit me to introduce Dr. Conaty." Archbishop Martinelli then revealed his little surprise. Rising at his seat, he raised his hand for silence, and said, with a smile: "Pardon me, but it is no longer Dr. Conaty. It is now Monsignor Conaty."

The announcement was a complete surprise, but the Archbishop then explained that he had the day before received word from Rome of the elevation of Dr. Conaty.[6]

---

[4] BCA, 95-M-9, M. Card. Rampolla to J. Card. Gibbons, Rome, April 15, 1897. The original letter is in Italian from which this translation has been made.

[5] BCA, 95-N-3, M. Card. Rampolla to J. Card. Gibbons, Rome, April 22, 1897. The original letter is in Italian from which this translation has been made.

[6] New York *Tribune*, June 30, 1897.

The ceremony of investiture took place on October 30, 1897, before a large gathering of the clergy[7] among whom was Archbishop Keane. The first rector of the University spoke most flatteringly of his successor:

When providential events made it necessary for the prelates of the Church to look for another rector they easily singled out from all the priests of the United States Dr. Conaty. He had three qualities that made him particularly desirable. He was a pastor of a most flourishing parish in a most flourishing diocese. He was a typical American priest . . . . he was a representative American worker for the modern elevation of American youth . . . he was a representative model educator. His success with the summer schools and his popular methods of education had demonstrated this fact.
Since he had gone to the University every word and every act proved that the prelates had made no mistake.[8]

It is fortunate that at least some honor should have come to strengthen Conaty, for within a short time he would need all the encouragement he could get to continue in his position. In November, 1897, the resentment that had been swelling up since the hasty removal of Keane found a release in the campaign to have Monsignor Joseph Schroeder dismissed from the University. Together with this, another incident was developing that reached its climax after the Schroeder case had received its widest publicity. The Reverend Daniel Quinn had been appointed professor of Greek in 1891, but before actually beginning work in the University, he had spent two years in further study in Europe. His department was never really in a flourishing condition, having in it at most three students a year. In 1897 he decided that the Department of Greek should be expanded, and he, therefore, offered two schedules for the school year of 1897-1898, one of which he could handle by himself. The alternative course would require two men, himself and his brother, John Quinn. When Father Quinn found that he was not destined to receive much support from the rector for obtaining an assistant, he did not press the point, although Conaty was able to formulate the opinion later, that:

It was very evident to me that he was bitter in criticism of the past Rector and of his Faculty, as also dissatisfied because the University did not

---

7 *The Church News* (Washington), October 23, 1897.
8 Boston *Pilot,* October 30, 1897.

broaden out the work of his department at an expense entirely out of proportion to all possible needs.[9]

On November 15, 1897, the professor of Greek offered his resignation to take effect at the end of the scholastic year, "unless the University desire to immediately fix an earlier date." [10] Conaty acknowledged the proffered resignation on November 24, promising that he would submit the matter to the proper authorities. The following morning the newspapers found another topic of interest and speculation to present to their readers. After recounting what had previously transpired, the Washington *Post* went on to say:

Dr. Quinn has declared his intention of going back to the University of Athens and resuming his work along the lines which he was pursuing before he joined the Catholic University corps. Three other professors, it is said on good authority, are now making plans for severing their connections. . . . . The trouble between Dr. Quinn and the University authorities is principally centered in his inability to conform himself to the methods now dominating the course of studies. The contentions over the Schroeder case, it is understood, simply hastened him in his determination to leave the institution.[11]

The New York *Journal*, ever on the alert for a bit of sensationalism, was more explicit although less accurate, when it reported:

University circles here today were surprised by the report that Dr. Daniel Quinn, the eminent Greek scholar, of the Catholic University, and the president of its Hellenic Academy, had resigned on account of friction with Dr. Edward Pace.

Owing to a long train of incidents and a constant friction, Dr. Quinn, on the 15, instant, notified Monsignor Conaty, the Rector, that he felt himself compelled to sever his relations with the Catholic University at the close of the present scholastic year, or immediately if it better suited the convenience of the administration. . . .

It is rumored that three other professors—Dr. Hyvernat, the eminent Orientalist; Dr. Greene, the great American botanist, and Charles Warren Stoddard, the essayist and teacher of English literature—will shortly follow

---

[9] NYAA, G-24, Thomas J. Conaty to M. A. Corrigan, Washington, December 4, 1897. This is an explanatory letter on a full report of the Quinn case submitted to Corrigan, a member of the executive committee, by the rector. Professor Quinn who was receiving a salary of $2,300, had asked for a salary of $700 for his brother; he had in his class for the school year 1897-1898 one student.

[10] NYAA, G-24, Daniel Quinn to Thomas J. Conaty, Washington, November 15, 1897, copy.

[11] Washington *Post*, November 25, 1897.

Dr. Quinn's example. Indeed, the report goes so far as to say that they are now considering how far their loyalty binds them to continue during this year.[12]

The three professors who were named as planning to resign, quickly denied the assertions made concerning them. Henri Hyvernat immediately informed the rector:

I attach very little (next to none) importance to newspaper talk and as a rule do not take the trouble to deny any false statement they make about me. If I wanted to take any such step as resigning from my office you would be the first to know it. Therefore not only may you deny that I have spoken to you of resigning, but you will oblige me greatly by doing so.[13]

Charles Warren Stoddard laconically denied the statement with two short sentences,[14] while Edward L. Greene more emphatically expressing his indignation, retorted, "No public rumor could seem to be more absolutely unfounded, or more entirely of the nature of a fiction, than that which says I am contemplating a withdrawal from the Catholic University." [15]

Because of this unfavorable publicity, "which could not have been known and given to the press except by Dr. Quinn himself," [16] Monsignor Conaty quickly formulated an opinion as to how the case should be handled. He explained to the Archbishop of New York:

This discourteous and unprofessional act on the part of Dr. Quinn, especially after the very kind treatment which he had received from the University, and particularly from Archbishop Keane, it seems to me demands that, he be taken at his word, and that the board fix an earlier date for his resignation than the last of September.[17]

---

[12] New York *Journal*, November 25, 1897, under a Washington dateline of November 24, 1897.

[13] NYAA, G-24, H. Hyvernat to Thomas J. Conaty, Washington, November 29, 1897, copy.

[14] NYAA, G-24, Chas. Warren Stoddard to Thomas J. Conaty, Washington, November 25, 1897, copy.

[15] NYAA, G-24, Edw. L. Greene to Thomas J. Conaty, Washington, November 27, 1897, copy.

[16] NYAA, G-24, Thomas J. Conaty to M. A. Corrigan, Washington, December 4, 1897.

[17] *Ibid*. Keane expressed his opinion of the Quinn case in a letter to Philip Garrigan, Rome, January 3, 1898 (ACUA, Garrigan Papers), by saying, "Once more thanks be to God for the happy solution of the Schroeder difficulty. The price you had to pay for the final riddance was cheap enough. In some measure one can not help saying the same thing with regard to poor Dr. Quinn."

To Dr. Quinn himself the rector made the notification in direct language:

Under all the circumstances I deem it for the interest of the University that it [the resignation] should take place as soon as possible, and hence I shall recommend to the Executive Committee to whom the matter is referred to fix the date as the first of February, 1898.

I intended to confer with you on this matter before announcing my conclusion, but as you decline all oral discussion I give you this formal notice in writing.[18]

Rather than wait for the University deadline, Quinn resigned earlier, and Conaty officially notified the academic senate of the fact on January 11, 1898, and at the same time announced that George M. Bolling had taken over Quinn's classes.[19] That the matter of Quinn's resignation was not a unique bit of newspaper gossip, but part of a general readiness to give publicity to any possible University scandal is shown by another published rumor of the same period:

Hon. Hannis Taylor was expected and advertised to give his second lecture in the public course on Thanksgiving afternoon, but was prevented from doing so by an acute bronchial trouble, which appeared on his late visit from New York. . . . Coincident with this, a rumor spread through the newspapers that the Spanish Government had, through its Minister, De Lome, [sic] sent in a strong request to the Apostolic Delegate to prevent, or use his influence to prevent, Mr. Taylor from lecturing in the Catholic University; and that the latter was to lecture on Cuba. Even your Boston Herald did its share in circulating this silly rumor. . . . Neither the Delegate nor the University has had any intimation of disapproval from the Spanish Embassy here, and I do not believe it would have any influence whatever on the parties concerned if such disapproval

---

18 NYAA, G-24, Thomas J. Conaty to Daniel Quinn, Washington, December 3, 1897, copy.

19 ACUA, RRTTS, January 11, 1898. Conaty had informed Corrigan when the news of Quinn's intended resignation became public: "I hope you pay no attention to newspaper stories about disaffection of Professors in the Faculty of Philosophy. It is a piece with much of the irresponsible newspaper work of today. Prof. Quinn has expressed his intention of resigning because his Dept. is not a success and he wants us to do more than we can afford or his needs will warrant. . . . The University is moving along happily and there are no contending Elements except as they are found in discontented minds of correspondents who want sensational items." NYAA, G-24, Thomas J. Conaty to M. A. Corrigan, Washington, November 30, 1897.

were made known. The plain facts in the case are: Mr. Taylor was to lecture on "Parliamentary Government as It Now Exists," not on Cuba.[20]

Conaty made up on the outside for the time he had to spend at the University during the first months of his rectorship. In January, 1898, he lectured on education at the Catholic Winter School in New Orleans. While there he enjoyed a flattering experience, as the *Catholic University Bulletin* recounted:

A very pleasant incident of his visit was the reception tendered to him by the Admiral of the French warship Le Dubourdieu and the commander of the Austrian schoolship Donau, which were in the harbor. All the courtesies of the navy were extended to him, and each ship gave him the naval salute of nine guns as he was leaving it.[21]

Again in June and July Conaty was on a lecturing tour, but this time it was much more extended, including Nazareth, Kentucky; Chicago, Dubuque, Milwaukee, Worcester and ending up in Philadelphia. It was while in Philadelphia that he gave the Fourth of July oration at the Temperance Fountain in Fairmont Park, at which Archbishop Patrick J. Ryan was also present.[22] One invitation, the acceptance of which by his predecessor had caused the lifting of several episcopal eyebrows, Conaty refused, and that was an invitation to preach at Harvard. Francis Peabody had written to Monsignor Conaty in June, 1898:

I take the liberty in behalf of this University of reminding you that a year ago, when I had the privilege of inviting you to preach in the chapel of the University, you intimated that at some later date you should feel inclined to accept such an invitation. Is it possible you may do us the kindness of preaching and conducting worship in our chapel during the

---

[20] Boston *Pilot,* December 4, 1897. Taylor had been the American Minister to Spain. Conaty's opinion of newspaper reports is revealed in a letter of a later date: "As far as the University is concerned, we send from the University to you, as to many of the Catholic papers, a letter twice a month, giving all the information that anyone can get about the University. I have done this to prevent gossip being sent as information, and distorted reports as happenings. . . . . You cannot be too careful in receiving reports from Washington, which are often created from street gossip, or the disposition of local reporters to fill out columns for the daily papers. . . . As to the University, we will furnish you with all its news." ACUA, Thomas J. Conaty to Jeremiah Dunlevy, Catholic Publishing Co., Washington, October 11, 1900, copy.

[21] "University Chronicle," *CUB,* IV (April, 1898), 289-290.

[22] "University Chronicle," *CUB,* IV (October, 1898), 528-529.

108

course of the next academic year? If it is not too remote for an engagement may I suggest Jan. 22 or Jan. 29, 1899? It will be a pleasure for us if you can see your way to accept this invitation.[23]

The rector of the University, wary of the imputations of liberalism and laxity that certainly would have come his way, found that he must refuse the invitation. Edward Hale expressed the disappointment of the interested parties at Harvard by informing Conaty: "I am very sorry that you find it not possible to preach in Appleton Chapel this year, and I know that Professor Peabody will share in my regret and disappointment." [24]

Even though Thomas Conaty escaped criticism by declining to preach at Harvard, his critics found an opportunity to exercise their ingenuity when his *New Testament Studies* [25] was published. When Conaty was writing to the Archbishop of New York for an *imprimatur*, he explained the origin of the work:

While in parish work I had an advanced class of children under my personal direction, engaged in studying the Life of Christ from the New Testament narrative. The lessons appeared monthly in the little Magazine which I published and afterwards were issued as Leaflets and circulated among our schools, academies and convents. I have completed the series since I came to the University, led to it by the demand of many who followed the courses as they appeared. I have been frequently solicited to publish the series in manual form in the hope that it would supply to some extent at least a want in our school text books. Fr. Grannan has given very careful examination to the *lessons* and urged me to publish them as in his judgment they would be of great benefit. I have consequently given them to the Benzigers who will seek an imprimatur.[26]

Although the book was given a favorable review by the *Catholic University Bulletin*,[27] the *Herold Des Glaubens* and the *Review*, both German-American newspapers of St. Louis, were decidedly hostile. The *Herold Des Glaubens* gave the first notice:

Benziger Brothers have recently published "New Testament Studies," by Right Rev. Mgr. Thomas J. Conaty, D.D. According to the circular

---

[23] ACUA, Francis Peabody to Thomas J. Conaty, Harvard, June 30, 1898.

[24] ACUA, Edward Hale to Thomas J. Conaty, Harvard, October 26, 1898.

[25] Thomas J. Conaty, *New Testament Studies* (New York, 1898).

[26] NYAA, G-28, Thomas J. Conaty to M. A. Corrigan, Washington, May 8, 1898.

[27] "Book Reviews," *CUB*, IV (October, 1898), 498-499.

this book is intended for schools, and is written in catechetical form. We have seen only the specimen pages of this new book. These five pages show clearly enough the catechetical unfitness of the author. Not one of these answers is catechetically correct. In the answers all the catechetical rules are ignored or violated. . . . If the other pages of this schoolbook are no better than these five specimen pages, this work of Mgr. Conaty's must be set down as an unsuccessful catechetical work, which is still worse than his Latin. It may be mentioned as an excuse for Mgr. Conaty that as a pastor he had no parochial school, and that therefore he had very little experience in catechetical work. Therefore, he should have spared us with [sic] this unsuccessful performance, as well as with [sic] his Latin.[28]

The *Review* went even further and accused the author of incipient Nestorianism, but the value of both these book reviews was very doubtful in view of the prejudices that were involved.

Some encouragement was brought to the University rector by the visit on October 30, 1898, of its principal benefactor, a visit which occurred shortly after the release of the unfavorable book reviews. The *Bulletin* gave an account of the day, which it graced with the name of Founder's Day:

The Marquis and Marquise des Monstiers de Merinville, accompanied by Mrs. Donnelly, the aunt of the Marquise, were the guests of the University Sunday, October 30. It is eight years since Mary Gwendoline Caldwell, now the Marquise de Merinville, visited the University, and it was the first visit of her husband. . . . Solemn High Mass was celebrated at 10 o'clock, and the illustrious guests occupied places of honor. . . . . After the Mass, the Marquis and Marquise held a reception in the parlors of Caldwell Hall for the Faculties and Divinity School students. The occasion was made memorable by the presentation to the Marquise of a set of beautiful diamonds by Mgr. McMahon. The Rector entertained his visitors at dinner, to which the Deans of the Faculties were invited. The Marquise visited all parts of the Divinity building, and expressed herself as delighted with the progress of the work.[29]

---

[28] NYAA, G-28, Translation inserted in a letter of Benziger Brothers to M. A. Corrigan, New York, September 22, 1898, who in describing it stated: "We know of only one other unfavorable criticism, that of Mr. Preuss in the REVIEW." Preuss was a close friend of Schroeder and of Pohle, and hardly favorable to anything connected with the University. In the review quoted there is a reference to the parochial schools, of which the Germans in the United States were strong proponents. Monsignor Schroeder had been noted for his ability to write and speak Latin.

[29] "Founders' Day at the University," *CUB,* IV (October, 1898), 493-495.

The further results of this visit the rector made known to the Archbishop of New York:

It was a great consolation and encouragement for us to have an opportunity of expressing to her the gratitude of the University for her great act of generosity in the founding of the Divinity Building. Our kind reception touched her very deeply and renewed her first fervor in University work. As you may have seen from the newspapers, her first manifestation of interest was the establishment of a Scholarship of $5,000 in the School of Divinity in the name of her young nephew, Waldemar Conrad Baron von Zedtwitz, the son of her sister, Lina Caldwell Baroness von Zedtwitz. A second indication of her renewed interest was shown on Saturday following the establishment of a Fellowship of $10,000 also in the Faculty of Divinity. The latter foundation was done in conjunction with her sister, who cabled from Paris her willingness to thus aid the University. To have these two first friends of the Institution again identify themselves with its work and bestow upon it their generosity is of itself sufficient to show their opinion as to the satisfactory condition of University matters, and must give confidence and encouragement to all friends of the University.[30]

This was not the only benefaction to the University from this source during the rectorship of Conaty, for in April of the following year the marquise presented to the University library a collection of thirty-four volumes of French classics.[31] Again in 1901, the chapel in Caldwell Hall was the recipient of a set of vestments which were the handiwork of the donor herself.[32] Further encouragement came at this time from the letter of the Cardinal Secretary of State, which informed the chancellor that the Holy Father was very pleased by the manner in which the University was being conducted.[33]

The lecture tours of Conaty continued during 1899 and 1900, throughout New England, the Middle West, as well as in Canada. While all these travels were in progress, the name of Thomas Conaty was being mentioned several times for various bishoprics. One of these was Columbus, Ohio, which had become vacant on April 17, 1899, with the death of John A. Watterson. That there was some foundation for the rumors was shown by a letter written after the

---

[30] NYAA, G-28, Thomas J. Conaty to M. A. Corrigan, Washington, November 19, 1898.

[31] "University Chronicle," *CUB*, V (April, 1899), 292.

[32] "University Chronicle," *CUB*, VI (July, 1901), 390.

[33] BCA, 96-T-3, M. Card. Rampolla to J. Card. Gibbons, Rome, November 16, 1898.

meeting of the consultors and irremovable rectors of the diocese by one who had attended. He wrote to Conaty:

I wish you to remember two things in connection with the late nomination for the Bishop of Columbus: (1) That one vote was excluded, viz, that of Dean Hartnedy, who was absent. (2) That one who voted had no vote and I protested against his vote and yet the Vicar General who knew he had no vote allowed him to vote. This was by Rev. P. M. Husy of Dennison. Again, the Archbishop did not, as was his duty, enquire into or challenge any man's vote. The whole business was irregular and I know that the vote cast was a purely party vote. The man of the first choice would not have been chosen only for me and I changed my vote to prevent an enemy of the late bishop and a most unworthy man from getting in to the first place. . . . You had four votes and we needed only what we were deprived of to elect you.[34]

Conaty was also among the many mentioned as coadjutor for the troublesome See of Chicago although a more probable candidate seemed to be the Bishop of Peoria, John Lancaster Spalding. A faithful correspondent who kept Denis O'Connell informed of all the developments, both of fact and of fiction, in the Archdiocese of Chicago, notified him in 1900:

It is rumored that the Germans are particularly active, and I fear the demoralized condition of affairs gives them a favorable opportunity. Vigilance is necessary, but there is no one here to exercise it.

In speaking to you about the possible candidates I left out one that no doubt will be considered if the Consultors are brought together. I mean the present rector of the Catholic University.[35]

Again a year later, the same priest wrote:

About Coadjutor. Spalding would be welcomed by all except the Archbishop. Riordan of San Francisco would be acceptable to many who realize that perhaps Spalding would not come. Conaty of the University has been frequently mentioned. Glennon of Kansas City Mo. has many friends.[36]

---

[34] ACUA, B. M. O'Bozlan to Thomas J. Conaty, Newark, Ohio, May 18, 1899. O'Bozlan, as was to be expected in a preponderantly German section, was definitely opposed to the German element, as he revealed in other letters to Conaty dealing with the dismissal of Schroeder. The man chosen for Columbus was Henry Moeller, who on April 27, 1903, became the coadjutor, *cum jure successionis,* of William H. Elder, Archbishop of Cincinnati. He succeeded to the See of Cincinnati on October 31, 1904.

[35] RDA, H. P. Smyth to D. J. O'Connell, Evanston, Ill., July 7, 1900.

[36] RDA, H. P. Smyth to D. J. O'Connell, Evanston, Ill., June 25, 1901.

If the rector was not to be named to either of these sees, he was very shortly to receive at least a titular bishopric. On July 18, 1901, the New York *Tribune* carried the information:

Monsignor Thomas J. Conaty, rector at the Catholic University at Washington, D.C., who is delivering a course of lectures before the Catholic Summer School at Cliff Haven this week on "Christian Education," has received a cable dispatch from Cardinal Gibbons, announcing that the Pope has elevated the monsignor to a bishopric.[37]

This rather surprising bit of information was judged by the *University Bulletin* to be "not only a commendation of the many merits of the Rt. Rev. Rector, but a proof of the constant watchfulness of the Holy See for the interests of the University." [38] The preparations for the consecration were speedily begun, and since the rector desired to make the ceremony a University event, plans were made to hold it in the University chapel.[39] However, due to the large number who signified their intention of attending, the ceremony was transferred to the Cathedral of the Assumption in Baltimore.[40] The brief of appointment arrived from Rome on October 28, 1901, naming Conaty titular Bishop of Samos, a port in the Ionian archipelago, under the jurisdiction of the Archbishop of Rhodes.[41]

Honors sometimes attract their kind. The first honor to come to the newly-appointed bishop was an invitation to address St. Joseph's College in Philadelphia, and to receive an honorary degree at the same time. After refusing twice, since the date scheduled was immediately after the consecration, the rector finally agreed to be present in Philadelphia, although he did refuse the honorary degree:

As to the matter of degree, of which you speak, I would rather you would not mention me in connection with it, for the simple reason that it would look like piling on the agony just at present. I appreciate more than I can say the kindness of the thought which prompted the suggestion, but please let me out of that also. The University is so unalterably opposed to honorary degrees, that I fear it would place me in a position to be misunderstood in university circles, and for the present, at least, I think it wise not to be considered. You will readily understand how I feel about

---

37 New York *Tribune,* July 18, 1901.

38 "University Chronicle," *CUB,* VII (October, 1901), 507.

39 ACUA, RRTTS, October 8, 1901.

40 New York *Tribune,* November 24, 1901.

41 New York *Tribune,* October 29, 1901.

the matter, and I think everything considered you will do me a favor by not honoring me at this moment.[42]

The rector entered into the preparations for his consecration in a conservative spirit. He wrote to his jeweler:

I fear a little bit the expense of a seal, when I really have no official documents to which the seal should be attached. Could you not copy the coat of arms on the ring and thus have it serve all the purposes that present themselves to me at present? So many things crowd on me that I am anxious to save myself as much extra trouble and expense as possible.[43]

The preparations for the consecration also prevented the bishop-elect from attending the reception tendered to the Irish envoys, but this could not prevent an expression of love for his native land:

Will you kindly express my good wishes to the Envoys, and assure them that everything that tends to the advancement of our people, at home and abroad, meets with my heartiest good will and cooperation. I shall never be satisfied until the people of Ireland enjoy to the fullest extent the benefits of freedom under an independent government of its own. May God speed the day.[44]

The consecration of Conaty, which took place on November 24, appealed to the Baltimore *Sun* for its colorfulness, and a rather full coverage was given to the story. The sermon was preached by Thomas J. Shahan before well filled pews, while many others stood in the rain outside for a glimpse of the procession:

This procession was an imposing spectacle. Headed by the cross bearer and numerous altar boys in red cassocks, the students from St. Mary's and St. Joseph's Seminaries followed. Then came the priests in their black cassocks and white surplices. These were followed by the faculty of the Catholic University in academic robes. The bright colors of the University men contrasted brilliantly with the black and white of the priests and seminarians. Monsignors and bishops in their purple robes came next, and then the nine archbishops, each of whom was attended by

---

[42] ACUA, Thomas J. Conaty to C. Gillespie, S.J., Washington, November 9, 1901, copy.

[43] ACUA, Thomas J. Conaty to J. H. Buch, Washington, November 8, 1901, copy.

[44] ACUA, Thomas J. Conaty to T. Kehoe, Washington, November 13, 1901, copy. The so-called Irish Envoys were John Redmond, member of Parliament, chairman of the Parliamentary Party and the United Irish League formed by the reconciliation of the Dillonite, Healyite and Parnellite factions at the 1900 session of Parliament; P. A. McHugh, the Mayor of Sligo, recently released from a

two priests as chaplains. The bishop-elect, accompanied by Bishops Maes and Beaven, followed, and then the officers of the mass. The procession ended with Cardinal Gibbons in his robes of office. . . .

One of the interesting incidents of the consecration occurred toward the end when the new bishop had been presented with the Episcopal ring, crozier, and mitre. Starting down the main aisle to give his blessing he paused at the first seat on the gospel side, where an aged gentleman bent over the extended hand and kissed the ring. It was an impressive sight, and thrilled all who witnessed it. It was the meeting of father and son after that son had been consecrated a bishop, and the aged parent, who is Mr. Patrick Conaty, of Massachusetts, afterward bowed his head, overcome with emotion.[45]

The ceremony was followed by a dinner at St. Mary's Seminary, which, for a temperance man like Conaty, was not without its human interest, as he informed a friend:

I am deeply grateful to you for all the kind things you said in your letter and particularly grateful to you for the information concerning Samos and the bottles of Samos wine, which you were so thoughtful to send me. I was very proud to have been able to use the wine at the banquet at Baltimore, and thus give my friends, especially those around the Cardinal, a taste of my diocesan production.[46]

The ceremonies could not entirely overshadow the disagreeable situation that had arisen at the University with the decision of the Board of Trustees not to reappoint the Reverend Richard Henebry as associate professor of Gaelic.[47] This move, although long anticipated,

---

six months' sentence for complaining about jury packing in Ireland; and Thomas O'Donnell, member of Parliament. These men had come to America to arouse interest in the United Irish League and to gain financial support. In 1896 John Dillon sought Conaty's support in working out this conciliation. He wrote, "I was very glad to see your handwriting again after such a long time. I hope you will come over & attend the National Convention in Dublin on the 18th September. . . . A few good speeches from men like you would have an incalculable effect in inducing our people to abandon the many factions which have raged for the past 6 years—and to unite once more for the old cause. . . . So I hope you come along & strike another blow for the old cause for which you have already done so much." ACUA, John Dillon to Thomas J. Conaty, House of Commons, London, July 11, 1896.

[45] Baltimore *Sun,* November 25, 1901. Cf. New York *Tribune,* November 25, 1901.

[46] ACUA, Thomas J. Conaty to Captain John Furey, Washington, December 18, 1901, copy.

[47] ACUA, MMBT, November 20, 1901.

served to stir up a torrent of protests from Irish-American organizations. The Gaelic chair had been given to the University on October 22, 1896, during the dark days following the departure of John J. Keane. The Ancient Order of Hibernians had been collecting for the chair since 1892, urged on by the first rector and by Thomas J. Shahan, who had originated the idea.[48] The man chosen to assume the duties of the chair was the Reverend Richard Henebry, who had been a professor of Irish in Maynooth College, Ireland, in 1891 and 1892,[49] and had acquired a fair reputation for his interest and work in Gaelic. In June, 1896, he wrote accepting the terms of his contract, saying:

Your rule to enter into probationary contracts seems just and practical. Seeing that your staff material has to be drawn from so many and so distant sources it was a necessity that some easy, fitting arrangement be adopted for material accommodations. In my own case, however, I trust that the term of trial will be as short as possible.

Initial contracts for three years only as part of that rule are to be held fair and reasonable.[50]

Henebry's intention to come at once to the United States was, however, frustrated, since it was thought best that he should have some additional preparation as well as possess a degree, before entering upon his work at the University. On this point he wrote:

I received your letter containing a proposal that I should visit Germany for a course of study and a degree. . . . The suddenness of the idea, when

---

[48] Boston *Pilot,* October 31, 1896. Bishop McQuaid of Rochester had caustic comments and an inaccurate prophecy to make about this proposed chair when writing to Denis O'Connell on January 16, 1892 (RDA): "Bp. Keane's calling on the A.O.H. to found a chair in his University is another added to the many scandals growing out of the shocking liberalism spreading over the country. Another specimen was given by Bp. Foley, when he allowed himself to be dubbed Chaplain of this miserable secret society. Such men as Kenrick of Baltimore, Wood of Philadelphia, Hughes of New York condemned these societies. That the Molly McGuire's [*sic*] of Pa. & the A.O.H. are even one and the same society cannot be denied. This fact was demonstrated beyond gainsay at the trials of the Molly Maguires for brutal murders. This new University Chair ought to be labelled the 'Murderers' Chair'. This well earned appellation will never be given to it because the chair will never exist." For secret societies, Cf. Fergus MacDonald, C.P., *The Catholic Church and the Secret Societies in the United States* (New York, 1946).

[49] *Year Book of the Catholic University of America, 1899-1900* (Washington, 1899), p. 14.

[50] ACUA, Richard Henebry to John J. Keane, Portlaw, Waterford, Ireland, June 2, 1896.

I was bent so on going to Washington, gave me a little shock at first, but I acknowledge the wisdom of your reasoning and now heartily approve of the plan glad that I shall have an opportunity of hearing the great masters expound *their* learning. I leave for Freiburg i/B in a couple of days. . . . My attention will be devoted to Sanskrit Philology and Irish.[51]

In October, 1898, Henebry came to the University after receiving his Ph.D. degree from the University of Greifswald, and he quickly entered into Irish-American activities in this country. In 1899 he was elected president of the Gaelic League of America at their first convention, an honor which he continued to hold as long as he remained at the University.[52]

Ill health overtook Dr. Henebry in 1900 and forced him to spend a year of recuperation in Colorado. Very little was heard from him at the University, and the problem of what to do about fulfilling the obligations of the Gaelic chair troubled the rector.[53] A leave of absence for a year was obtained for the sick professor from the Board of Trustees,[54] and plans were laid for the following year. Arrangements were made with Dr. Frederick N. Robinson of Harvard University to give a course of five lectures in April, 1901, so that at least something could be offered to satisfy the requirements of the Gaelic chair.[55] The question of salary brought the first rift between the University and its Gaelic professor, for Henebry wrote from Denver in January, 1901, asking for what he considered was due to him:

I forgot to make arrangements with you about my salary. Dr. Gargan [*sic*] told me that the Board of Trustees had left the matter in your hands. In that case I have no apprehension that I shall be short of money. My September salary I have not yet drawn. Advise me of your intentions in this matter, and let me have a check at this address, for I am running awfully low and soon will not have enough to peg out a placer claim unless I get someone to grub-stake me.[56]

The rector replied by sending him the $166.66 that was due the

[51] ACUA, Richard Henebry to John J. Keane, Portlaw, Waterford, Ireland, August 25, 1896.

[52] "University Chronicle," *CUB*, VI (January, 1900), 133.

[53] ACUA, RRTTS, October 5, October 9, 1900.

[54] ACUA, MMBT, October 10, 1900.

[55] ACUA, RRTTS, November 13, December 11, 1900; "University Chronicle," *CUB*, VII (January, 1901), 128; *ibid.*, (July, 1901), 390.

[56] ACUA, Richard Henebry to Thomas J. Conaty, Denver, January 2, 1901.

Gaelic professor from his salary of the previous year. He also informed him:

> With regard to salary this year: as you have not been on duty, and are not at present doing any work of the University's, you can readily see that the University is not to be expected to pay you any salary. As I told you when you were talking with me, the University was more than just last year, because you were here, and willing, but unable to do such work as you might be called for. I cannot see my way to approve any bill for salary during your absence. The Board of Trustees had a very decided opinion about such matters, and instructed me along those lines. . . . I shall be very glad to learn that your health is improving, and pleased to welcome you back at any time during the year when your health will permit you to do the work of your department.[57]

The three-year contract which Henebry had signed upon his arrival in Washington in 1898 was about to expire. When the matter of his reappointment was brought before the academic senate, they voted in the negative.[58] Conaty advised Henebry of this fact in July:

> It is my duty to inform you that as the term of your engagement at the University closes with this year, the Faculty of Philosophy was called upon to make recommendations concerning the Chair of Celtic, and they recommended in view of the responsibility of the University to this Chair endowment, your health did not warrant a recommendation of reappointment. This action of the Faculty was approved by the University Senate, and it becomes my duty to make this report to the Trustees at their annual meeting.
>
> In answer to the inquiry concerning reports from you, I was obliged to answer that I had received no communication from you since last November, and consequently I knew nothing officially from you.[59]

Henebry sent an immediate reply asserting that his health had greatly improved; in fact, that he was entirely well, and he added that he would like to see the faculty reverse its decision.[60] But it was to no avail.[61]

---

[57] ACUA, Thomas J. Conaty to Richard Henebry, Washington, January 10, 1901, copy.

[58] ACUA, CHF, Faculty of Philosophy Governing Board Records, I, 55, May 20, 1901.

[59] NYAA, G-28, Addenda, Thomas J. Conaty to Richard Henebry, Washington, July 5, 1901, copy.

[60] NYAA, G-28, Addenda, Richard Henebry to Thomas J. Conaty, Bennett, Colorado, July 11, 1901, copy.

[61] ACUA, RRTTS, October 8, 1901: "This request was presented by the Rector to the Faculty at their first meeting in October, and the governing board

118

To replace Henebry, John J. Dunn, instructor in Romance languages and literature at the University, was made a fellow in Gaelic and sent to Harvard to begin his training.[62]

Dr. Henebry was determined not to take his dismissal from the University without a struggle, and he had many friends. In October, 1901, the president of the Ancient Order of Hibernians, John T. Keating of Chicago, wrote to the rector in rather direct terms stating that the A.O.H. had helped to pick Henebry for the position he had occupied, and that they wanted him to remain in that post. He also asked that some accounting be given for what had been done with the funds of the foundation.[63] In the following month, with the trustees' meeting drawing near, Keating wrote in the same vein to Archbishop Corrigan of New York, as well as sending along a copy of the letter he had written to the rector.[64] The newspapers also entered into a full discussion of the case, among them the San Francisco *Examiner* which reviewed the situation in the following manner:

Unfortunately, however, the Catholic University of Washington appears to be under the domination of the Anglo-Saxon spirit. Mr. [*sic*] Henebry came there when it was running very high. The German Dr. Schroeder had been dismissed after a campaign which alienated and still alienates the whole German Catholic population of America. Dr. Henebry was too much indebted to German science to be intolerant of the German clergy,

---

reported unanimously that the Rector's letter offered no special reason for reconsidering their past action. This information was forwarded to Dr. Henebry, who was told by the Rector that he 'no longer belonged to the teaching corp of the University'." ACUA, CHF, Faculty of Philosophy Governing Board Records, I, 58, October 2, 1901.

[62] ACUA, Thomas J. Conaty to John J. Dunn, Washington, September 30, 1901; ACUA, RRTTS, October 8, 1901.

[63] NYAA, G-28, Addenda, John T. Keating to Thomas J. Conaty, Chicago, October 3, 1901. Keating was disappointed in his effort to secure the co-operation of Michael Cudahy, a member of the Board of Trustees, in carrying out his plans. Cudahy informed him: "With reference to your communication of the 7th inst., will say I don't wish to take any part in the matter you refer to. I think the Rector is a very competent, fair and just man and from my knowledge of the matter, think Father Hennebry [*sic*] has done very little in all the time he has been at the University. I made inquiries over two years ago. If the Ancient Order of Hibernians have no other interests in the matter than to get the best results and most efficiency from the chair, I would advise they leave it to Monsignor Conaty." ACUA, CHF, Henebry Case, Michael Cudahy to John T. Keating, Chicago, November 13, 1901, copy.

[64] NYAA, G-28, Addenda, John T. Keating to M. A. Corrigan, Chicago, November 7, 1901.

and too much of a scholar to take any interest in ecclesiastical politics. In consequence he was not looked on with favor by those who run the institution.

The local authorities had chosen a young man [Dunn] entirely unacquainted with Irish, had given him the Celtic chair and had sent him to Europe to study the Romance languages, with Celtic on the side. On his return the money of the Ancient Order of Hibernians is to be used to teach French and Italian, and the Celtic is to be relegated to a subordinate place.[65]

A protest meeting was held on November 10 by all the Gaelic societies of New York, together with the Gaelic League, who after sending a list of their resolutions to the newspapers, sent the printed copy to the rector.[66] The many protests served only to strengthen the resolve of the University authorities, and the rector reported to the senate:

The Senate is no doubt aware of the campaign which Rev. Dr. Henebry is apparently waging against the University, as we fear that he is largely responsible for it. It seems to be a determination on his part to excite against the University those who have been its best friends, and particularly the organization of the Ancient Order of Hibernians. It is strange that reasonable men should believe all that he says and allow themselves to be used by him without hearing the other side or giving us credit for reasonable judgment.[67]

In a like vein, and calling on his background for substantiation, Conaty answered the letter of the president of the A.O.H.:

I must confess that nothing has pained me more than to see your letter to me figure in the New York Journal of this morning. I certainly need no one to go sponsor for me, with regard to my loyalty for all the aspirations of my race. If you do not know me personally, I can appeal to the service of a lifetime in devotion to the ideals that you love dearly. I have too much respect for our people to think that they will be led to believe that the men who for the last twenty-five years have stood by all their interests can by any possibility stand in the way of an advance of either the race or of its language, in which they have as great a pride as that of any one who boasts of the same lineage.

---

[65] ACUA, Undated clipping of the San Francisco *Examiner* published shortly before the meeting of the trustees on November 20, 1901, included in the Henebry case file.

[66] NYAA, G-28, Addenda, Edward McCrystal to Thomas J. Conaty, New York, November 15, 1901, copy.

[67] ACUA, RRTTS, November 12, 1901.

.... At present all that I can say is that I am pained beyond expression at what is happening, not so much for myself as for the people to whose interests I have been devoted, and to whose interest I shall remain devoted as long as I live.[68]

The meeting of the Board of Trustees took place on November 20. The trustees followed the example of the faculty of the School of Philosophy and the senate, and decided against the reappointment of Henebry.[69] The meeting also issued a statement on the case, telling of the unanimous decision not to reappoint Dr. Henebry, while also promising to hold sacred the trust given to them by the A.O.H. foundation.[70]

The case of Henebry was by no means finished with the action of the trustees in not renewing the contract. A great many members of the A.O.H. and other Irish-American organizations still felt aggrieved at the University, but the pettiness of Richard Henebry was revealed by himself in the statement of the case which he presented in March, 1902:

In March, 1895, I was approached by the University with an offer of

---

[68] ACUA, Thomas J. Conaty to John T. Keating, Washington, November 12, 1901, copy.

[69] ACUA, MMBT, November 20, 1901. An interesting sidelight on the way that the board meetings were conducted, and the manner in which Keane thought they ought to be directed was given in a letter of Keane to the third rector. "I always considered myself the responsible Executive; and in the meetings of the Board I never dealt with them as a Bishop with fellow Bishops, but as the Executive of the Univ'y dealing with its over-Senate.

Such too seemed always to be Dr. Conaty's view. He really *bossed* our every meeting, and we were all glad that he did, for it was the only way to have deliberation & action strictly *ad rem*.

Allow me to take the liberty of a loving old friend, and say that you have not seemed to take this view,—that you have not sufficiently bossed our meetings,—that in your actions on these occasions there has been too little of *initiative,* of *direction* of debate, of shaping our conclusions. Your answer, that you were 'a simple priest' don't [*sic*] seem to me to meet the case at all. It is *not* as "a simple priest" that you were there, but as the *Executive of the Univ'y,* bound to be acquainted with every detail of its life & its needs, far beyond what any of us could be, and bound as such and as member of the Board, to be not only outspoken, but the leader in all debate & the most potent influence in all action. Your view, or your action, has been, as we used to say in olden days, 'too *subjective.'* More *objectivity,* regardless of *personality,* is what will bring you up to the full level of your situation. That with patience, tact, considerateness, which circumstances so demand, cannot but win." ACUA, O'Connell Papers, John J. Keane to D. J. O'Connell, Dubuque, April 2, 1906.

[70] ACUA, Statement on the Henebry Case, November 20, 1901.

the Gaelic Chair. On accepting I received a contingent appointment *to be made absolute upon payment of the Endowment Fund by the A.O.H.*

While awaiting that event, I was requested to prepare to teach Sanskrit also. I protested as my contract was to teach Gaelic only, and because at the time I was totally ignorant of the Sanskrit language.

After the fund was paid in 1896, I was sent to Germany by the Trustees to perfect myself in my studies. . . .

On reporting myself ready for work I received a letter instructing me how to acquit myself on reaching America. Amongst other things *it contained a caution to say nothing about the Anglo-American alliance.*

A little after my arrival in Washington, Doctors Shahan and Conaty being together present with me told me somebody had asked a public question why I had been sent to learn Irish from "the Dutch," and that to allay ignorant protest they had found it necessary to publish that I had gone to Germany not for study but to consult manuscripts. *And they requested me "not to give them away"* (exact words).

I had been repeatedly asked to be "loyal to the University." My wonder at this disappeared when I learned the meaning attached to loyalty, and then I felt ashamed. For loyalty has a highly technical meaning there. Towards the end of my first year Dr. Shahan commented with bitterness at the dinner table upon somebody's want of loyalty to the University. *He added that they had got rid of Professors before and they would do so again.* Shortly afterwards he took back from my room a number of books he had given my department, and his manner to me was cold ever afterwards. The reason I never discovered. . . .

When the Gaelic League and the A.O.H. conventions were held concurrently in Boston, I applied to Dr. Conaty for permission to attend, and *he refused me leave of absence for the purpose.*

After recounting his sickness and his year's leave of absence without pay, he continued:

I presented myself on the opening day of the University in good health ready to resume work. On attending a meeting of my Faculty as usual, Dr. M. F. Egan, Chairman, stood up, and before the assembled members enquired my business. And he immediately produced a document from the Rector which showed I was no longer a member of the Faculty. Whereupon I withdrew. Dr. Conaty sustained that contention by arguing that the term for which I had been appointed by the Trustees expired on October 15th. I urged that I held my appointment granted by the Trustees until they formally withdrew it; and that in any case *my contract was for three years teaching with salary,* and only two such had elapsed.

I learned at the University that Dr. Dunn, a native of New Haven, Conn., the Instructor in Romance Philology, had been appointed to take my place. *He had been sent to Harvard to make his Keltic studies there.* That was of a sort with the hasty orders addressed to me to put myself

122

in order for the teaching of Sanskrit. . . . The professors with whom I had parted on good terms on my way to Colorado, appeared almost uniformly to regard me with suspicion and *feared to be seen talking with me.* I secured Dr. Conaty's permission to absent myself and withdrew from the University.[71]

Within a short time a change of sentiment began to take place among the Hibernians, and a friend was able to encourage the University with the words:

I have heard from New York from a gentleman of unquestioned veracity, also a warm friend of the University and a leader among the Hibernians, that "the New York and Chicago Gaelic League people have turned on Dr. Henebry," and that they now begin to see him in an entirely different light than they did when he first posed as martyr. My friend who writes me from New York asks me to say to Dr. Conaty that everything will be all right, and that the threatened trouble is rapidly subsiding.[72]

The accuracy of this statement was borne out by a letter from John Keating of Chicago, asking the rector for an appointment to talk over matters concerning the Gaelic chair, to which he added:

I take this opportunity to say that I sincerely regret the attitude taken last November relating the Henebry controversy, as far as Dr. Henebry is concerned.

. . . . Recent events have proven that Dr. Henebry was not the individual fitted for so important a position. However, in connection with the controversy, I trust you will understand that I did not directly or indirectly countenance or consent to the use of Newspapers or the publication of any matters relating to the controversy.[73]

The conference held on April 22 turned out favorably for the University. It still remained the duty of the rector to face the A.O.H. convention in Denver during July in which he felt sure "that there is a nasty campaign on hand, which may have this effect at least of creating a little bad blood." [74] The result was better than Conaty had anticipated, as he informed the Dean of the School of Law:

You will be pleased to know that my visit to the A.O.H. Convention at Denver resulted in a complete triumph for the University. I never met

---

[71] San Francisco *Leader,* March 8, 1902. Cf. ACUA, CHF, Henebry Case.

[72] ACUA, P. J. Haltigan of the *National Hibernian* to P. J. Garrigan, Washington, March 28, 1902.

[73] ACUA, John T. Keating to Thomas J. Conaty, Chicago, April 7, 1902.

[74] ACUA, Thomas J. Conaty to John J. Dunn, Washington, July 7, 1902, copy.

with such enthusiasm, as followed my address to the Convention. I did not refer to the Henebry matter; but confined myself exclusively to the relations of the University with the A.O.H., and Father Yorke who represented the opposition was completely humiliated on a test question of striking out the words "completely satisfactory" from the vote of thanks.[75]

The possible break with a very influential element of the Catholic population was avoided and the stigma of discrimination against the Irish professors, unlike that against the Germans, was not placed upon the University.

Dr. Henebry was not the only member of the faculty to have difficulties with the University. There was a somewhat parallel case in that of Charles Warren Stoddard. This well-known lecturer and travel writer had been on the original staff of the University,[76] but he had the misfortune to fall into ill health in 1900. He had been forced to take some time off because of a kidney ailment during April and May of that year. Drawing a comparison between Harvard and other institutions that granted their professors a sabbatical year, Stoddard felt justified in asking for a year's leave of absence with salary to recuperate after the eleven hard years he had put in at the University.[77] However, because of the financial condition of the institution, his request had to be refused.[78] The question of salaries for professors during their absence from the University was submitted by Monsignor Conaty to the senate, but no definite plan was evolved.[79] In November the senate did decide:

The Recommendations of the Governing Board of the Faculty of Phil. were taken up, and it was voted, that in accordance with the recommendations of the Govn'g Board of the Faculty of Philosophy, of date Nov. 11, 1901, the Academic Senate recommend to the Board of Trustees that the services of Chas. W. Stoddard, Professor of English Literature, be terminated at the end of this academic year, September 30, 1902, because

---

[75] ACUA, Thomas J. Conaty to William C. Robinson, Washington, August 7, 1902, copy.

[76] Cf. Ahern, *op. cit.,* 25.

[77] ACUA, Chas. Warren Stoddard to Thomas J. Conaty, Kendal Green, Massachusetts, April 17, 1900. "I must live; I must be provided for. Without the salary it would be a choice of two fates—the final collapse in harness, or the final collapse out of it."

[78] ACUA, Thomas J. Conaty to Chas. Warren Stoddard, Washington, April 28, 1900, copy.

[79] ACUA, RRTTS, May 8, 1900.

the present University conditions no longer require them; and that the Rector present this recommendation to the Board of Trustees.[80]

Such a course was not required of the rector. Stoddard submitted to him the desired resignation, which was presented to the board on November 20, 1901,[81] and accepted to take effect as of September 30, 1902.[82]

Two other members of the staff also severed their connections with the University in that same year of 1901, both of them members of the School of Law. Both of these men had obtained positions in the Philippines through the activity of Monsignor Conaty. In May, 1901, the General Superintendent of Schools for the Philippines wrote from Manila to Dr. Conaty authorizing him to select three teachers for the Philippines, who would receive a salary of $1,000 plus their necessary travelling expenses.[83] Two names presented for approval were those of Charles H. Goddard[84] and Edmund B. Briggs.[85] These men were both instructors in law whose services in the University had not been too enthusiastically received. Edmund Briggs sent in his resignation from the University in August, saying in part that "It is not necessary for me to say this step is taken with regret. You are aware of the love I bear to the University; and of the career that has so suddenly been opened to me. 'Ich Dien'!"[86] Briggs had had an interesting career, having attended Seton Hall College, where he formed the acquaintance of Father Michael A. Cor-

[80] ACUA, Senate Records, II, 230, November 12, 1901, Cf. ACUA, CHF, Faculty of Philosophy Governing Board Records, I, 59, November 11, 1901.

[81] ACUA, MMBT, November 20, 1901. ACUA, CHF, Chas. Warren Stoddard to Thomas J. Conaty, Washington, November 18, 1901: "As this is my thirteenth year of routine work at the Catholic University; as the climate of Washington does not agree with me; as there has been no year during the last twelve in which I have not suffered more or less illness; and as this illness seems to be increasing with the years; I deem it wise for me to seek the change I stand so much in need of: Therefore, I tender my resignation from the Chair of English Literature in the Catholic University of America, the same to take effect at the end of the present Scholastic year—that is, on Sept. 30th, 1902."

[82] ACUA, RRTTS, December 10, 1901.

[83] ACUA, Thomas J. Conaty to Lt. Col. C. L. Edwards, Washington, October 8, 1901, copy.

[84] ACUA, Thomas J. Conaty to Lt. Col. C. L. Edwards, Washington, May 29, 1901, copy.

[85] ACUA, Thomas J. Conaty to Lt. Col. C. L. Edwards, Washington, August 11, 1901, copy.

[86] ACUA, E. B. Briggs to Thomas J. Conaty, Washington, August 7, 1901.

rigan, later the Archbishop of New York. He received his bachelor of laws degree from Georgetown in 1875, after which he entered into practice, to interrupt this by a very unsatisfactory year as United States consul to Santos, Brazil, during 1885-1886. In 1895 Edmund Briggs was appointed a fellow in law at the University and succeeded in getting his master of laws and doctor of civil law degrees in 1897.[87] When Bishop Keane was removed and the new rector appointed, Briggs was worried about his position in the University. In writing for support to the Archbishop of New York, he revealed something of the spirit of the institution during those trying days, as well as part of his own character:

If you can, without in any way compromising yourself, you might well assist me, just now, by saying a kind word or two for me to our new Rector, Dr. Conaty. I have been content, in the main, to do any work, knowing that it was being well done; and I am willing to stand upon my record as an instructor. At the same time I have not hesitated, upon occasion, to speak out my heart in defence of Seton Hall, Your Grace, and Bishop McQuade [sic]: not that any of the three could be benefited much by ought that I could say; but that my heart is still young enough not to have forgotten the past.[88]

A few weeks later he wrote again to Archbishop Corrigan, this time in a much more candid manner:

There is an old trite saying, not very elegant, to the effect that "kissing goes by favor;" and I fear it is not entirely inapplicable to that "August Body," our "Senate". It would be a severe blow to me if, in June, I should find myself "dropped", even with a Doctor's Diploma in my hand. It is upon this particular point that I pray for Your Grace's powerful intercession and good offices.[89]

Although Dr. Briggs had sounded so enthusiastic for his new position when he offered his resignation to the University, he did not long remain in that frame of mind. When he had been in the Philippines less than a month, he wrote to the rector:

Since my arrival in the Philippines, Oct. 10th last, I have met two, just *two* gentlemen, to wit: Mr. Frank A. Brannegan, [sic] and Rev.

---

[87] ACUA, University History, Biography, submitted by members of the faculty for insertion in the *Year Book*.

[88] NYAA, G-24, E. B. Briggs to M. A. Corrigan, Washington, January 29, 1897.

[89] NYAA, G-24, E. B. Briggs to M. A. Corrigan, Washington, February 16, 1897.

Edw. H. Fitzgerald. Father McKinnon I have not yet seen; and Judge Taft has been ill since my arrival. There *may* be others.

Your Lordship was so good to say to me that, if the conditions here did not suit, I might return to the University.

Well, I have been made a victim of the "A.P.Aism" which controls the Public School system here; and am going back to a free country.

We expect to sail for San Francisco by transport Hancock, Nov. 15th or 16th; and I want to *withdraw* my resignation of my Ass't Professorship.[90]

The speedy return of his former law instructor was somewhat of an embarrassment to Conaty, especially due to Briggs' shouting of A.P.A. charges against the administration. Conaty was still willing to help him, but in a limited way, as the rector informed William C. Robinson:

On my return from the West I have learned that Dr. Briggs has created a little ferment in Government circles, and, as far as I know, he has asked for reinstatement, as also a release of his baggage which is held at San Francisco, as also from some $180. in debt contracted in the Commissary department on his return home. I really pity the poor fellow, and would like to do what I can to help him out. I think that it is foolish for him to expect the Administration to do anything for him in his attempt to force an issue on his position. I would be willing to see the Department and try to have his baggage released, and, perhaps, the remission of his indebtedness. Of course, I do not know whether I could succeed in this, but I am willing to try; provided, however, that he keeps out of the papers and ceases to make trouble for the Administration.[91]

The activity on the part of Conaty for Briggs was by no means the only political activity in which the University rector was engaged. In the period of American expansion towards the East and the conflict with Spain, there was bound to be a greater Catholic interest in the functions of government. The question of Church lands in the Philippines and Cuba was a very touchy one politically in a nation that was undergoing a wave of bigotry because of the activities of the A.P.A. The situation was not eased by the increasingly influential immigrant vote. To protect themselves, and to attain any justice in the matter, it was essential that political leaders maintain some contact with Catholic leaders in America. John Ireland was, perhaps, the most outstanding example of Catholic participation in government policies, but there were others whose opinion was sought and sometimes heeded. Conaty was instrumental in the removal of the naval commander of

[90] ACUA, E. B. Briggs to Thomas J. Conaty, Manila, November 5, 1901.

[91] ACUA, Thomas J. Conaty to W. C. Robinson, Washington, August 7, 1902, copy.

Guam, who had shown strong prejudice against the Spanish friars on the island. The commander had even gone so far as to order them to leave the territory.[92] Thomas Conaty was also of assistance to the Church in Cuba, interceding with the President and the Secretary of War for a just settlement of property claims.[93] He was aided by the fact that the Secretary of Navy, John D. Long, had been an old friend of his from Massachusetts days, as well as the fact that McKinley was not antagonistic to Catholic claims, although he was cautious of the power of anti-Catholic elements. The attitude of President McKinley was well demonstrated by Archbishop Corrigan's report of an interview with him, which he submitted to the former Apostolic Delegate, Cardinal Satolli:

Regarding Manila, the case is different, and the President recommends urgently that the Holy See obtain every proper concession from Spain NOW, before the treaty of peace is signed; as after that date, the United States will act simply on its principle of separation between Church and State, and grant no concessions to Catholics, more than to Presbyterians or any other denomination.

The President hopes all this can be arranged quietly and harmoniously before the signing of the treaty, so as to preclude all sectarian clamor, etc. This is the substance of his message which was entirely unsought on my part, and which probably is not new to Your Excellency, or to other Prelates. I merely refer the matter to you, to unburden my conscience— more than once in the interview, the President expressed his hope of QUIET and satisfactory arrangement with Church authorities, and his

---

[92] ACUA, Thomas J. Conaty to John Crane, Washington, undated, but in January of 1901, copy. "It gave me pleasure to receive your letter on Friday and to make immediate arrangements to call on the President and talk with him about the matter suggested. The President received me Saturday afternoon, and gave me an opportunity for more than half an hour of going over the whole situation. He was very much pleased with your letter, and said that he had presented it to the Secretary of the Navy, and will cause investigation to be made immediately."

[93] ACUA, Thomas J. Conaty to Bonaventure F. Broderick, Washington, October 17, 1900, copy. "I had a long interview with the President yesterday, and we talked over your matters as well as others. He is awaiting the return of General Wood. I feel satisfied that the President's disposition is excellent in the matter." *Ibid.*, November 3, 1900, copy, "I had a half hour's talk with the Secretary this morning, and went over the whole matter with him. He has no official notice of the decision of the Commission, and probably would not until General Wood returned to Cuba. He thinks it not wise to take immediate action."

desire to help us, as far as his position and what are known as "American principles" permit.[94]

The consideration of McKinley in this matter, since it was unknown to the public, did not help him to any extent with the Catholic voters in the 1900 election. Hence the report circulating that the American army in the Philippines had systematically looted the churches there had to be either disproved or verified. Conaty, with the urging of Ella Loraine Dorsey, the daughter of the well-known Catholic novelist, did what he could to remove this aspersion.[95] Again, the Secretary of the Navy consulted the Rector of the University on the matter of appointing a Catholic chaplain for the Navy. In this matter, Conaty informed his own bishop, Thomas Beaven of Springfield:

> Secretary Long sent a message to me, and I went to see him yesterday. The purpose of his enquiry was to find which one of the candidates for the Navy among the Catholic priests would in my judgment be the best to appoint. He left it entirely with me, and said that without further enquiry he would immediately appoint; detailing, however, what he would wish to find, and what he would wish to have in the man.[96]

The influence of Conaty in Washington political circles was

---

[94] NYAA, G-21, M. A. Corrigan to F. Card. Satolli, New York, August 21, 1898, copy. During 1898 most of the relations with Rome dealing with American political affairs had been carried on through the Archbishop of St. Paul, John Ireland. On Ireland's relation to the McKinley administration, Cf. "Archbishop Ireland and Manifest Destiny," by John T. Farrell, *CHR*, XXXIII (October, 1947), 269-301. Contemporaneous Catholic opinion on the question of church lands and their treatment by the United States may be found in the *American Ecclesiastical Review*, "Conferences," "The Friars Question," XXVII (August, 1902), 205-206; H. J. Heuser, "Catholic Journalism and the Friars Question," XXVII (September, 1902), 266-273; "Studies and Conferences," "The Philippine Controversy," XXVIII (March, 1903), 343-346; Thomas C. Middleton, O.S.A., "Report of the Philippine Commissions (of 1899-1900) on Religious and Educational Matters," XXVIII (March, 1903), 262-302; "Studies and Conferences," "The Philippines Commissions' Report," XXVIII (May, 1903), 572-577; and Bryan J. Clinch, "The Work of the Philippine Commission, *ACQR*, XXVI (October, 1901), 625-643.

[95] ACUA, Ella Loraine Dorsey to Thomas J. Conaty, Washington, October 19, 1900, with which was included a document referring to Monsignor Conaty for substantiation of the good action of the army in the Philippines as far as Catholics were concerned, R. C. Kerens to Ella Loraine Dorsey, September 28, 1900, copy. The same document was also sent to Archbishop Corrigan by Miss Dorsey, NYAA, G-29, Addenda, Washington, October 8, 1900.

[96] ACUA, Thomas J. Conaty to T. D. Beaven, Washington, April 23, 1901, copy.

lessened with the death of McKinley and the inauguration of Theodore Roosevelt. He so informed a friend writing for help in a personal matter: "I have not the honor of as close an acquaintance with the present President as with his predecessor, and would have to move slowly in the matter." [97]

Besides the departure of Dr. Briggs, there was another member of the University family who was called away a few months later, whose loss was felt much more deeply by the rector. The news that Philip J. Garrigan had been appointed to the new See of Sioux City was released on January 28, 1902. Conaty thus lost the able assistant who had aided him so much during the stormy years of his administration of the University.[98] Philip Garrigan had long been a friend of Conaty. Like the rector, Garrigan had been born in Ireland, coming to America while young, and had been called to the University from parish duties in the Diocese of Springfield.[99] That Conaty was sorry to see him leave is clear from the words of praise he gave his vice-rector when formally announcing the fact to the academic senate:

Dr. Garrigan's resignation, as Vice-Rector, has been placed in the hands of the Rector. . . . Dr. Garrigan's resignation closes fourteen years of faithful and disinterested service to the University. Loyal to all its interests, patient and attentive to all the details of his office, he has presided over the buildings erected, and has contributed to the growth and development of the University. As a faithful officer, a conscientious guardian of everything entrusted to him, Dr. Garrigan deserves the gratitude of the University and the good wishes of all who have been associated with him during his University life.[100]

The consecration of the new bishop took place in St. Michael's Cathedral in Springfield on May 25, 1902, with the sermon being preached by Garrigan's new metropolitan and his former superior at the University, John J. Keane of Dubuque.[101] The story behind the choice of the new ordinary of Sioux City was told by John Keane in his diocesan diary:

May 30th, 1901. Have this day rec'd notice from the Apost. Delegate that the Holy See is now ready to take action for the erection of a new

---

[97] ACUA, Thomas J. Conaty to Marion Lindsay, Washington, October 22, 1901, copy.

[98] Baltimore *Sun,* January 28, 1902.

[99] Cf. Ahern, *op. cit.,* 9.

[100] ACUA, RRTTS, May 13, 1902.

[101] Boston *Hibernian,* July 2, 1902.

See in the western part of this Diocese, — & asking names of candidates, to be presented *only by the Bishops of the Prcvince,* in order to avoid complaints if the present consultors & C. were permitted to send a list. Have summoned the Suffragans.

June 1st. Meeting of the Bishops of the Province held, to prepare list of candidates for the new see. Sent the names of Rt. Rev. Thomas M. Lenihan Bishop of Cheyenne, first; Rev. James M. Cleary of Minneapolis, Minn. second; Very Rev. Philip J. Garrigan, D.D., Vice Rector of the Catholic University of America, third.

December 15th. Today Bishop Lenihan of Cheyenne died at the residence of his Rev. brother at Marshalltown, Iowa. . . . We are informed that he would surely have been appointed to Sioux City. In consequence, Very Rev. Dr. Garrigan, Vice Rector of the Cath. University, has been chosen first Bp. of Sioux City.[102]

The previous woes of Bishop Conaty in his position as rector appear as trifles compared with what lay before him. The Schroeder incident and the Henebry trouble paled before another event that had its official beginnings at the meeting of the Board of Trustees on November 20, 1901, just four short days before the consecration of the rector was to take place in Baltimore. On the motion of the Bishop of Peoria it was moved:

that a Special Committee be appointed by the Chairman, which shall have full authority to examine into the actual condition, financial and academic, of the University and to report with suggestions to a meeting of the Board of Trustees to be held the Second Wednesday after Easter next, April 9th, 1902. The motion was carried unanimously. The Cardinal appointed as said Committee: Archbishop Keane of Dubuque, Bishop Spalding of Peoria and Bishop Maes of Covington.[103]

Behind this motion there was the work of a disgruntled professor of the University, Charles P. Grannan. Grannan had been friendly with the rector at first. With the passing of the years, and without a known reasonable cause, he turned against Conaty. Edward Pace, Thomas Shahan and Charles Grannan had been close friends of Denis O'Connell. In his frequent letters to this friend in Rome, Grannan would frequently refer to the three professors and O'Connell as "The Chumps". Pace and Shahan, however, remained loyal to the rector, and thus Grannan was left to himself in the rather miserable

---

[102] DAA, "Record of the Administration of John J. Keane, Archbishop of Dubuque," pp. 25-34. Although dated, the entries seem to have been made at a later period.

[103] ACUA, MMBT, November 20, 1901, p. 95.

task of undermining the work that Conaty was trying to do. Writing consistently—it could hardly be called faithfully—to Denis O'Connell in Rome, the professor of sacred scripture revealed his blind prejudice against the rector as well as what he was doing to keep life in the University far from peaceful. The definite turning against Conaty was first shown by Grannan in March, 1901.[104] By June he was writing to O'Connell, "I never saw such a lot of indignant men as there are here,—indignant at the administration for doing absolutely nothing,—but blundering." [105] By October of that year, Grannan had really worked himself up to a state of great excitement, and he informed O'Connell of his interpretation of what was going on in the University:

"There is no place like home",—for everlasting wrangling. It is clear that there will be the devil to play here in a short time, unless something is done. The Keane Hall, called the Dormitory, has only *four* students, and *five* Professors. . . . All of the Professors, five of them, are already looking for other quarters, in town or elsewhere, and by Christmas, I suspect that Keane Hall will be closed and padlocked. That will be the beginning of the end. But you must not think that our pair of administrators will be content at that, — no, not so long as one building is open. Garrigan expects to go, & is crazy to go, to Sioux City. Rect. Conat. Bulls are now here. I believe that the University will pay the expense of the Consecration and of the Banquet. And if so in this case, there is no reason why it should not pay for Garrigan's also. You know we are so rich; we have debts by the hundreds of thousands, and can afford some more.

I understand that the Delegation does not make itself responsible at all for Conat's [*sic*] appointment to the Episcopal office. James did it all. No one has ever mentioned to me the measly letter on the Varsity that James brought home with him. When I asked about it, every one smiled a sad smile. One wicked man regretted the blessing at the end of the letter. One result of the letter is that this year we have fewer students, by a great sight, than we ever had before. . . .

Rearden [*sic*], Spalding, Maes and some others are in possession of all the facts and are MAD. N. York and Philadelphia will be innoculated again in about one week, so that the fever may take. James and Conat will endeavor to put everything off, to some future time. The latter will,

---

[104] RDA, "#$%&%$#" to Doktor [Grannan to O'Connell] (postmarked Washington, March 3, 1901).

[105] RDA, "#$%&%$#" to Doktor [Grannan to O'Connell] (About June, 1901).

THOMAS J. SHAHAN

EDWARD A. PACE

no doubt, make a flamboyant, flim-flam report, wherein all will be painted in roseate colors. If the Trustees believe him, it will not be my fault.[106]

John Ireland seemed to be in partial agreement with the views of Grannan, or else he was merely reflecting some of them, for the Archbishop of St. Paul wrote to O'Connell in Rome in November, 1901:

The University is in a perilous condition. This is understood by the Directors: and the next meeting, at which Spalding leads will be most important. It must reform things—else, the University goes down. The elevation of Mgr. Conaty renders the situation more difficult: it was a mistake.[107]

After the meeting of the trustees, Dr. Grannan again supplied a caustic commentary to O'Connell:

Dr. Charles Warren Stoddard has given in his resignation. . . . The Faculty has demanded, with one dissentient vote, i.e., that of Dr. H. H. H. that the Senate recommend him to the Board for dismissal; and the Senate, without one dissentient voice, did recommend him to the Board for dismissal. However, on hearing of what was in store for him, Charles Warren asked to be allowed to resign, which was allowed. To relieve any of the members of the Faculty of Philosophy of the odium of moving that one of their number be dismissed, Rev. Dr. Grannan, of the Faculty of Theology, made the motion, which was carried unanimously. I am informed by an eye-witness, that the only one who was opposed to the dismissal was the Rector of the University. But he has become a worse poltroon, since he has been named a bishop, than ever before. . . .

A committee was appointed by the Board to investigate the condition (financial, disciplinary, academic, and m. . . l,) of the Varsity. It consists of John Joe of Dubuque [Keane], Spalding and Maes. I tried hard to get them to put Riordan on as Chairman, but he was not here, and he lives so far away that they did not dare to put him on. Though John Joseph is wedded to his blunders, yet it is hoped that Spalding and Maes— two good men—will be able to dominate him. The Committee will sit in January for two weeks, if necessary, and will cite every Professor who has any ideas to give out. I have been informed by himself that Dr. G-----n put it into the heads of the Trustees to leave out of this Committee both the Rector and the Cardinal, so that the meetings would be certainly

---

[106] RDA, "#$%&%$#" to DOC [Grannan to O'Connell] (postmarked Washington, October 28, 1901). The expenses of Conaty's consecration were not met by the University. James was one of Grannan's names for Cardinal Gibbons. The "measly letter on the Varsity," was that of Leo XIII to Cardinal Gibbons, Rome, June 13, 1901, in which the Holy Father praised the University.

[107] RDA, John Ireland to D. J. O'Connell, New York, November 6, 1901.

called, and so that the Professors would feel themselves free to talk as they choose. The present Committee was made up before-hand, so that the Cardinal would not have the option in the choice of the members. Dr. G-----n advised that the names be inserted into the motion so as to go along with it. It was so done. . . .

The Professors have their hand in and are willing to continue to bounce the drones from the hive, as soon as they can. Look out for the heads of Professors Viridis [Greene], Raucher [Rooker], and Hibernator [Hyvernat]—next Spring. . . .

My Dear Dok. You see that we have much to suffer "In questi tristi tempi che scorrono". I feel it in my bones that much of this trouble comes from the machinations of two CHUMPS who met some time ago on the shore of one of the most beautiful of all the Swiss lakes.[108]

The appointment of Charles P. Grannan to the Biblical Commission, and the congratulations he publicly received from the rector,[109] in no way assuaged his temper. Although the meeting was postponed until February, and he could not get the support of the other two "chumps," Grannan was not pessimistic when he again wrote to Denis O'Connell:

Some will face the music and tell all they know and all they think. Others are cowards and poltroons. Chump T.J.S..h.n [Shahan] has retired into his shell and sees nobody. The Bulletin is his craze. He is writing furiously and paying no attention to what is of general interest to the others. Chump no. 2, E. P.c. [Pace], is busy, persuading all the fellows not to say anything against the mismanagement of things here. He is incomprehensible to me. . . . Some others, however, have much fight in them and I am encouraging them. . . . Spalding wants to wipe out everything except Theology and Philosophy. So at least t'is said. Broad John [Keane] wants to add to the expense. He says that our debts, like the debts of England, is [sic] our pride and glory.[110]

With such a background of intrigue, the rector could hardly be expected to appear in a favorable light at the committee meeting held in

[108] RDA, "J-E-S-H-U-R-U-N." to Dok [Grannan to O'Connell] (postmarked Washington, November 24, 1901.) The practice of speaking of himself in the third person is common in the letters of Grannan to O'Connell. "Dr. H.H.H." referred to Henri H. Hyvernat, professor of Semitic languages and biblical archeology. The "two CHUMPS" mentioned at the end of the quotation were Grannan and O'Connell.

[109] ACUA, RRTTS, January 14, 1902; Cf. "University Chronicle," CUB, IX (April, 1903), 311.

[110] RDA, Jeshurun to Doktor [Grannan to O'Connell] (postmarked Washington, January 29, 1902).

Caldwell Hall from February 7 to 14, 1902.[111] With tongue in check, the University *Bulletin* reported, "the Committee was pleased with all that it saw and heard. . . . Everybody at the University was delighted to see this manifestation of deep interest on the part of the Trustees." [112] With more truth O'Connell's Washington correspondent wrote: "I, of course, do not know what was the impression made on the members of the investigating Committee; but judging by what the boys said, the impression ought to be that the present incumbent ought to pack up and get out." [113]

The first result of the investigation was the voluntary resignation of Frederick Zadock Rooker, the secretary of the Apostolic Delegation and lecturer in ethics in the University. His letter of resignation was a masterpiece of sarcasm which effectively reduced the force of all the arguments which might be used to recommend the abolition of the lectureship in ethics—one of the recommendations of the committee.[114] At the same time, he pointed out that it was purely a personal motive that prompted his removal from the University, and in such a case, he could no longer remain with the institution.[115] Aside from questions of personality, it was on the financial side that the committee made the more important findings. As a preview for what would take place at the special meeting in April, the Bishop of Peoria wrote to Cardinal Gibbons:

I sincerely hope that the Waggaman business will be settled in a thoroughly satisfactory manner by the 9th of April, as any doubt on this point would make anything we might propose futile. Abp Williams and yourself will of course make a thorough investigation. Dr. Conaty, it

---

[111] Such was the date given in *CUB,* VIII (March, 1902), 259, although Spalding in his report gave February 4 to 10.

[112] "University Chronicle," *CUB,* VIII (March, 1902), 259.

[113] RDA, Jeshurun to Doktor [Grannan to O'Connell] (postmarked Washington, February 11, 1902).

[114] This recommendation had in turn been received from the governing board of the faculty of philosophy, composed of Maurice F. Egan, John J. Griffin, Edward L. Greene, Henri Hyvernat, Charles P. Neill, Edward A. Pace and Daniel W. Shea. ACUA, CHF, Faculty of Philosophy Governing Board Records, I, 64-65, (March 5, 1902). "It was voted to recommend to the Rector & the Academic Senate:—. . . . IX. That the existing lectureship in Ethics be abolished; and that Dr. W. J. Kerby be appointed instructor in Ethics for the year 1902-3."

[115] ACUA, FBT, Envelope 28, Frederick Z. Rooker to Thomas J. Conaty, Washington, March 3, 1902; March 22, 1902. Cf. Appendix D.

seems to me, laks [sic] business capacity, though I do not wish to say this to any one but yourself.[116]

At the meeting of the trustees on April 9, the investigating committee reported on the question of finances:

The Committee finds that in the management of the University funds there has been not only a lack of business method and of competency, but an almost culpable negligence. . . . It is recommended:
1. That steps be taken at once to provide for the complete safety of the University funds, the revenue derived therefrom being of secondary importance. An examination of the securities in which these funds are invested, led the Committee to the conviction that they were insufficient and in every way unsatisfactory.[117]

The remainder of the report covered matters within the University itself, defining what work was required of a professor, suggesting Dr. McMahon as a special collector for the University, asking for a native-born English-speaking Sulpician to be the President of Divinity College. But the principal burden of this section of the report was directed toward what the character of a university rector should be. The results of the investigation met entirely the approval of Grannan and his coterie, and, with the exception of the development of an Institute of Pedagogy, the trustees' committee brought about a period of retrenchment in the University. The newspapers, which always seemed to find the institution a newsworthy source, did not ignore the latest developments. The Baltimore *American* asserted that Conaty had no desire to attempt a second term at the University, and that the trustees were each grooming possible candidates to take over the financially embarrassed institution.[118] The Baltimore *Sun* did not mention the possibility of a new rector, but it did, inaccurately, lump together all who left the University during the year, and ascribed the reason to the financial condition of the University which had led the trustees to dispense with their services. It gave as the basic reason, "For more than two years it has been apparent that the American Hierarchy did not support the university with the steadfast loyalty

116 BCA, 99-M-6, J. L. Spalding to J. Card. Gibbons, Peoria, March 14, 1902. Thomas E. Waggaman was the treasurer of the Board of Trustees and in charge of the investments.

117 ACUA, FBT, Envelope 27, Report of Special Committee, April 9, 1902. The accuracy of these reports was shown a few years later by the failure of Waggaman with a tremendous financial loss for the University.

118 Baltimore *American,* April 12, 1902.

which Pope Leo XIII expected when he made this apostolic foundation." [119] The *Freeman's Journal* came strongly to the defense of Bishop Conaty, asserting that he would be the unanimous choice of the trustees for the next rectorship, and analysed the troubles by saying "Strong friction and disagreement of views develop a proper spirit of endeavor." [120] It also explained away the departures of professors by stressing the fact that there were only sixteen lay students at the University; therefore, prudence and good discipline would require care that the institution be not overstaffed. At the commencement of 1902, the cardinal chancellor felt it necessary to defend the institution and to retort to the widely circulated rumors by remarking:

From time to time during the year false statements have been circulated throughout the press concerning the finances of the university. . . . As the chancellor, and speaking for the trustees, I wish to give our people to understand that there is no truth whatever in these rumors. . . . It is a young institution and has made wonderful strides. Why should it not be encouraged instead of calumniated? Let there be no fear as to its future. The Holy Father loves it with great intensity. I saw him a year ago and I know how deeply interested he is in its success.[121]

The school year of 1902-1903 opened with anticipation of the trustees' meeting scheduled for November 12, at which the *terna* for the next rectorship would be determined. The meeting did just that, but to understand properly much that happened during the years of Conaty's rectorship, and especially to give the true evaluation to this particular trustees' meeting of November, 1902, the University must be fitted into its place in the general history of the Church in the United States in these same years.

[119] Baltimore *Sun,* April 24, 1902.
[120] New York *Freeman's Journal,* May 3, 1902.
[121] Washington *Evening Star,* June 4, 1902.

Chapter V

AMERICANISM AND THE UNIVERSITY

The Catholic University of America and the disturbance known as "Americanism," which rocked the Church of the United States during the 1880's and 1890's, were intimately related. The story of the one cannot be separated from the other without a loss of the true understanding of each. Neither can be divorced from the general background of the conflicting characters of the period. To report this in its entirety, however, is an impossibility, due to lost, destroyed, or inaccessible archival material, as well as to the limitations of space. The best that can be achieved here, therefore, is an account which will endeavor to trace some few strands of the tangled web, to recount one important phase of an extensive movement that has yet to find its definitive historian.

Thomas T. McAvoy in his article on "Americanism, Fact and Fiction," [1] presented an accurate description of the background of the general subject of Americanism. He drew the distinction between the three types of Americanism, political, theological and, if it may be called such, practical Americanism. Political Americanism and theological Americanism will enter here only in passing, in so far as they affect the third type, practical Americanism. Practical Americanism is a rather elusive term, a name tagged on to the efforts made to accommodate the immigrant groups to the American culture. Because of the number of foreign-born, and their immediate descendants, in her flock, the Catholic Church, with the European and reactionary tinge that some associated with her, bore the brunt of the difficulties accompanying this Americanizing process. These difficulties occasioned a practical, if not admitted, rift between various elements

[1] *CHR*, XXXI (July, 1945), 133-153. This article gives in an admirable way the general background of the conflicting personalities and the incidents which occasioned most of the troubles. It also treats of the European aspects that were expressed in the newspaper controversies in France and Italy, the theological and political productions that were mainly responsible for the letter of Pope Leo XIII on Americanism, the *Testem benevolentiae*. The part of the Paulists, and especially the theological doctrines of Isaac T. Hecker, is treated by Vincent F. Holden, "A Myth in 'L'Americanisme,'" *CHR*, XXXI (July, 1945), 154-170.

within the hierarchy.[2] In time the leaders of the liberal and conservative parties could be determined, although there was a constant wavering on the part of the less involved hierarchical partisans.

John Ireland, Archbishop of St. Paul, was easily identified as the leader of the progressive party. Bishop John J. Keane, Rector of the Catholic University of America, and Monsignor Denis J. O'Connell, Rector of the American College in Rome, were in consistent and active co-operation with Ireland. On crucial occasions the support of Cardinal Gibbons could be relied upon, as the cardinal's almost constant sympathy was with the general trend of ideas as espoused by Ireland and his friends. Less obvious and less consistent support came from Archbishop Patrick W. Riordan of San Francisco, Bishop Camillus P. Maes of Covington, and Archbishop John J. Kain of St. Louis. Bishop John Lancaster Spalding of Peoria, while agreeing in general with the Ireland group, led an independent existence, acting in concert with it only when his own social views coincided with those of the Americanizers.

The conservative party had its leader in Michael A. Corrigan, Archbishop of New York, continuously urged on by his equally outspoken suffragan of Rochester, Bernard J. McQuaid. Richard Gilmour, Bishop of Cleveland, and Patrick J. Ryan, Archbishop of Philadelphia, both gave indirect aid to the conservative group. The German-American bishops proved active auxiliaries, notably Frederick F. X. Katzer, Archbishop of Milwaukee, Ignatius F. Horstmann, Bishop of Cleveland after the death of Gilmour in 1891, and Sebastian G. Messmer, Bishop of Green Bay, and former professor of canon law in the University. It is impossible to draw any hard and fast line through the hierarchy of those days which would put the

[2] The reprinted sermon of a Baptist minister, F. L. Anderson, quoted from the Rochester *Union and Advertiser,* of December 3, 1894, by Frederick J. Zwierlein, *Life and Letters of Bishop McQuaid* (Rome, 1927), III, 234, gives a representative picture of the ordinary American view of the situation. ". . . . there are two distinct and hostile parties in the Roman Catholic Church in America. One is led by Archbishop Ireland. It stands for Americanism and a larger independence. It is sympathetic with modern thought. It believes the Roman Catholic Church should take its place in all the great moral reforms. It is small, but progressive, vigorous, and brave.

"The other party is led by the overwhelming majority of the hierarchy. It is conservative, out of touch with American or modern ideas. It is the old medieval European Church, transplanted into the Nineteenth Century and this country of freedom, interesting as an antiquity and curiosity but fast losing its power and growing in bitterness."

conservatives on one side and the liberals on the other; for many, such as Archbishop John J. Williams of Boston, refused to involve themselves, while others would pass from side to side as each new subject of controversy arose. One of the most influential ecclesiastics who completely shifted his allegiance was America's first apostolic delegate, Archbishop, and after 1896, Cardinal Francesco Satolli, who throughout the entire episode remained a power to be reckoned with, both in the United States and in Rome.

The Catholic University of America had opened in 1889 only after a long and sometimes acrimonious struggle between the two parties of the hierarchy.[3] The University had been born in contention and, during the early years of its life, it seemed destined to live in contention. Opposition to the University came less from the idea and purpose of a university than it did from the personalities involved, and the fostering of private plans. McQuaid and Corrigan had both been instrumental in the development of Seton Hall College at South Orange, New Jersey, and it was only natural that when the site for the new university was shifted from Seton Hall to Washington that they should view it with a somewhat jaundiced eye. Moreover, Bishop McQuaid was busy during the late 1880's and the early 1890's with plans for what became his prime love, St. Bernard's Seminary, and this helped to solidify his opposition to the projected university. When the university became a fact, McQuaid proceeded with the development of St. Bernard's, convinced that the University would shortly be a failure. With that in view, he eventually succeeded in obtaining from Rome the right for his seminary to grant theological degrees equal to those of the University.[4]

[3] Cf. John Tracy Ellis, *The Formative Years of the Catholic University of America* (Washington, 1946), for the complete account of the interesting factional struggle that finally resulted in a victory for Spalding, Keane, and Ireland and the establishment of the University.

[4] The document granting this right may be found in "Analecta," *AER*, XXV (July, 1901), 59-61. In the same issue in "Conferences," pp. 69-71, there is a section on "Academic Degrees in the Rochester Theological Seminary," which carries a letter from McQuaid to his fellow bishops telling of the advantages of the Rochester seminary and using the number of students already enrolled to draw an indirect comparison with the University, favorable to Rochester. McQuaid wrote an article, "Our American Seminaries," *AER*, XVI (May, 1897), 461-480, telling of the advantages, the life and education offered at St. Bernard's. It is noteworthy for its pointed lack of references to the University and the higher degrees offered there.

Archbishop Corrigan also had a seminary project in mind, as well as having Fordham in his see city, but his main objection seems to have been more personal. John J. Keane, the Rector of the University, was, in his estimation, a meddler who had tried to interfere in the case of Dr. Edward McGlynn. While Keane was in Rome in 1887 on university business, he had written to McGlynn, at the request of Cardinal Simeoni, in an endeavor to have the New York priest make his peace with his archbishop. Although Keane's letter was of no avail in reconciling McGlynn with the archbishop on the question of the single tax doctrine, it was not without results. About these results Keane wrote to Denis O'Connell:

Just before his Jubilee, Abp. Corrigan wrote in reference to that letter of mine from Rome, which he has hitherto ignored. I responded most affectionately, giving explanations for peace' sake [sic]. A correspondence has ensued, showing a bitter spirit in him. His last clearly shows that my first reply to him was at once sent to la Signora [sic], & that she has vigorously canvassed all available parties, from Card. Simeoni down, to prove that I was regarded as a meddler in the affairs of the Abp. of N.Y. This will doubtless raise embarrassments & hinderances in my way in Rome. *Personally,* I do not care, — but I regret the obstacles thus thrown in the way of what I firmly believe to be the work of God & His Church.[5]

Probably not unrelated to the Keane letter to McGlynn was the resignation—much to the dismay of the chancellor, Cardinal Gibbons—of Corrigan from the Board of Trustees of the University, giving as his reason that "the care of my Diocese requires all my time

[5] RDA, John J. Keane to D. J. O'Connell, Baltimore, November 2, 1888. La Signorina meant Miss Ella B. Edes, a newspaper woman in Rome, who frequently acted as Roman agent for Corrigan and McQuaid. The letter of Keane to Corrigan, Chicago, September 16, 1888, NYAA, E-k, presents a review of Keane's stand and is a full explanation of why he became involved in the case. He protests that he gave no encouragement to McGlynn: "That the unfortunate priest should have answered me, as he has, only by insult and misrepresentation, I could very quietly let pass without feeling it; but that I should have been suspected and accused of acting against you, and abetting disaffections towards you, has indeed been a sorrow to me." In all there is a series of six letters from Keane in answer to those of Corrigan, dated from September 11 to October 31, 1888, after which Corrigan decided to say no more, even if he was not completely satisfied. New York *Freeman's Journal,* June 18, 1887, carried an interview with Keane in which he related his attempts to save McGlynn.

and attention." [6] By July 1888, however, he had returned to the board and Gibbons must have been encouraged to hear from O'Connell:

Your news about Abp. Corrigan's return to the Board did not surprise me; was in fact what I expected, and part of what I intimated to you some time ago. In a late audience with the Holy Father I said that the University was getting on well, but of course it had its enemies. "*Si*" he replied, "*quello Corrigan.*"[7]

The final establishment of the University, however, did not bring peace to the American Church. The School Controversy of the early 1890's called the opposing groups to their posts once more. Corrigan, McQuaid, and the German-American bishops hit at the Faribault-Stillwater plan of John Ireland, aided as they were, by several Jesuit writers, and by Monsignor Joseph Schroeder, professor of dogmatic theology in the Catholic University of America. This group had, at least, the implied approbation of Archbishop Ryan of Philadelphia, through the pages of the *American Ecclesiastical Review,* published in his see city.[8] Ireland was able to call on the talents of Thomas Bouquillon, professor of moral theology in the University. In two pamphlets Bouquillon ably set forth the moral principles which, under certain conditions, justified the participation of the State in the education of its subjects, and answered the objections of the opposing faction.[9] Keane, in various newspaper interviews, gave his support

[6] BCA, 83-T-6/1, M. A. Corrigan to J. Card. Gibbons, New York, November 28, 1887. Gibbons wrote to Corrigan asking him to change his mind but in a letter of December 17, 1887 (BCA, 83-V-4), Corrigan reasserted his intention, and so Gibbons reluctantly accepted his resignation on December 23, 1887 (NYAA, C-15).

[7] BCA, 84-T-7, D. J. O'Connell to J. Card. Gibbons, Rome, July 25, 1888.

[8] Cf. Daniel F. Reilly, O.P., *The School Controversy (1891-1893)* (Washington, 1943), for an extensive treatment of the subject. *The American Ecclesiastical Review,* Vols. VI and VII for 1892, has many articles, all of which support the anti-Ireland side of the case. Schroeder played a more reserved part, but was definitely active in the affair, writing a book on the subject, entitled *Une dernière phase de la question scolaire aux Etats-Unis,* and reviewed in the *American Ecclesiastical Review,* XI (July, 1894), 72-74. The most outstanding Jesuit writers were René I. Holaind, James Conway, Salvatore M. Brandi, and D. T. O'Sullivan.

[9] *Education: To Whom Does It Belong?* (Baltimore, 1891); *Education: To Whom Does It Belong? A Rejoinder to Critics* (Baltimore, 1892). McQuaid commented on the situation by writing to O'Connell on January 16, 1892 (RDA): "Just now, Bouquillon, in the name of his Superiors, has set the American Catholic World agog on the school question, apropos to the Fairbault

to Bouquillon. Satolli, recently arrived in the country as ablegate of Leo XIII, and after a month's visit in St. Paul, presented his fourteen propositions [10] at the meeting of the archbishops in New York on November 17, 1892. Satolli's efforts were an attempt to bring peace to the American scene. His endeavors succeeded only in stirring further discussion. A doubtful peace was won only after Gibbons had appealed to Rome and was answered on May 31, 1893, by Pope Leo XIII who confirmed the *tolerari potest* for Ireland's school plan as originally stated by Satolli the previous November.

In the same eventful meeting of November, 1892, another question had arisen, namely, the participation in the World's Parliament of Religions at the Columbian Exposition of 1893 in Chicago. A somewhat hesitant approval was given to Catholic participation and Keane was appointed to represent the American Church in the preparations. Gibbons, Ireland, and Keane were active in the Chicago congress, motivated by a desire of church union, but a union based on a return to the "old Catholic Universal Church." [11] The conservatives were highly incensed at this seeming co-operation with Protestants, Mo-

---

[*sic*] arrangement. If these imported Europeans, with their old world motives, would only keep quiet, until they had found out where they were, it would conduce greatly to their comfort. . . . The newspapers tell us that Ireland will soon leave for Rome. As it is not his visit *ad limina,* we wonder what takes him there. He is the head and the front of the new liberalistic party in the American Church. If he would stay at home a little more, and mind his own diocese the latter would be the gainer. He is away from his diocese only a little more than Cardinal Gibbons." John Ireland informed Keane of the results of his Roman visit when he wrote in April, 1892: "The matter is summed up in the Faribault plan being allowed—Dr. Bouquillon's brochures shall certainly not be examined—Moreover the whole theological world of Rome is coming over to him—outside of the Jesuits. . . . The worst enemy of the University is Card. Mazzella. He has ever a sneer for it. The University will have to gird its loins, & fight: then it will win. . . . We must make it thoroughly American— lock out all traitors. If you cannot freeze out Schroeder I lose confidence in you. Mgr. Corrigan must not be allowed to boss the directors & exclude from chairs men whom he dislikes. I do not forgive you the loss of Mivart. Don't be afraid of good sound liberalism. Confidence in self, & the support of the American people will carry us always through. I can find no professor of Canon Law. You must educate your professors, & then hold on to them—making bishops only of those who are not worth keeping as professors." ACUA, CHF, John Ireland to John J. Keane, Rome, April 26, 1892.

[10] Cf. Reilly, *op. cit.,* pp. 271-276.

[11] John Henry Barrows (Ed.), *The World's Parliament of Religions* (Chicago, 1893), I, 182. This gives the final speech of Keane at the closing of the

hammedans, and pagans. John Keane wrote an accurate prophecy when he said:

> I think he (Satolli) looks askance at our part in the Parliament of Religions, as do, no doubt, all the ultra conservatives. I got into it, first at the urgent solicitations of Abp. Ireland, — then at the request of the Abps. at their meeting in N. Y. — and I am confident that the result is an enormous advantage to the Church. But I take it for granted that I shall be denounced for it. So be it.[12]

The New York election of 1894 produced a further source of difference, when John Ireland spent several weeks before the election in New York City in close contact with Republican leaders. This was all the more aggravating since in the spring of the same year, McQuaid had been defeated as a candidate for the office of regent of the University of the State of New York by Sylvester Malone, a Brooklyn priest, and a *persona non grata* to both Corrigan and McQuaid, and this supposedly through the Republican influence of Archbishop Ireland. A series of charges and countercharges were dispatched to Rome by Corrigan and Ireland, and McQuaid could not remain passive in the fray. On November 25, 1894, he entered the lists with a sermon, delivered in the Rochester cathedral, attacking the interference of Ireland. Satolli, still the friend of Ireland, and amazed at a public denunciation of this kind by one bishop of another, sent the sermon to Rome and also admonished McQuaid. In answer to a request for an explanation of his extraordinary conduct to be offered to Rome, McQuaid found the opportunity he had been awaiting, and he unburdened himself of charges he had been cherishing for years. His position was summarized in one of his statements:

> Of late years, a spirit of false liberalism is springing up in our body under such leaders as Mgr. Ireland and Mgr. Keane, that, if not checked in time, will bring disaster on the Church. Many a time Catholic laymen have remarked that the Catholic Church they once knew seems to be passing away, so greatly shocked are they at what they see passing around them.[13]

---

congress. The two-volume work of Barrows gives a chronicle of the congress and the papers presented during the gathering. Cf. Zwierlein, *op. cit.*, III, 235-240.

[12] RDA, John J. Keane to D. J. O'Connell, Washington, October 10, 1893.

[13] Zwierlein, *op. cit.*, III, 224. A long account of the McQuaid-Ireland relations, definitely colored by Zwierlein's obvious affection for McQuaid, may be found in this work, Chapter XXXII, pp. 160-251.

So far as the present writer has been able to determine, no definite conclusion was brought to this particular episode, although it could hardly be without influence on later happenings.

John Ireland must have been strengthened in his liberal course by the news that Keane had brought back from Rome in the preceding summer of 1894, and by the audience which the University rector had with Leo XIII; of which Keane had written to Gibbons:

. . . . we got at the University. First I explained our success and presented an album of photographic views. Then we came to our difficulties, and discussed fully the opposition 1. of the Germans, 2. of the Jesuits, 3. of N.Y. — 4. of all opposed to Mgr. Satolli and his policy, with which they identify the University. The last point launched us into the discussion of the delegation and Mgr. S. Here is where the Pope is most determined, because the delegation is simply an element in his "policy," which is, the breaking down of the influence of the Triple Alliance, — which means monarchism, militarism, and the oppression of the Papacy, —by enhancing the influence of democratic France and democratic America — an influence which presages democratic Italy, or Federated Italy, with the Pope in a position suitable to him. On this policy he is inflexibly bent.[14]

In spite of this encouragement for the Americanizers, a portent of what lay before Keane came in June, 1895, when Denis O'Connell sent to Gibbons his resignation as Rector of the American College in Rome, an action which was intended to go into effect in October.[15] For years O'Connell had acted as a general agent at Rome for all members of the American hierarchy, although in spirit he had been a follower of Ireland and Gibbons. In the later years of his rectorship, he came to act more particularly as the agent of the Ireland faction and his correspondence with Corrigan and McQuaid slackened. By 1895 O'Connell was definitely identified in the minds of many as a member of the Ireland party. That his resignation had been requested by the Holy See is certain.[16] Precisely why it was asked is still a somewhat open question. One of the most plausible explanations was that given by Salvatore M. Brandi, S.J., one of the editors of the *Civiltà Cattolica*, in a confidential letter to Archbishop Corrigan:

14 BCA, 93-J-7, John J. Keane to J. Card. Gibbons, Pegli (near Geneva), July 31, 1894.

15 BCA, 93-V-4, D. J. O'Connell to J. Card. Gibbons, Rome, June 7, 1895.

16 Cf. BCA, 94-B-4, J. Card. Gibbons to D. J. O'Connell, Baltimore, October 11, 1895, copy: "And it is sad to think that this excellent condition of the College was not taken into consideration, as well as your own personal high char-

Dr. O'Connell's resignation has surprised no one in Rome. It was given *spinte* and not *sponte* at the demand of the Holy Father, to whom complaints against the Rector had been made by the Cardinals of the Propaganda. The principle [*sic*] complaints were, first, neglect of duty by frequent and long absences from Rome, second, want of confidence in the Rector on the part of the great majority of American Bishops. Besides these reasons, the Holy Father, I think, was displeased with the Rector because of his relations with Miss McTavish of Baltimore. . . . Miss McTavish, at the request of the Rector, and the day *after* the pontifical audience was received at the Quirinal by the queen. Such conduct gave offence at the Vatican. . . . I have heard a very eminent personage express the hope that the Archbishops, to whom it belongs to make the terna for the new Rector, would propose to the Holy See only those men who enjoy their full confidence and allow no clique to take the upper hand.[17]

At any rate, his resignation was the beginning of an exile of over seven years which O'Connell endured in Rome. Although he still retained his former friends to a great extent, especially the two Cardinals Vannutelli and others of the *Concilionisti*,[18] he remained in the bad graces of the Pope and of Satolli. Gibbons made O'Connell the vicar of his titular church, Santa Maria in Trastevere. Thus he remained in the Eternal City, acting in so far as he could as the agent of the Gibbons and Ireland party and from time to time making trips to Germany and other countries in Europe in their behalf.

The resignation of Denis O'Connell was but a breeze compared to the tornado stirred up in September of the following year, when the resignation of John J. Keane as Rector of the Catholic University of America was announced.[19] This bit of news marked the end of

---

acter & reputation, before your resignation was peremptorily demanded." In 1888, the Pope himself had declared that O'Connell was indispensable for the American College when he had been urged for the See of Richmond. Cf. BCA, 85-L-9, John J. Keane to J. Card. Gibbons, Rome, December 18, 1888.

[17] PFA-A, S. M. Brandi, S.J., to M. A. Corrigan, Rome, July 8, 1895 (photostat). The rumor that a reference by O'Connell to the relations between Leo XIII and Satolli was the cause of his dismissal seems to be proved false by a letter from Ireland in 1894 to O'Connell, which placed the origin of the remark with Corrigan. Cf. RDA, John Ireland to D. J. O'Connell, New York, April 29, 1894.

[18] "Cardinals Who May Be the Next Pope," *CW*, LXIX (July, 1899), 433-448. The *Concilionisti* were those who wished to arrive at some *modus vivendi* with the Italian government.

[19] Cf. Ahern, *op. cit.* This study gives an extensive account of Keane and the University during those years, as well as the part that Keane played in the controversies of the day.

the first phase of the Americanism conflict, with an apparent victory for the conservatives. The great surprise came in the sudden change of Satolli, who formerly was most favorable to Keane and Ireland, but who had made a *volte-face* on the eve of his return to Rome in 1896. There he was to receive the red hat and afterward assume his duties as Prefect of the Congregation of Studies. The press gave wide coverage to Keane's dismissal, and was almost unanimous in its sympathy for the dismissed rector, with the exception of some German language newspapers and the *Western Watchman* of St. Louis, edited by Father David S. Phelan.[20] The two most frequently mentioned causes for the dismissal were the differences of Keane and Satolli and the efforts of certain German-Americans, centering in Monsignor Joseph Schroeder of the University faculty, to remove this temperance advocate and Americanizer from the scene.

McQuaid was exultant, and he hastened to communicate his joy to his friend, the Archbishop of New York:

The news from Rome is astounding. The failure of the University is known in Rome at last, and the blame is thrown on Keane. Much of it is due to him, but other causes are there. These causes are irremediable now. The failure implicates the Holy Father, who was made to father the undertaking from the beginning.

What collapses on every side! Gibbons, Ireland, and Keane!!! They were cock of the walk for a while and dictated to the country and thought to run our dioceses for us.[21]

Some weeks later he expressed his feeling of reassurance at the trend which had overtaken the party of the opposition:

They are not talking now of knocking your mitre or mine off our heads. They had things their own way for a long time.[22]

Newspaper accounts foretold the dismissal of several professors in the University, and they even went so far as to say that Gibbons and Ireland were in danger of being removed from their positions because

---

[20] The New York *World,* October 8, 1896, offered an interesting sample: "The Jesuits are the ones wholly responsible . . . . probably he might be found in Rome in the College of Cardinals, and in the person of the German Jesuit, Andreas Steinhuber Schroeder's Ordinary. Events will prove whether American Catholics will tamely allow Jesuitism to rule them."

[21] Zwierlein, *op. cit.,* III, 241. B. J. McQuaid to M. A. Corrigan, Rochester, October 3, 1896.

[22] NYAA, C-40-M, B. J. McQuaid to M. A. Corrigan, Rochester, November 13, 1896.

of liberalism.[23] However, a letter from Leo XIII reassured the wondering victims.[24] Keane was called to Rome, where, among other official positions, he became a canon of the Basilica of St. John Lateran, of which Cardinal Satolli was archpriest, as well as being made Archbishop of Damascus. Unofficially, he joined with O'Connell as a second representative of the Americanizers in Rome. In spite of all this, John Ireland was not cheerful:

> Of course Bp. Keane's presence in Rome will be a wonderful help. Our enemies did not know what they were doing when they had him removed from Washington. Was not Satolli's letter sweet? I frightened him in my last interview in Brooklyn. Nothing but stern courage on our part will avert disaster from us. We are timid children, & we are treated as children. Our enemies are not timid.
>
> The University is dead: nothing can revive it. The Jesuits have triumphed here—for good.[25]

But John Ireland did not remain discouraged. He was not of the timid brand of men; he was a battler, and he was soon prepared for the "War of 1897." [26] The battlefield was an old one, the first major skirmish having taken place simultaneously with the Roman negotiations for the founding of the University. Ireland and Keane from Rome at that time had been able to gather almost unanimous support from the non-German-American bishops to remove the danger from the petition for national churches in America on an equal footing with the English-speaking parishes. This request had been submitted to Rome by the Reverend P. M. Abbelen, with the backing of a group of St. Louis priests.[27] The second attempt to obtain a better position for the Germans in America, the so-called Lucerne Memorial of the St. Raphael's Society, presented to the Pope on April 16, 1891, by Peter Paul Cahensly, brought equally speedy and almost unanimous

[23] New York *Tribune*, November 14, 1896.

[24] BCA, 94-U-2, Sebastian Martinelli to J. Card. Gibbons, Washington, December 2, 1897.

[25] BCA, 94-U-1, John Ireland to J. Card. Gibbons, St. Paul, December 2, 1896.

[26] RDA, Thomas J. Shahan to D. J. O'Connell, Washington, February 21, 1898. "Ireland is here these days, very happy. We have lived over the War of 1897."

[27] John J. Meng, "Cahenslyism: The First Stage, 1883-1891." *CHR*, XXXI (January, 1946), 389-413. The two articles by Meng in the *Review*, the one mentioned above, and "Cahenslyism: The Second Chapter, 1891-1910," XXXII (October, 1946), 302-340, give the general picture of the German problem in the American Church, of which the present article forms but an incident. This

opposition from America.[28]   It resulted in a deepening of distrust between the Americanizers and their opponents. Cahensly was unsuccessful in his attempts, but Joseph Pohle and Joseph Schroeder of the University faculty were prominent at the St. Raphael's Society's next convention which took place in Mainz at the end of August, 1892. Schroeder spoke words of high praise for Cahensly in a speech which also lauded Corrigan, Katzer, and Ireland's most aggravating suffragan, Bishop Otto Zardetti of St. Cloud, for their defense of the parochial school.[29]

This incident was not the only thing that put Schroeder into disfavor with the liberals. He, in common with the majority of the Germans and other immigrant groups, was not hesitant in expressing his views on the question of temperance and on the manner of observing Sunday. On these two points the liberals took a conservative stand, Keane and Ireland especially being strong protagonists for total abstinence. They were naturally opposed, therefore, to the saloons and beer-gardens doing business on Sundays. In this they had the strong support of many temperance societies which were then, perhaps, at the height of their influence and popularity. The Germans and the conservative school of thought generally favored neither the "Puritan Sunday" nor the confusing of temperance with total abstinence,[30] and their attitude furnished the cause for some of the strongest opposition to "Americanization."

---

encounter was not speedily forgotten, as a letter of John Ireland written in 1890 demonstrates: "I do not know whether you read the German papers. The old question has been revived, and is being discussed with a great deal of rancor. Father Abbelen has published a phamplet [sic] and distributed copies of it to the German Priests of the country. It contains both our documents, his own memorial, an introduction in which he states that he had the full approval of the Archbishop of Milwaukee, and that he was defeated only by our representations. The translations of our documents are poorly made, and often incorrect." ACUA, CHF, John Ireland to John J. Keane, St. Paul, March 3, 1890.

28 Cf. Meng. op. cit., pp. 402-413. The figures on the losses of immigrants to the faith after arriving in America led the St. Raphael's Society, in conference at Lucerne, to ask for national churches for immigrants, with priests speaking their own language, and the preservation of the national tongue in the schools and churches as a means of preserving the immigrant's faith.

29 Meng, "Cahenslyism: The Second Chapter, 1891-1910," op. cit., p. 329.

30 Father George Zurcher, pastor of St. Joseph's Church in Buffalo, a Germanophobe and temperance fanatic, presented an interesting account of the part temperance played in the conflicts of the day and the active role taken by Schroeder, Keane, and others in the question of Sunday observance and tem-

The first result of the Mainz convention was an endeavor to rid the University of the two German professors, who had made themselves so disliked by the "liberals." Cahensly was worried over such a possibility, for he wrote to Corrigan in his somewhat shaky English:

I also know from very good authority, that Msgr. Ireland, during his stay in Rome, passed unfair remarks about Msgr. Dr. Schroeder and Dr. Pohle, professors at the Catholic University in Washington, saying, that they must quit their chairs. He now will surely, use all his endeavors with his friend Msgr. Keane, in order to get these men removed as soon as possible. . . . In the interest of the Catholic Church of America would I be sorry, were these learned men to get lost to the University.[31]

Schroeder himself realized what was before him, and he did not hesitate to tell Archbishop Corrigan:

Meanwhile the day which will decide my fate and that of Dr. Pohle draws near. I have many reasons to believe that my silence in the controversies of the day was not enough for Mgr. Keane or his friends and they are still determined to have their victim. . . . Nevertheless, those gentlemen of the University are badly mistaken if they think that I am going to resign without being forced to do so.[32]

The tenacity of Schroeder irked Keane, for he wrote to O'Connell: "Schroeder holds on, & there is no way to oust him as yet, but he sees he has to be quiet." [33] Again in January, 1894, after Pohle had been invited to accept the chair of dogmatic theology at Münster, Keane wrote to O'Connell: "Pohle leaves us for a chair of Dogma in Münster. Would that Schroeder would do the same. He stands his ground, and the Board won't take action. But it won't last long so." [34]

The spring meeting of the Board of Trustees of the University in 1894 took place on April 4, during which a document of impor-

---

perance. Although highly prejudiced in his interpretations, he did show the agitation of the day by quoting widely from German-American newspapers and other scattered sources. His work, published after the dismissal of Keane, entitled "Foreign Ideas in the Catholic Church in America," appeared in the *Roycroft Quarterly,* I (November, 1896).

[31] NYAA, C-41, P. P. Cahensly to M. A. Corrigan, Limburg a. d. Lahn, October 31, 1892.

[32] NYAA, Catholic University of America File, Jos. Schroeder to M. A. Corrigan, Staten Island, June 23, 1893.

[33] RDA, John J. Keane to D. J. O'Connell, Atlantic City, October 10, 1893.

[34] RDA, John J. Keane to D. J. O'Connell, Washington, January 5, 1894.

tance was presented. Pohle, in a long letter, tendered his resignation, taking this occasion to justify the stand of Schroeder and himself. Schroeder, he said, had been abused because the professors of the University had been mixing in public questions of the day and taking a stand which he and Schroeder felt bound to oppose. He stated further:

I pass a similar judgment upon his (Schroeder's) attitude in the s.c. movement against Cahenslyism. Whilst condemning in common with him the policy falsely ascribed to Mr. Cahensly, I have publicly protested in common with him against such a scandalous crusade, based upon calumnious misrepresentations. I do not regret it; I even declare that this unchristian agitation influenced not a little my determination to leave America. Certain parties have accused us of a narrow national spirit, from which we were and are still far removed, perhaps more so, than our accusers themselves.[35]

At any rate, Pohle's resignation was accepted by the board and Schroeder was left alone, if not in peace, at least not in open warfare. Except for a request from Cardinal Gibbons that Schroeder should contribute to the University *Bulletin,* to which he agreed,[36] the campaign to remove Schroeder was suspended until after the dismissal of Keane. Meanwhile Schroeder continued active in German-American circles, notably in the first convention of the Union of German Roman Catholic Societies of the State of New York, at which the title of "protector" was offered to Archbishop Corrigan. To encourage him to accept the title, it was mentioned that: "It may please Your Grace to learn . . . that Very Rev. Mgr. Schroeder, D.D., was actively guiding the meetings in their debates and in formulating the resolutions that were passed." [37]

With the removal of Bishop Keane as rector in September, 1896, the suspended campaign against Schroeder was taken up with a new vigor, and this time under a more personal aspect. It was believed by some that Schroeder had spent the summer of 1896 in Rome for the purpose of working against Keane, through the instrumentality of Andreas Cardinal Steinhuber, S.J., and other German and pro-

[35] BCA, 93-D-9, Jos. Pohle to the Board of Trustees, Washington, end of March, 1894.

[36] BCA, 94-L-10, J. Card. Gibbons to Jos. Schroeder, Baltimore, April 23, 1896, copy; BCA, 94-L-13, Jos. Schroeder to J. Card. Gibbons, Washington, April 26, 1896.

[37] NYAA, G-19, J. Schaefer, Secretary, to M. A. Corrigan, New York, July 17, 1896.

German ecclesiastics. Schroeder made frequent denials that such had been the purpose of his visit, and he gave an interview which was reported in the press:

In conversation with his holiness, Mgr. Schroeder discussed the affairs of the university, and especially the foundation of the chair of Germanic literature. In regard to this the Pope complimented the German Catholics very highly, both for their Americanism and their devotion to the church. He expressed his wish that the chair of Germanic literature be founded, and commissioned Mgr. Schroeder to convey that wish to the German Catholics in this country.

Mgr. Schroeder laughed at the report that he was the head of the opposition among the professors at the university to the rector. "I am the only German here," said he, "and if I head the party, I am also the whole of it."[38]

The choice of the new rector of the University, in December, 1896, in the person of Thomas J. Conaty, had its interesting aspects for the problems then at issue. Conaty was a priest of the Diocese of Springfield and a pastor in Worcester, Massachusetts, an active temperance worker as well as Irish by birth, Irish in outlook, a member of a number of Irish organizations. His appointment would have been regarded as a direct blow to the German-Americans, if it were not for the fact that he was also a friend of Corrigan. The friendship of Conaty with the Archbishop of New York had arisen mainly through the Catholic Summer School near Plattsburg, New York, of which Conaty had been the president. In general, Conaty was looked on as a compromise candidate, although he had previously attracted the favorable attention of Satolli for his summer school work. Several German-American papers looked on his appointment as a victory for the Keane faction; one was puzzled by Satolli's action: "It is strange that Satolli, a partisan of the German element and one who has crossed the American party, should have recommended Conaty's appointment." [39] They were not the only people puzzled in their efforts to

---

[38] Washington *Post,* October 7, 1896. The German Roman Catholic Central Society, composed of German Catholic Benevolent Societies, at their convention in Detroit in September, 1896, had determined to raise $50,000 to found a chair for German language and literature in the University, before Keane's dismissal had become known. Cf. NYAA, G-25, Anton Bickle to M. A. Corrigan, Milwaukee, April 5, 1897. While there had been German opposition to the University from the beginning there also had been German support, for at no time did the Germans form a solid block.

[39] *Morgan Journal* (New York), November 21, 1896.

determine the motives that prompted Satolli's action in that year of 1896.

When the first stunning effect of Keane's removal had worn off, the forces began to assemble against Schroeder. By September, 1897, after a summer in which O'Connell could meet some of the University professors in Europe and prepare the way in Germany for support there, Archbishop Ireland was ready to make the meeting of the University Board of Trustees his battleground for the "War of 1897." It would be the first move to win back the ground lost by Keane's removal. He did not enter the battle alone, as he told O'Connell:

> Abp. Riordan will spend a week in St. Paul on his way to Washington. . . . He & I are hot against Schroeder: he will lead the fight. The obstacle is C. Gibbons, who talks of giving a monitum to Schr. I wish you would at once write to the Cardinal a very strong letter, giving him an idea of the support we have in Germany. . . . If Maes stands with us, I have hopes: Corrigan and Ryan will vote to gain friends—and not for the University; Williams & Gibbons will want peace.[40]

Neither did he enter the battle unopposed, for Bishop Horstmann of Cleveland had written to Corrigan, "I depend on you to be present at the meeting of the University Board Oct. 20 to support me if any action is taken against Monsy. Schroeder." [41]

In the meeting of the trustees, at the conclusion of the rector's report, Conaty spoke concerning the internal condition of the institution. He presented the charges against Schroeder and, for the welfare of the University, as rector, he demanded that his resignation be requested. The battle was on, with Horstmann, Corrigan, and Ryan arrayed against Ireland, Maes, Riordan, Placide L. Chapelle, and Keane. Keane returned yearly from Rome to attend the meetings, for, while his resignation as rector had been accepted, the board would not allow him to resign from his trusteeship. The charges in general were that Schroeder had taken practically no part in University life during the past years and that he was a source of contention among the faculty. After heated discussion a resolution was drawn up which asked for Schroeder's resignation. Gibbons, the chancellor, then had to read a cablegram which he had received from Cardinal

[40] RDA, John Ireland to D. J. O'Connell, St. Paul, September 13, 1897.

[41] NYAA, C-40-h, Ign. F. Horstmann to M. A. Corrigan, Cleveland, September 29, 1897. Horstmann had prepared the defense with Schroeder before February, 1897. Cf. ACUA, CHF, Ign. F. Horstmann to Thomas J. Conaty, Philadelphia, February 26, 1897. Cf. also Appendix A.

Rampolla, the papal Secretary of State: "The Holy Father has given Schroeder of the Cath. Univ. to understand that it would be better for him not to resign. Now it appears that the Board of Bishops intend to force him to do so. Y. E. will, if occasion requires, with delicacy and prudence call their attention to the unfittingness of such a measure." [42] When the vote on the resolution was taken, the result was ten to four in favor of dismissal, but it was also voted to delay action until the reasons for Schroeder's dismissal could be laid before the Holy Father. This ended the first session. When the trustees assembled the next morning, Gibbons stated that things might be settled more easily if some assurance could be received that Schroeder would resign. Horstmann agreed to do what he could to secure such assurance. In the afternoon session he was able to produce a letter from Professor Schroeder, in which, after an explanation of all the circumstances including the fact that he had returned to the University in the fall of 1897 only at the insistence of the Pope and of Cardinal Steinhuber, Schroeder stated that he would be ready to resign whenever the Pope would give permission. With this statement, the entire case was forwarded to the Holy See and temporarily allowed to rest in America. [43]

Through some unknown source the charges presented against Schroeder leaked out to the newspapers, which published on October 21 and 22, accounts of the affair that were highly uncomplimentary to Monsignor Schroeder. As a result Schroeder made his own letter to the Board of Trustees public, and informed Gibbons of the fact. [44] Although Schroeder had not yet resigned, enough had been accomplished for the friends of Keane to rejoice, and to warrant revealing definitely that arrangements had previously been made to effect the removal of Schroeder. Archbishop Chapelle wrote to O'Connell:

The University meeting and the Conference of the Metropolitans have been held & I take the first opportunity to inform you that I have *kept my*

---

[42] ACUA, MMBT, October 20, 1897, p. 73, Cardinal Rampolla to J. Card. Gibbons, Rome, October 16, 1897.

[43] ACUA, MMBT, October 21, 1897, pp. 74-76. These are the official minutes as presented by Horstmann. However, a letter from Maes in the files of the trustees, written to Conaty on November 19, 1897, from Covington, gives a slightly different account, although it is not in conflict with what is presented in the text above. For the report of the rector to the Board of Trustees, as well as the Gibbons' report to Rome, Cf. Appendix B, C.

[44] BCA, 95-U-7, Jos. Schroeder to J. Card. Gibbons, Washington, October 22, 1897.

154

pledges to the very best of my ability. Schroeder has been practically ousted & I did my best by word and vote to reach that happy consummation. Card. Steinhuber's interference alone prevented absolute and final action on the part of the Board.[45]

Thomas J. Shahan, professor of church history in the University, also joined the list of those writing to O'Connell in exultation:

It was a terrible siege. Of a great battle nothing was wanting but the guns and the smoke. For the rest, feeling and passion just raged behind the doors of the senate-room where it all went on, in McMahon Hall. You know all up to our departure. As soon as we came back we started in, and secured sufficient evidence.[46]

Another member of the University faculty, most probably Charles P. Grannan, professor of sacred scripture, added his version to Monsignor O'Connell:

The battle is over & we remain to tell the tale. We tore him up root, trunk & branch. . . . It was a test of strength of the two parties. While the *battle* is over, the *war* is not yet ended. . . . You can see that the promises made in the "Hotel Engel" have been kept. Even the Pontifical bombshell exploded in our camp on the 20th inst., did not make me budge one inch or lose one particle of hope.[47]

But all the interested parties in the meeting were not in a happy mood, for Horstmann wrote to Gibbons:

Poor Schroeder! I pass over the whole long conspiracy against him. I felt sure that if I secured from him the assurance that he would leave at the end of this year that all proceedings against him would drop, but it seems that as far as they can they are determined to crucify him. . . . I am sick of the whole affair but convinced also that he will find Justice in

---

[45] RDA, P. L. Chapelle to D. J. O'Connell, New York, October 23, 1897.

[46] RDA, T. J. S. [Shahan] to D. J. O'Connell, Washington, October 23, 1897. The gathering of evidence had included the preparation of affidavits signed by prominent Washington citizens to attest the fact that Schroeder frequented saloons. Looked at objectively, it was a conflict of mentalities. Schroeder, with the German and European attitude could hardly see anything wrong in drinking a glass of beer in public. The temperance men of the opposition did see something very reprehensible in this. Again, this was a clash of American customs, puritanical though they might have been, with German customs.

[47] RDA, ——————— to D. J. O'Connell, Philadelphia postmark, October 25, 1897. This is one of a very interesting series of letters in the Richmond archives, which are either anonymous or are written over the names of Jeshurun, Grapeshot, Grapes, G. P. S. T., or C. P. G., all of which point definitely to Charles P. Grannan as their writer.

Rome. I know and he realizes and did realize last year that Drs. Shahan and Grannan would never rest until he left.[48]

Cardinal Rampolla finally transmitted Leo XIII's permission for Schroeder to resign, provided his good name be preserved. The Rampolla letter arrived at the Apostolic Delegation in Washington at the end of November.[49] After some reports that Schroeder would join Monsignor Joseph Jessing at the Pontifical College Josephinum near Columbus, Ohio, it was announced from Berlin on December 5 by the Prussian Minister of Education and Ecclesiastical Affairs that Schroeder had been appointed to the Catholic Academy of Münster. This allowed a graceful means for Schroeder to tender his resignation from the University on December 29, the day after he received his official appointment.[50] After a farewell dinner at Columbus, Ohio, before forty-five German-American priests from all over the United States, with a final jab at the American liberals, Schroeder departed in February, 1898, to take up his new position at Münster.[51]

The most dignified summation of the entire incident was given by the first rector. He had written to Dr. Garrigan in December, 1897:

Now the University has ended the chapter of its first and greatest difficulties. It was happily closed by the action of the Board of Directors at their last meeting. As you are already aware, their action has been fully endorsed by the Holy Father. Even before the official documents of the Cardinal and the Rector reached him, he was already convinced especially by the statement of the Apostolic Delegate that he had been led into an untenable position and with simple dignity he stepped out of it. Henceforth there ought to be nothing but unity, harmony, and concerted energy for the highest purposes in the work of the University. The institution may still feel for some time the results of the storm through which it has passed, but it has weathered the storm. Thank God, and now it need not be long till every vestige of it shall have disappeared. If every man do his full

---

48 BCA, 95-U-12, Ign. F. Horstmann to J. Card. Gibbons, Philadelphia, October 27, 1897.

49 BCA, 95-V-7, M. Card. Rampolla to Sebastian Martinelli, Rome, November 13, 1897. Cf. BCA, 95-V-14, M. Card. Rampolla to J. Card. Gibbons, Rome, November 29, 1897.

50 BCA, 95-V-1, Jos. Schroeder to J. Card. Gibbons, Washington, December 29, 1897. He had promised his resignation before the first of the year in a letter to Gibbons on December 14, Cf. BCA, 95-W-4.

51 New York *Tribune*, February 11, 1898.

duty at his post, and this I am certain they will do, the Providence which started the Institution will ensure its future success.[52]

Meanwhile Archbishop Ireland was able to sit back and review his "War of 1897" with complacency. His cohorts had worked well, and he gave special commendation to Monsignor O'Connell for his efforts:

Your letters from Germany were intensely interesting—as your work there was surprisingly effective. . . . Your work in Rome during our Washington meeting & since then gave us a victory. . . . The downfall of Schroeder is the end of the anti-liberalism, & of Cahenslyism, and a great defeat for Corrigan.[53]

Shahan stated, "It has taken a 'Combinazione' to secure justice, but it has worked, and the results must be appalling to the other side."[54] Ireland also had his own opinion about Schroeder's appointment to Münster which he confided to O'Connell:

The "Germania" comments on the promptness with which the Centrum & the Prussian Minister took up Schroeder. You see, Germany is grateful to him. He was doing her work in America. He was a Cahenslyite— but the last of the Mohicans. The greatest and last battle of the war has been fought and won.[55]

It appeared that Ireland was correct, that he had won the fight, and that he had vindicated the philosophy of life which he had expressed in 1889:

Success is not the test of valor or merit. If we never venture, we never win. The conservatism which wishes to be safe is dry-rot. . . . The timid move in crowds, the brave in single file. . . . The Church in America must be, of course, as Catholic as in Jerusalem or Rome; but so far as her garments may be colored to suit environment, she must be American.

There is danger: we receive large accessions of Catholics from foreign countries. God witnesses that they are welcome. I will not intrude on their personal affections and tastes; but these, if foreign, shall not encrust themselves upon the church.[56]

---

52 ACUA, Garrigan Papers, John J. Keane to P. J. Garrigan, Rome, December 16, 1897.

53 RDA, John Ireland to D. J. O'Connell, St. Paul, December 3, 1897.

54 RDA, T. J. Shahan to D. J. O'Connell, Washington, December 19, 1897.

55 RDA, John Ireland to D. J. O'Connell, St. Paul, January 8, 1898.

56 John Ireland, *The Church and Modern Society* (Chicago, 1897), I, 71-73. These excerpts are from "The Mission of Catholics in America," a sermon delivered by Ireland in Baltimore at the centennial of the American hierarchy on November 10, 1889.

157

With the removal of Joseph Schroeder, Ireland thought that the battle was over. Yet it was merely the lull before the storm, for soon the Archbishop of St. Paul would be fighting one of his greatest struggles, a struggle that would bring either justification or an absolute condemnation of most of the principles upon which he had based his public policy and his career as an American churchman.

While Ireland was fighting the "War of 1897", a new battle was being prepared against him. The removal of O'Connell and Keane had been but skirmishes in the major attempt that was soon to take place. Apart from the modernism in theological circles which was developing in France, the political situation in France, Germany, and Italy was responsible for a growing interest in the democracy of the United States and especially in the Catholic participation in that democratic life.[57] The unification of Germany, under the direction of Bismarck, and the opposition of the Catholic Centre Party in the German Empire to the Kulturkampf, had intensified German interest in Catholic activities in America. This interest continued to be stimulated by Denis O'Connell through Father Franz Xavier Kraus,

[57] The letter of an American student in Rome in 1889 gave an interesting comparison of two approaches to this subject, the more interesting since Bishop Keane had, and still retains, a reputation as an outstanding American orator. "Last evening Claudio Jannet gave us a conference from 7-8 pm on the science of Economy. He is a charming speaker and told the boys some plain truths soberly & modestly. The world is marching he said, towards the American system of Church & State, & of State alone, where every man irrespective of religion has the same rights before the law. . . . Those who think that society can be brought back to the old regime, lose their time & prove that they do not remark by what laws society tends to such a state of things. He admired the old systems, even admitted that there was more charity & more virtue formerly than now, but the Church's duty now was to accept the state of things & moderate them & guide them. . . . We will all sooner or later have to become good republicans in France, let the curé associate less with the "Seigneur du chateau" & more with the people & we will get along better in France. In these terms he spoke. Very modestly, with love for the past & confidence for the future. He convinced about seven times as easily, as Bishop Keane, who was up not long ago. The boys did not easily concede what the Bishop affirmed simply because the Bishop has a kind of "loud" or "spread eagle" way of stating the question. . . . He's not a speaker, as Ryan, nor an essayist like Spalding, & I don't think he has the intellectual ability of either, but he's practical, outspoken, unpretending and is the best man in my humble opinion they could have at the head of the University." ACUA, Hyvernat Papers, James R. Mahoney to James Driscoll, Rome, February 28, 1889. The Hyvernat Papers were put at the disposal of the writer through the kindness of the Reverend Theodore C. Petersen, C.S.P., of the Department of Semitic Languages.

the ecclesiastical and art historian, and liberal political journalist, who was in frequent correspondence with O'Connell, and who received from the latter American newspaper clippings as well as letters of encouragement and instruction.[58]   Italy was still deeply stirred by the rapid rise of the house of Savoy and the limitation of the temporal power of the Pope.   The *Concilionisti* followed American activities with the view to their offering, perhaps, a pattern for the settlement of the difficulties between the Vatican and the Italian government.[59]   But it was France that was to be the main battleground, with America brought into the conflict between the conservative monarchists and the liberal republicans.   Ireland, reputedly at the request of Leo XIII, had, in June, 1892, lectured in France on the American democracy and the necessity of co-operating with the spirit of the age.   It was an attempt to gain the monarchists to participate in the government of France, and thus instill Catholic principles and philosophy into the policies of the republic.   For this effort Archbishop Ireland became, naturally enough, *persona non grata* to the French monarchists.

The French adaptation of Elliott's *Life of Father Hecker*,[60] with an introduction by John Ireland and a thirty-five page preface by Abbé Felix Klein of the Catholic Institute of Paris, was a serious matter for the French conservatives.   Klein, as the London *Tablet* wrote, "rather out-Heckers Hecker," [61] for he had improperly emphasized Hecker's doctrine on individualism, the seeming minor importance of the vows of religious, and the greater dependence on the direct action of the Holy Spirit. This was seized upon by the conservatives, "Martel" and "Saint-Clement", through the pages of *La Vérité*.   Keane, in

[58] These clippings were gathered in the United States by Grannan of the University faculty and others, sent to O'Connell, and relayed to Kraus.   Kraus had taken part in the campaign against Schroeder, and was supposedly influential in changing German opinion, as the O'Connell letters (from Grannan and Ireland as well as many letters from Kraus to O'Connell), in the archives of the Diocese of Richmond, show.

[59] Especially was this shown by the continued friendship of Serafino Cardinal Vannutelli and his brother Vincenzo Cardinal Vannutelli, noted *Concilionisti*, with O'Connell, Keane, and Ireland.

[60] *Le Père Hecker. Fondateur des "Paulists" Américains 1819-1888,* par Le Père W. Elliott de la même Compagnie.   Traduit et adapté de l'Anglais avec autorisation de l'auteur.   Introduction par Mgr. Ireland.   Préface par l'Abbé Félix Klein (Paris, 1897).

[61] The *Tablet* (London), March 18, 1899.

January, 1898, thought things were peaceful in Rome,[62] but Abbé Alphonse Magnien, the Baltimore Sulpician who was one of Gibbons' closest advisers, was then in Paris. Thus nearer to the scene he could write to Edward Dyer, S.S.:

Just now there is in the french [sic] clergy a certain amount of excitement raised by Fr. Hecker's life translated into french by Abbé Klein: of course the Jesuits are the men who condemn loudest. . . . One of them spoke against it in the pulpit of St. Sulpice to the great disgust of the American and even many french Seminarians. I hear from very reliable sources that they exert themselves to have the book put on the index: Would not this be a very skillful way of reaching Abp. Ireland who wrote the preface?[63]

By April, 1898, Keane had identified "Martel" and "Saint-Clement" of *La Vérité*. To encourage Walter Elliott of the Paulists he wrote:

The article in the Verite was written by a priest named Maignen,[64] who made himself notorious some years ago by his attacks on the Count de Mun for having accepted the direction of the Holy Father in regard to the action of Catholics in France. He is noted as hot-brained and unscrupulous. He has as his partner in this business Dr. Peries whom we removed from his post as professor of Canon Law in the University, and who is trying to take the revenge which he threatened. He writes in the Verite also under the name of St. Clement.[65]

In that same year of 1898 the articles of Maignen were published in book form under the title of *Etudes sur l'Américanisme, le Père Hecker: est-il un saint?* [66] The strong vitriolic tone of these articles, which in book form bore the *imprimatur* of Albert Lepidi, O.P., Master of the Sacred Palace in Rome, meant that, as Keane again remarked, "the enemy overreached themselves astonishingly, and gave us an opportunity to enter protests in the Vatican. . . . we have spiked their guns." [67] To make certain that the guns remained

---

[62] BCA, 96-A-10, John J. Keane to J. Card. Gibbons, Rome, January 24, 1898: "Thanks to the French 'Life of Father Hecker' and Mgr. O'Connell's Essay on Americanism, more attention is of late being expended on these subjects than ever before. That spirit of narrowness of course manifests itself, but the bulk of sentiment is on our side."

[63] SMSA, A. Magnien to Edward Dyer, Paris, December 6, 1897.

[64] Abbé Charles Maignen of the Congregation of the Brothers of St. Vincent de Paul.

[65] PFA-A, John J. Keane to Walter Elliott, Rome, April 19, 1898.

[66] Charles Maignen, *Le Père Hecker—Est-il un saint?* (Paris, 1898).

[67] PFA-A, John J. Keane to Walter Elliott, Paris, July 4, 1898.

spiked, Cardinal Gibbons wrote a long letter in August to Cardinal Rampolla, protesting that to the uninitiated, the *imprimatur* of Lepidi on Maignen's book, might well appear as papal approval of the attacks on certain members of the American hierarchy contained therein.[68] On September 13, Ireland congratulated Gibbons on the stand he had taken, offering the Cardinal of Baltimore encouragement by saying:

I believe the Vatican is disposed to regret the "Imprimatur." I have received a very full letter from Card. Rampolla, in which he expresses the Pope's "vivo desiderio" that I do what I can for the protection of Catholic interests in the countries lost to Spain's domination—and in which also he reiterates his assurance that I may very safely leave the "Maignen" book to the Pope who will in his good time speak and act.[69]

On September 23, Rampolla addressed a letter to Gibbons and assured him that Lepidi had meant no insult to any member of the American hierarchy, and that "in regard to the teachings of P. Hecker His Holiness will himself write Your Eminence a personal letter." [70]

In spite of McQuaid's warning to Corrigan that the Paulists "should not be made scapegoats to cover Ireland, Keane & Co.," [71] the Archbishop of New York, in the October, 1898, meeting of the American metropolitans, merely read the strong and convincing memorial of Father George Deshon exonerating the Paulists, and moved that the archbishops not interfere, since Leo XIII was preparing an encyclical

[68] BCA, 96-M-6, J. Card. Gibbons to M. Card. Rampolla, Baltimore, August 27, 1898. In the French rough draft, although crossed out later, Maignen's collaborator is identified as "Dr. Peries whom we were obliged to send away from our University where he was teaching Canon Law." The gravity of the affair was summarized by Gibbons: "Knowing that their main author, Father Maignen, was a worthless individual and little appreciated in his own country, I paid no attention to the articles. But the situation is completely changed today. The *imprimatur* granted that libel by the Master of the Sacred Palace gives it the importance of a serious and trustworthy piece of work. It is on account of that *imprimatur* that I believe it is my duty to write to Your Eminence in such a fashion as this." The original French draft was written in the hand of the Baltimore Sulpician, Abbé Magnien.

[69] BCA, 96-N-4, John Ireland to J. Card. Gibbons, St. Paul, September 13, 1898. This was the period immediately after the Spanish-American War, which Ireland had sought to prevent by diplomatic measures.

[70] BCA, 96-N-6, M. Card. Rampolla to J. Card. Gibbons, Rome, September 23, 1898.

[71] NYAA, C-40-M, B. J. McQuaid to M. A. Corrigan, Rochester, August 30, 1898.

on the matter.[72]   Ireland, who was absent from the meeting, expressed his disdain for this cautious action and he outlined his future plans in a subsequent letter to Elliott:

You, no doubt, have heard how your cause was treated at the meeting. The Archbishop of New York timidly and as acting under protest, offered a paper from the Paulists—& added at once his own opinion, which was that the hierarchy of America should lie low in this war.   No voice bellowed out in the name of justice—and all was over.

It is as well: I like to fight—and to conquer with few allies.   You owe nothing, or but little, when the victory is won.

We are going to win—The last letter I have from Card. Rampolla, written on the field itself—in the Vatican, is most encouraging.   Besides I shall soon invade Africa and either Lepidi or Ireland will go into winter quarters.   I expect to be in Rome about Christmas.[73]

Before John Ireland departed for Rome in January, 1899, favorable accounts of the situation there were sent by Keane and O'Connell. Keane told Gibbons of an audience that Cardinal Serafino Vannutelli had with the Pope:

The Pope then went on to say: "They (without saying *who*) have been urging me to be *severe* with the Americans; but I am convinced that gentle measures will do more good." . . . Then he gave him the points of the Encyclical now being prepared for us: 1. Church & State; 2. Individualism; 3. The vows. As to each, only the familiar warning not to represent the contingently useful as the *ideal*.   So we may hope there is no danger ahead.[74]

---

[72] Holden, *op. cit.,* pp. 165-168.   Cf. PFA-A, containing a note by Elliott dated November 23, 1913, which stated: "In one of my interviews with Archp. Corrigan during the Americanism troubles he said squarely to me: 'The main trouble with your life of Hecker at Rome is due to your connection with Archp. Ireland & Bishop Keane, who are in great disfavor there.   If you publicly repudiate them all will go well.'   I told him that we could not do that."

[73] PFA-A, John Ireland to Walter Elliott, St. Paul, November 6, 1898.   In a letter of the same day to Father A. Magnien, S.S., Ireland further expressed his feelings: "I incline to believe the truth of the Associated Press cablegram, according to which the Pope had ordered silence on American questions.   I do not see what else the Pope could have done—if letters from Card. Gibbons & myself have weight any longer. . . . Did you read that extract from a letter of Satolli, which I sent to the Cardinal?   He & many others in Rome are simply mad about Freemasons—I am of the opinion that he thinks we all are Freemasons."   ACUA, Bouquillon Papers, John Ireland to A. Magnien, St. Paul, November 6, 1898.

[74] BCA, 96-S-8, John J. Keane to J. Card. Gibbons, Rome, November 9, 1898.

A month later O'Connell told Father Elliott that the complaints from America "shook" the Pope, and that Leo XIII had then reserved the entire matter to himself.[75] Although Ireland hurried to Rome to prevent it, the *Testem benevolentiae* letter of the Holy Father was issued on January 22, 1899, before he arrived.[76] The greatest surprise, and a grave obstacle which Ireland found in Rome, was the letter which Corrigan had written to Lepidi congratulating him and approving of the course he had taken in giving the *imprimatur* to Maignen's book. Although Archbishop Ireland readily submitted to the Pope's letter, he privately felt "Fanatics conjured up an 'Americanism'—& put such before the Pope. Lepidi & Mazzela [*sic*] wrote the body of the letter—I cannot pray that God forgive them." [77] The Archbishop of St. Paul received some encouragement from Cardinal Rampolla who hinted at an approach to the delicate situation which Ireland quickly seized upon and promoted. He gave an account of what was happening in Rome to Father George Deshon, and he said that Rampolla had softened the letter in the beginning and the end in deference to him (Ireland) and "that the words of the letter allow us

[75] PFA-A, D. J. O'Connell to Walter Elliott, Rome, December 10, 1898.

[76] The exact date of the issuance of the letter is hard to determine, as two letters from John Keane will indicate: "The war on 'Americanism' and 'Heckerism' is not over yet. I trust, however, that any Papal utterance the adversaries may succeed in extorting will not be such as to do harm.
"Abp. Ireland reached here last Thursday [January 26, 1899], and is, of course, as busy as a beaver, and his work must do good." ACUA, Garrigan Papers, John J. Keane to P. J. Garrigan, Rome, February 2, 1899. "The sky is full of *storm* these last two weeks. Ten fold efforts were made, and the letter is gone! And gone under circumstances which show that they dodged and deceived Ireland. Rampolla told him it had not been sent:—but between that evening and Ireland's seeing the Pope three or four days later, it had been sent! We have done our utmost, as you know, even now to hinder its publication,—but all signs indicate that they will be obstinate and we will fail. We have the consolation of knowing that we did our full duty—the blow will, I fear, be a sad one for the Paulists & for the memory of Hecker,—and a blow to the Cardinal and Ireland who wrote in their behalf. We must simply make the best of it, and carry on our game of explaining away to the American people the administrative blunders of our superiors.
"Times are so critical that, even should I be asked to go to America in the Spring and begin the work for the Univ'y, I would not dare to leave Europe at present,—nor as long as Ireland is in Europe; for I believe the attacks & the need of standing on the defensive will last as long as he is over here." ACUA, Bouquillon Papers, John J. Keane to A. Magnien, Rome, February 11, 1899.

[77] PFA-A, John Ireland to George Deshon, Rome, February 24, 1899. Cardinals Mazzella and Satolli formed the first investigating committee.

to say that the things condemned were never said or written in America not even by Hecker—but were set afloat in France—as 'Americanism' . . . & he added I should do my best to spread this view." [78] This became the line of thought that Ireland followed in his letter of submission to Leo XIII and it was the line taken by a majority of the American secular press.

However, the pattern of reception for the letter suggested by Rampolla, and encouraged by the Archbishop of St. Paul, was not followed unanimously in the United States. Corrigan wrote the Pope to thank him for the letter which would help save America from the threatened heresy. The bishops of the Province of Milwaukee went a step further. In their joint letter, besides thanking the Holy Father, they condemned those who, following the letter of the papal document rather than the spirit, excused themselves from ever having been guilty of the errors therein condemned. McQuaid, in a sermon in the cathedral of Rochester on June 25, 1899, put the capstone on the arguments against those who were excusing themselves by saying: "Yet there was a species of 'Americanism' which the Holy Father had condemned prior to his encyclical of last February." [79] He mentioned four points especially which were "specimens of 'Americanism';" the participation of the liberals in the Chicago World's Parliament of Religions; their stand on the Faribault School Controversy; their defence of certain secret societies;[80] and:

The fourth exhibition of advanced Catholic Americanism came before the American public when a Catholic ecclesiastic took his stand before a non-Catholic university in his clerical robes to advertise to the community the new born liberalism of the Catholic church in entering into the halls and chapels of non-Catholic universities.[81]

George Peries, too, had a final thrust at his opponents, an account of which was given to Archbishop Ireland by Abbé Magnien of Baltimore:

Peries, in his triumph, thought of being witty and sarcastic at my expense: he sent me by mail his card with the following.

---

[78] *Ibid.*

[79] Rochester *Union and Advertiser,* June 26, 1899.

[80] Referring indirectly to the Knights of Labor and the Ancient Order of Hibernians.

[81] Rochester *Union and Advertiser, loc. cit.* This is a reference to Keane's delivery of one of the Dudleian lectures at Harvard University on October 24,

"Abbe G. Peries . . . . found out already last year, about the unfavorable remarks M. Magnien made concerning him and, if he delayed telling him of the little attention he paid them, it is because he preferred waiting for the manifestation of the Holy Father's opinion on Americanism. Therefore, today he offers St. Mary's Superior the assurance of his fitting regards and of his sympathetic congratulation."

In answer I sent my card as follows:

"Very Rev. A. Magnien . . . assures M. Peries that he does not feel himself the least bit affected by the condemnation of Americanism. The Holy Father very justly stigmatizes, not what exists in America, but what the double-dealing and hatred of certain individuals called Americanism. St. Mary's Superior offers M. the ex-professor of the Catholic University of Washington, the congratulations he deserves for the important part he took in that glorious campaign and assures him that his sentiments in his regard remain the same as ever."[82]

This bit of repartee between the two French priests influenced the next part of the campaign. On June 17, 1899, the *New Era* of London, under the heading "The Real Author of 'Americanism'," issued an exposé of Peries as the "Saint-Clement" of the articles which were being written at the time against Archbishop Ireland, who was then lecturing in France. The account told of Peries' dismissal from the University and also charged: "It is this ex-professor who was, at least in the initial stages, the inspirer of what is popularly known as the Anti-American campaign in France—a combination which for two years past has saddened the Catholic world." The *New Era* went further, and supplied Peries' motive by giving extracts from the minutes of the autumn, 1896, meeting of the University's Board of Trustees, quoting from Peries' letter to Horstmann:

I do not want any scandal, but I must warn you that if something is

---

1890. An example of earlier German-American imputation of Americanism in the University may be found in the San Francisco *California Volksfreund*, April 16, 1898: "That Americanism was from the beginning interwoven with the plan for the establishment of a Catholic University in America, was clear enough from the beginning, and therefore, the conservatives withdrew steadily from it. . . . We want a Catholic University with CATHOLIC professors, and indeed, capable ones who are to be found without distinction of nationality. We want a Catholic University in which the doctrine of the *Catholic*, and not of an *American* Church, are taught. We want a Catholic University in which the young are formed and educated in genuine Catholic spirit, and not chiefly and before all, in Americanism and Patriotism, and nothing else."

[82] RDA, A. Magnien to John Ireland, Baltimore, March 9, 1899. In the original the quotations were given in French.

made against me, the country at large and the Roman competent congregations will know what has been the spirit of this house, and I will do that, not in view of a mean revenge, but for the interests of the Church.

I hope, nevertheless, that nothing will be necessary and that I will not be obliged for the honor of my name, and the defence of my interests to enter a struggle which would prove disadvantageous for several, and for the great aim we have in view for this Institution.[83]

This publication of the London journal, as it received wide notice, did much to discredit the sincerity of those who were opposed to the so-called Americanism. In the estimation of the New York *Tribune,* "The interest of the document lies in this—it proves that the agitation which has so moved the Church, both in France and in America sprang from a source contaminated by a purely personal quarrel." [84]

An interesting sequel to this exposé was supplied in the next three meetings of the Board of Trustees of the University. In the October, 1899, meeting Bishop Horstmann, the secretary, rose on a question of privilege, and demanded an explanation of how the *New Era* had obtained its information, since he, as secretary, had been responsible for the minutes. Archbishop Riordan of San Francisco moved that a committee of two be appointed to study the question and thus the matter was delayed for another year.[85] At the autumn meeting of the board in 1900 Gibbons explained that "a very worthy Ecclesiastic applied to the University authorities in the name of a member of the Board of Trustees for the extract of the Minutes." [86] The Bishop of Cleveland thereupon asked that the name of the board member who had made the request be made known, but his request was voted down since the presumed prelate was absent. The question came up once more at the next meeting, when Horstmann again insisted that the member's name be given, but "he declared himself satisfied when Archbishop Ireland acknowledged, readily, that it was he who used the letter of Dr. Peries and published it in the papers. Incident closed." [87]

John Ireland could be sure of himself then, for by this time he was

[83] *New Era* (London), June 17, 1899.

[84] New York *Tribune,* June 29, 1899.

[85] ACUA, MMBT, October 11, 1899, p. 85.

[86] ACUA, MMBT, October 10, 1900, p. 91. Bishop Maes of Covington began acting as secretary this year and he continued in this office for several years.

[87] ACUA, MMBT, November 20, 1901, p. 95.

back in favor in Rome and had so informed Mrs. Bellamy Storer in August, 1900:

Well, "mon accueil" could not possibly be better. It surprises me. The evident purpose is to make me understand beyond a possible doubt that I am in high favor, that they are all delighted with me that need my co-operation, and are resolved to have [it].

The Pope told me to forget that letter on Americanism, which has no application except in a few dioceses in France! [88]

This favorable impression continued in Rome, for Bishop Thomas O'Gorman of Sioux Falls, former professor of church history in the University, was able to report to Gibbons nearly two years later that, "On all sides it is proclaimed that Americanism, which was supposed to be our defeat, has been turned into a glorious Victory. We are surely on top." [89]

The Americanizers were at last victorious, at least in their own understanding of the situation. That was not enough. The first phase of the Americanism struggle had ended with the victory of the conservatives in the dismissal of Keane. The second phase had appeared as a defeat for the Americanizers with the publication of the *Testem benevolentiae*, but it had resulted ultimately in their vindication. The third phase was to be the public approval of the Americanizers. Denis O'Connell was still enduring his Roman exile, but it was an exile that would soon be terminated and that in a way to bring a change, too, at the University in Washington.

The final campaign was begun in the University by one who was a friend of Monsignor O'Connell; by a professor who had to come to entertain a strong dislike for Bishop Conaty, the rector. Charles P. Grannan, professor of sacred scripture in the University, began his campaign in June, 1901, by arranging to meet O'Connell in Europe during that summer. In July he was in Switzerland, supposedly for his health, but as he wrote O'Connell, "Between ourselves, I am not at all a sick man, as you will soon see, but am here, not because I am sick, but lest I should become sick. . . . The conclusion is that I can get out of here almost any time and meet you wherever you choose." [90]

[88] Maria Longworth Storer, *In Memoriam Bellamy Storer* (privately printed, 1923), pp. 46-47. John Ireland to Mrs. Storer, Rome, August 5, 1900. The support of Ireland was needed in the question of the Church lands in the Philippines and Cuba.

[89] BCA, 99-R-6, Thos. O'Gorman to J. Card. Gibbons, Rome, May 17, 1902.

[90] RDA, [C. P. Grannan] to D. J. O'Connell, Tarasp, Switzerland, July 5, 1901. This letter is unsigned but it is in Grannan's hand.

The first meeting came off and the groundwork was laid for the final struggle. When Grannan returned to Washington he seized every opportunity to expose the defects in the administration of the rector of the University, and defects there were. Grannan kept up a steady correspondence with O'Connell, feeling safe in so doing since the letters were all signed with false names, many of them written as if from a third person, all of them sharply critical of Conaty. Many statements made in the letters were inaccurate, all of them breathed a biased spirit, and several of them carried the instruction that they should be destroyed upon receipt. The fact that Conaty had been consecrated titular Bishop of Samos on November 24, 1901, and that the vice-rector, Philip J. Garrigan, had been appointed Bishop of Sioux City, Iowa, on March 21, 1902, served only to increase the bitterness of Grannan.

The University was, it is true, not in a flourishing condition in 1902. With all the conflicts into which it had been drawn, the clashing personalities within the Board of Trustees and within the faculty, the slight support the institution received from the country at large, and the very limited financial resources at its disposal, it was a wonder that it was able to survive at all, to say nothing of making progress. Conaty had worked to the best of his ability for the success of the University. He had organized the Conference of Catholic Colleges in 1899 to bring a much-needed integration to Catholic education. He had, perhaps a bit hesitatingly, been active in the Association of American Universities from its inception in 1900. He had formed a conference of seminary presidents in 1898 to set standards for seminaries that would establish the proper curriculum for seminary graduates to enter immediately into graduate work at the University. But he was not successful in producing funds nor in keeping peace in his faculty. Ignoring what he had done so well, Grannan stressed what Conaty did not do, and he made his own very considerable contribution to see that peace did not reign in the faculty. In January, 1902, he wrote a letter to the Dean of the School of Theology, emphasizing all the troubles within the University.[91] The letter, as Grannan intended, reached the special investigating committee of the Board of Trustees, which held a week long investigation at the University in

[91] ACUA, Trustees' file, Chas. P. Grannan to the Very Rev. Dean and Faculty of Theology, Washington, January 6, 1902. This letter was read at the meeting of the Faculty of Theology on February 3, 1902. ACUA, Faculty of Theology Records, October 2, 1901 - April 23, 1906, Session 197, February 3, 1902, p. 13.

February. The committee, composed of Archbishop Keane, Bishops Spalding and Maes, had in Grannan's mind, scored a success:

Success? Yes? Well! I should say so; humming success; thundering success; success all along the line. . . . One man's reputation as an administrator is torn to tatters. One rascal told everything. . . . The only question now asked is, who is going to succeed to his place?[92]

Professor Grannan went to Europe again in the summer of 1902 and there he held two important meetings, one with O'Connell and the other with Satolli. In January, 1902, Grannan had been appointed to the Pontifical Biblical Commission, and he used that fact as the reason for his trip to Rome. With the arrival of Grannan in Europe the campaign went into high gear. Cardinal Satolli was informed of the perilous condition of the University through the prejudiced account of Grannan. The cardinal, Prefect of the Congregation of Studies, promised to support Monsignor O'Connell for the rectorship when Conaty's first term of office should expire in January, 1903. Grannan then brought Gibbons, unsuspecting, into the fold and told him that Satolli favored O'Connell as the next rector of the University.[93] Although Gibbons was amazed that Satolli should now have changed over to favoring O'Connell after seven years of disapproval, he was pleased, for O'Connell had always remained a favorite of the Archbishop of Baltimore even when his fortunes were at the lowest ebb. Gibbons was unwilling, however, to leave Conaty unprovided for and forgotten. Keane, too, was surprised, but pleased, when he was informed of what was happening, and he wrote O'Connell, "A *soul* is needed for the institution; and you have it in you to be that. All will hinge on getting Conaty into some See—Los Angeles for example." [94] John Ireland and John Lancaster Spalding likewise favored the idea of O'Connell as rector of the University, and by the time of the meeting of the Board of Trustees in November, 1902, all that stood in the way of success was: what disposition was to be made of Bishop Conaty? Gibbons was under the impression that

---

[92] RDA, Jeshurun to Doktor [Grannan to O'Connell] (postmarked Washington), February 11, 1902.

[93] BCA, 99-W-5, Chas. P. Grannan to J. Card. Gibbons, Rigi-Scheidegg, Switzerland, August 20, 1902. Cf. RDA, Jeshurun to Doc [Grannan to O'Connell], Rotterdam, September 18, 1902. Cf. Appendix E, F.

[94] RDA, John J. Keane to D. J. O'Connell, Dubuque, September 26, 1902. Conaty was already on the *terna* for San Francisco, cf. BCA, 99-P-2, S. Card. Martinelli to J. Card. Gibbons, Washington, April 9, 1902.

only one name needed to be sent to Rome as the board's choice for rector. In that case he intended to insist on Conaty, but a hasty cablegram from Riordan, then in Rome after presenting the question of the Pious Fund to the Hague Tribunal, brought word that the Pope expected a *terna*.[95] Thus the embarrassment of a single name for the rectorship was removed. The *terna* put Conaty in first place, O'Connell second, and Thomas J. Shahan third, with the tacit understanding that Conaty would be passed over at Rome and O'Connell chosen. [96]

Archbishop Riordan of San Francisco returned from Rome in November, 1902, and from him Gibbons and Ireland had assurance that Conaty would definitely be appointed as Bishop of Monterey-Los Angeles. [97] The final step came on January 12, 1903, when Pope Leo XIII signed two papal decrees, one transferred the jurisdiction over the University from the Congregation of the Propaganda to the Congregation of Studies, presided over by Cardinal Satolli; the other appointed Monsignor Denis J. O'Connell rector of the University.[98] Bishop Conaty cabled "Sincere congratulations and welcome" [99] to his successor and did what he could to make the reception of the new

[95] BCA, 100-C-4, 100-C-4/1, P. W. Riordan to J. Card. Gibbons, Rome, October 29, 1902. The Pious Fund originated in donations given for missionary work in the Californias, and at the time of the Mexican War it was being administered by the government of Mexico. The claims of the American bishops in California for their just share in this fund remained unsettled for years. Cf. William E. McDonald, "The Pious Fund of the Californias," *CHR*, XIX (January, 1934), 427-436.

[96] ACUA, MMBT, November 12, 1902, p. 102 and RDA, unsigned letter of Grannan to O'Connell, no place or date given. Gibbons had written to O'Connell from Baltimore on September 1, 1902 (RDA): "Suppose that the Board would hesitate to remove till some place was provided for him [Conaty], I want to know from you privately would you accept the post of Vice-Rector ad interim with the understanding of obtaining the Rectorship as soon as the vacancy occurred?" O'Connell answered from Rome on October 6, 1902 (BCA, 100-B-3) and told of an interview with Satolli, in which the Cardinal Prefect of Studies was supposed to have said: "Let them get him [Conaty] a See or make him an Auxiliary or do anything they like; but if they put his name on the list, the Holy Father will know how to choose; nay, I would rather they put his name on the list, and then un' altro nome quolunque—(any other name whatever)— and yours; yours will come out."

[97] RDA, J. Card. Gibbons to D. J. O'Connell, Baltimore, November 29, 1902, and RDA, John Ireland to D. J. O'Connell, New York, December 7, 1902.

[98] Boston *Pilot,* January 17, 1903; BCA, 100-G-2, F. Card. Satolli to J. Card. Gibbons, Rome, January 14, 1903.

[99] RDA, Thomas J. Conaty to D. J. O'Connell, Washington, undated.

rector as pleasant as possible.[100] While waiting to depart from Rome Denis O'Connell notified the cardinal chancellor of his reason for delaying, as well as of his gratitude for what Thomas Conaty was doing for him:

I hope then to leave here next Wednesday, Mar. 4. I also had another desire in delaying my departure. I hoped that the news of Mons. Conaty's appointment to Los Angeles would be spread through the States before it was said that I had already departed. The appointment however was delayed because no Latin Congregation was held Feb. 3, but it is expected that the nomination will be made next Monday Mar. 2, so that will fit in very well.

I have nothing but feelings of the greatest appreciation and of thankfulness towards Mons. Conaty for his bearing towards me on this occasion. Nothing could surpass the unstinted and generous manner in which he offered his cooperation & assistance.[101]

On April 21, the second rector of the University bid farewell to the academic senate to whom he said:

As this is the last Senate meeting over which I will have the honor to preside, I wish to express in unmeasured terms my grateful appreciation of the kindness I have experienced as Presiding Officer of the Senate during the past six years. I express the hope that in the future, as in the past, the Senate will be the expression of the highest aims and noblest purposes of the University.[102]

At the meeting of the trustees on April 22, 1903, Conaty's resignation was accepted, prior to his departure for Los Angeles, and O'Connell was inaugurated as the third rector of the Catholic University of America.[103] The course was run.

100 ACUA, Thomas J. Conaty to the University Faculty, Washington, February 2, 1903, March 18, 1903.

101 BCA, 100-H-9, D. J. O'Connell to J. Card. Gibbons, Rome, February 28, 1903.

102 ACUA, RRTTS, April 21, 1903.

103 ACUA, MMBT, April 22, 1903, p. 106. Conaty was named to the Board of Trustees, but as there was no vacancy, and a doubt if the trustees could act in such a case, the matter was passed over for future action which never took place, ACUA, FBT, Envelope 29, Thomas J. Conaty to D. W. Shea, Worcester, May 2, 1903. At the expiration of O'Connell's rectorship, the Archbishop of San Francisco, P. W. Riordan, wrote to Gibbons on November 4, 1908 (BCA, 105-F): "In the case of Monsignore Conaty no provision was made or promised and had I not taken him up for the See of Los Angeles he would have no position whatsoever in the American Church. He has made a splendid Bishop here and

171

The years of struggle were over and peace had finally come to the Church in America. The Apostolic Delegation had been firmly established and the public press was no longer able to air the differences which arose among the leaders of American Catholicism. One warrior passed from the field on May 5, 1902, with the death of Archbishop Corrigan of New York. Ireland and McQuaid in time sheathed their swords, and Cardinal Gibbons, the conciliator, could relax his vigil as his years approached the traditional three score and ten. John Ireland, with his flair for apt phrasing, summed up the situation for O'Connell:

Farley is ostentatiously reversing in all points the Corrigan regime. He proclaims, "in plateis" his friendship for me. McQuaid, too, is my staunch admirer. Le monde est a rebours. Vive l'americanisme.[104]

And about six weeks later the Archbishop of St. Paul heralded the triumph in ringing words to his friend still in Rome:

The associated-press dispatch from Rome this morning tells us of the significance in Rome of your appointment. And the significance in America! . . . "O'Connell in Washington—Simply impossible." Well, he is here—Viva l'Americanismo! Viva sempre![105]

I took him for Los Angeles precisely because no provision had been made for the good man." Charles P. Grannan became vice-rector during the first years of O'Connell's rectorship. Cf. "University Chronicle," *CUB*, IV (October, 1903), 573-574.

[104] RDA, John Ireland to D. J. O'Connell, New York, December 7, 1902.

[105] RDA, John Ireland to D. J. O'Connell, St. Paul, January 14, 1903.

BIBLIOGRAPHY

MANUSCRIPT SOURCES

Archives of the Catholic University of America. The files of the Rector; of the Board of Trustees; of the Academic Senate; the Hyvernat Papers, in the custody of the Reverend Theodore C. Petersen, C.S.P.; and of uncatalogued and miscellaneous material.

Archives of the University of Notre Dame. Photostat copies of the Hudson Papers pertaining to the Catholic University of America.

Baltimore Cathedral Archives. The records of the Gibbons administration from 1895 to 1904.

Dubuque Archdiocesan Archives. A diocesan diary entitled "Record of the Administration of John J. Keane, Archbishop of Dubuque, 1900-1911."

New York Archdiocesan Archives. The Corrigan and Farley Papers, and newspaper clipping files.

Paulist Fathers Archives, New York. The general files as well as the file on Americanism.

Richmond Diocesan Archives. The Roman correspondence of Denis J. O'Connell.

St. Mary's Seminary Archives, Roland Park, Baltimore. The Maignen and Rex Papers.

Only those works are mentioned in the bibliography which entered directly into the preparation of this study. For a more complete bibliography, consult John Tracy Ellis, *A Select Bibliography of the History of the Catholic Church in the United States* (New York, 1947).

PRINTED SOURCES

Acta et decreta concilii plenarii Baltimorensis tertii. A. D. MDCCCLXXXIV, Baltimore, 1886. This work contains the acts and decrees as they were confirmed by Rome.

Acta et decreta concilii plenarii Baltimorensis tertii. IX Novembris usque ad diem VII Decembris, A. D. MDCCCLXXXIV, Baltimore, 1884. This work was printed immediately after the close of the council for private use.

(Eighth) Annual Report of the Rector of the Catholic University of America, October, 1897, Washington, 1897.

(Ninth) Annual Report of the Rector of the Catholic University of America, October, 1898, Washington, 1898.

(Tenth) Annual Report of the Rector of the Catholic University of America, October, 1899, Washington, 1899.

(Eleventh) Annual Report of the Rector of the Catholic University of America, October, 1900, Washington, 1900.

(Twelfth) Annual Report of the Rector of the Catholic University of America, November, 1901, Washington, 1901.

(Thirteenth) Annual Report of the Rector of the Catholic University of America, November, 1902, Washington, 1902.

(Fourteenth) Annual Report of the Rector of the Catholic University of America, November, 1903, Washington, 1903.

Concilii plenarii Baltimorensis II., in ecclesia metropolitana Baltimorensi. . . . decreta, Baltimore, 1868.

Constitutions of the Catholic University of America, Rome, 1889.

Inauguration of the Schools of Philosophy and the Social Sciences and Dedication of McMahon Hall, Catholic University of America, October 1, 1895, Washington, 1895.

Ireland, John, *The Church and Modern Society,* 2 Vols., Chicago, 1897.

Proceedings of the Seventh German-American Katholikentag, Held in Louisville, Ky., September 24-27, 1894, Louisville, 1894.

Report of the First Annual Conference of the Association of Catholic Colleges of the United States, held in St. James' Hall, Chicago, April 12 and 13, 1899, Washington, 1899.

Report of the Second Annual Conference of the Association of Catholic Colleges of the United States, held in St. James' Hall, Chicago, April 18 and 19, 1900, Washington, 1900.

Report of the Third Annual Conference of the Association of Catholic Colleges of the United States, held in St. James' Hall, Chicago, April 10, 11 and 12, 1901, Washington, 1901.

Report of the Fourth Annual Conference of the Association of Catholic Colleges of the United States, held in Chicago, July 9 and 10, 1902, Washington, 1902.

Storer, Maria Longworth, *In Memoriam Bellamy Storer,* Privately printed, 1923.

Year Book of the Catholic University of America 1897-'98, Washington, 1897.

Year Book of the Catholic University of America 1898-'99, Washington, 1898.

Year Book of the Catholic University of America 1899-1900, Washington, 1899.

Year Book of the Catholic University of America 1900-1901, Washington, 1900.

Year Book of the Catholic University of America 1901-1902, Washington, 1901.

Year Book of the Catholic University of America 1902-1903, Washington, 1902.

Year Book of the Catholic University of America 1903-1904, Washington, 1903.

SECONDARY WORKS

Ahern, Patrick H., *Catholic University of America, 1887-1896,* Washington, 1949.

Barrows, John H. (ed.), *The World's Parliament of Religions,* 2 vols., Chicago, 1893.

Bell, Stephen, *Rebel, Priest and Prophet,* New York, 1937.

Bouquillon, Thomas, *Education: To Whom Does It Belong?* Baltimore, 1891.

——————, *Education: To Whom Does It Belong? A Rejoinder to Critics,* Baltimore, 1892.

Coleman, J. Walter, *Labor Disturbances in Pennsylvania, 1850-1880,* Washington, 1936.

Conaty, Thomas J., *New Testament Studies,* New York, 1898.

Elliott, W., *Le Père Hecker. Fondateur des "Paulists" Américains, 1819-1888,* [Translated by the Countess de Revilliasc], Paris, 1897.

Ellis, John Tracy, *The Formative Years of the Catholic University of America,* Washington, 1946.

Maignen, Charles, *Le Père Hecker—Est-il un saint?* Paris, 1898.

MacDonald, Fergus, C.P., *The Catholic Church and the Secret Societies in the United States,* New York, 1946.

Nevins, Allan, *The Emergence of Modern America,* New York, 1935.

[Purcell, Richard J.], *The Catholic University of America—A Half Century of Progress,* Washington, 1939.

Reilly, Daniel F., O.P., *The School Controversy (1891-1893),* Washington, 1943.

Ward, Justine, *Thomas Edward Shields,* New York, 1947.

Zwierlein, Frederick J., *Life and Letters of Bishop McQuaid,* Vol. III. Rome, 1927.

ENCYCLOPEDIAS

Adams, Raymond William, "Isaac Thomas Hecker" *Dictionary of American Biography,* VIII, 495, New York, 1932.

Carroll, Patrick J., "John Augustine Zahm" *Dictionary of American Biography,* XX, 641-642, New York, 1936.

Cartwright, Richard S., "Walter Hacker Robert Elliott" *Dictionary of American Biography,* VI, 99-100, New York, 1931.

Cerretti, Bonaventure, "Legate," *Catholic Encyclopedia,* IX, 120, New York, 1913.

"Conaty, Thomas J.," *National Cyclopedia of American Biography,* XII, 407-408, New York, 1904.

Clement, Rudolph A., "Michael Cudahy," *Dictionary of American Biography,* IV, 584-585, New York, 1930.

Driscoll, John T., "Catholic Summer School," *Catholic Encyclopedia,* XIV, 334-335, New York, 1913.

Fitzpatrick, Edward A., "Frederick Xavier Katzer," *Dictionary of American Biography,* X, 261-262, New York, 1933.

Haynes, George H., "Samuel Hoar," *Dictionary of American Biography,* IX, 89-90, New York, 1932.

Howard, Francis W., "Catholic Educational Association," *Catholic Encyclopedia,* V, 305-306, New York, 1913.

Jepson, W. L., "Edward Lee Greene," *Dictionary of American Biography,* VII, 564-565, New York, 1931.

Kerby, William, "Thomas Joseph Bouquillon," *Dictionary of American Biography,* II, 481-482, New York, 1929.
"Thomas James Conaty," *Dictionary of American Biography,* IV, 337-338, New York, 1930.
"John Joseph Keane," *Dictionary of American Biography,* X, 267-268 New York, 1933.

Michels, Roberto, "Conservatism," *Encyclopaedia of the Social Sciences,* IV, 230-233, New York, 1931.

Purcell, Richard J., "Michael Augustine Corrigan," *Dictionary of American Biography,* IV, 450-452, New York, 1930.

"Philip Joseph Garrigan," *Dictionary of American Biography,* VII, 167, New York, 1931.

"Richard Gilmour," *Dictionary of American Biography,* VIII, 313-314, New York, 1932.

"John Ireland," *Dictionary of American Biography,* IX, 494-497, New York, 1932.

"Sister Julia," *Dictionary of American Biography,* X, 244-245, New York, 1933.

"Camillus Paul Maes," *Dictionary of American Biography,* XII, 193-194, New York, 1933.

"Sylvester Malone," *Dictionary of American Biography,* XII, 226-227, New York, 1933.

"Bernard John McQuaid," *Dictionary of American Biography,* XII, 163-164, New York, 1933.

"Sebastian Gebhard Messmer," *Dictionary of American Biography,* XII, 579-580, New York, 1933.

"Thomas O'Gorman," *Dictionary of American Biography,* XIV, 3, New York, 1934.

"David Samuel Phelan," *Dictionary of American Biography,* XIV, 520-521, New York, 1934.

"Patrick William Riordan," *Dictionary of American Biography,* XV, 619, New York, 1935.

"Patrick John Ryan," *Dictionary of American Biography,* XVI, 263-264, New York, 1935.

"Thomas Joseph Shahan," *Dictionary of American Biography,* XVII, 16-17, New York, 1935.

"Thomas Edward Shields," *Dictionary of American Biography,* XVII, 107-108, New York, 1935.

"John Lancaster Spalding," *Dictionary of American Biography,* XVII, 422-423, New York, 1935.

"John Joseph Williams," *Dictionary of American Biography,* XX, 276-277, New York, 1936.

Ruggiero, Guido de, "Liberalism," *Encyclopaedia of the Social Sciences,* IX, 435-442, New York, 1933.

Ryan, John A., "Edward McGlynn," *Dictionary of American Biography,* XII, 53-54, New York, 1933.

Sheldon, Henry D., "Granville Stanley Hall," *Dictionary of American Biography,* VIII, 127-130, New York, 1932.

Spaulding, E. Wilder, "Hannis Taylor," *Dictionary of American Biography,* XVIII, 326-327, New York, 1936.

Strover, Carl G., "Charles Warren Stoddard," *Dictionary of American Biography,* XVIII, 52, New York, 1936.

Tschan, Francis J., "Placide Louis Chapelle," *Dictionary of American Biography,* IV, 11-12, New York, 1930.

Walsh, James J., "John Murphy Farley," *Dictionary of American Biography,* VI, 273-274, New York, 1931.

Ware, Edith E., "Charles Rufus Skinner," *Dictionary of American Biography,* XVII, 197-198, New York, 1935.

Will, Allen S., "James Gibbons," *Dictionary of American Biography,* VII, 238-242, New York, 1931.

NEWSPAPERS

Baltimore *American,* April 12, 1902.
    Sun, November 18, 20, December 9, 1896; August 30, 1897; May 27, 1898; November 25, 1901; January 28, April 24, 1902.

Boston *Hibernian,* July 2, 1902.
    Pilot, July 3, 1886; May 11, 1889; June 13, July 4, 25, August 26, September 12, October 31, November 28, December 12, 19, 1896; January 2, 9, 16, 23, October 30, November 6. December 4, 1897; April 20, September 28, October 26, December 7, 1901; April 19, 1902; January 17, March 28, April 4, 1903.

Buffalo *Volksfreund,* November 27, 1895.

Columbus *Waisenfreund,* December 22, 1897; April 5, 6, 13, 1898.

Detroit *Stimme der Wahrheit,* July 15, August 19, 1897.

London *New Era,* June 17, 1899.
    Tablet, March 18, 1899.

Louisville *Katholischer Glaubensbote,* June 17, July 15, 1897.

Milwaukee *Catholic Citizen,* October 10, 1896.

New York *Catholic News,* December 24, 1893; December 2, 1896.
    Democrat, October 11, 1896.
    Evening World, October 8, 22, 1896; January 19, 1897.
    Freeman's Journal, June 18, 1887; November 3, 1888; October 8, 1898; May 3, 1902.
    Journal, October 20, November 25, 1897.
    Morgan Journal, November 21, 1896.
    Sun, January 29, February 14, August 7, 1893; July 30, 31, 1894; April 18, July 4, 1895; July 14, 1896.
    Tribune, October 15, 22, 23, November 13, 14, 20, December 4, 1896; January 20, June 30, October 21, 22, 23, 26, 27, December 6, 1897; February 11, June 6, November 19, 1898; February 25, May 30, June 29, 1899; July 18, October 29, November 24, 25, 1901; April 23, 1903.

Philadelphia *Catholic Standard and Times,* April 30, 1901.

Rochester *Union and Advertiser,* June 26, 1899.

St. Louis *Church Progress,* December 5, 1896.
    Herold Des Glaubens, August 11, 1897.
    Review, undated clipping.

St. Paul *Der Wanderer,* July 28, 1897.

Salt Lake City, *Intermountain Catholic,* December 2, 1899.

San Francisco *California Volksfreund,* April 16, 1898.
    Examiner, November, 1901.
    Leader, March 8, 1902.
    Monitor, October 30, 1897.
Washington *Church News,* October 23, 1897; January 1, 1898.
    Evening Star, August 5, 15, 1891; June 4, 1902.
    Post, October 7, 8, 1896; November 25, 1897.
    Times, May 29, 1899.
Worcester *Telegram,* May 27, June 1, 2, 29, August 29, 31, September 7, 9, October 5, 9, 26, December 9, 15, 30, 1896.

PERIODICAL LITERATURE

"Analecta," *American Ecclesiastical Review:*

Epistola Emi. Card. Rampolla ad Emum. Card. Gibbons de Novo Lycei Washingtoniensis Rectore Designando, XVI (February, 1897), 168-169.

Epistola Leonis XIII ad Archiepiscopos et Episcopos Foederatarum Americae Septentronialis Civitatum. (*Longinqua oceani*) XII (February, 1895), 156-167.

Epistola SS. D.N. Leonis PP. XIII ad Cardinalem Gibbons Cancellarum Magni Lycaei Washingtoniensis, Episcopos Exhortans ut Alumnos ad Lycaeum Mittant. XXV (August, 1901), 137-138.

Ex actis Leonis XIII et e secretaria brevium SS. Pontifex laudat commentaria quibus nomen La Civiltà Cattolica. XX (June, 1899), 623-624.

Litterae S.P. Leonis PP. XIII. De Universitate Washingtoniensi. XIII (September, 1895), 217-218.

Privilegium concedendi gradus academicos in seminario Roffensi. XXV (July, 1901), 59-61.

Becker, Thomas A., "A Plan for the Proposed Catholic University," *American Catholic Quarterly Review,* I (October, 1876), 655-679.

"Shall We Have A University?" *American Catholic Quarterly Review,* I (April, 1876), 230-253.

Blied, Benjamin J., "The Most Rev. Otto Zardetti, D.D., 1847-1902," *Salesianum,* XLII (April, 1947), 54-62.

Book Review, of *New Testament Studies,* in the *American Ecclesiastical Review,* XIX (October, 1898), 439-440.

Une dernière phase de la question scolaire aux Etats-Unis, in the *American Ecclesiastical Review,* XI (July, 1894), 72-74.

Brosnahan, Timothy, S.J., "President Eliot and Jesuit Colleges," a reprint from the *Sacred Heart Review,* January 13, 1900.

Burns, James A., C.S.C., "Catholic Secondary Schools," *American Catholic Quarterly Review,* XXVI (July, 1901), 485-499.

"Cardinals Who May be the Next Pope," *Catholic World,* LXIX (July, 1899), 433-448.

Catholic University Bulletin
    "Alumni Meeting," VII (July, 1901), 367-376.
    "Book Reviews," IV (October, 1898), 498-499.

178

Conaty, Thomas J., "The Catholic College of the Twentieth Century," VII (July, 1901), 304-319.

"Dedication of Holy Cross College," V (October, 1899), 518.

"Dedication of the Franciscan College," V (October, 1899), 515.

"Educational Conference of Seminary Presidents," IV (July, 1898), 397-405.

"Founders' Day at the University," IV (October, 1898), 493-495.

"Installation of the New Rector," IX (July, 1903), 436.

"Leo XIII and the Catholic University," VII (October, 1901), 509.

"Letters of Cardinal Martinelli and Cardinal Gibbons," VII (July, 1901), 386-387.

"The Mitchell Memorial Scholarship," IV (October, 1898), 481-492.

"The New Holy Cross College," V (April, 1899), 287-288.

"Ninth Alumni Association Meeting," IX (April, 1903), 293-297.

"Notes and Comments," VII (January, 1901), 101; VII (April, 1901), 244.

"The Pontifical Jubilee of Leo XIII (1878-1903)," IX (April, 1903), 282-292.

"The Progress of Trinity College," V (October, 1899), 517.

"Right Rev. Monsignor James McMahon," VII (July, 1901), 377-381.

"Rt. Rev. Thomas J. Conaty, D.D.," IX (July, 1903), 493-440.

"Solemn Opening of Trinity College," VII (January, 1901), 120-123.

"The Third Annual Conference of Catholic Colleges," VII (July, 1901), 382-385.

"Twelfth Annual Commencement," VII (July, 1901), 388-389.

"The University and the Apostolic Delegate," IX (January, 1903), 147.

"University Chronicle," IV (April, 1898), 289-292, (July, 1898), 423, (October, 1898), 527-539; V (April, 1899), 291-292, (October, 1899), 521-525; VI (January, 1900), 130-133, (July, 1900), 443; VII (January, 1901), 127-128, (April, 1901), 255-256, (July, 1901), 390, (October, 1901), 507; VIII (January, 1902), 124-131, (March, 1902), 257-259, (July, 1902), 400; IX (January, 1903), 170-176, (April, 1903), 311-312, (July, 1903), 444, (October, 1903), 573-574.

"Visit of President McKinley," VI (October, 1900), 449-451.

Clinch, Bryan J., "The Work of the Philippine Commission," *American Catholic Quarterly Review*, XXVI (October, 1901), 625-643.

"College Education," *Catholic World*, XXV (September, 1877), 313-321.

"Conferences," *American Ecclesiastical Review*:

"Academic Degrees in the Rochester Theological Seminary," XXV (July, 1901), 69-71.

"The Case of Boston College and Harvard University," XXIII (August, 1900), 173-175.

"Catholic Journalists and the Recent Encyclical," XII (March, 1895), 212-218.

"Catholic Teachers and Protestant Training Colleges," XXI (September, 1899), 296-301.

179

"The Educational Conference of Seminary Faculties," XIX (July, 1898), 83-84.

"The Friars Question," XXVII (August, 1902), 205-206.

J. McM. [Joseph McMahon] "The Clergy and the Summer School," XVI (April, 1897), 420-423.

"Leo XIII and the 'Civiltà Cattolica'," XX (June, 1899), 634-635.

"The Need of Catholic Normal Schools for Women," XXII (April, 1900), 409-412.

"The Philippine Controversy," XXVIII (March, 1903), 343-346.

"The Philippines Commissions' Report," XXVIII (May, 1903), 572-577.

"The Proposed Seminary for the Home and Colonial Missions," XXVI (January, 1902), 75-78.

"The Work of Our Parochial School Superintendents," XXV (December, 1901), 509-516.

Conlon, Noel, O.F.M., "Falconio—A Franciscan Portrait," *Provincial Annals,* IV (January, 1943), 17-30.

"Ecclesiastical Chronology," *American Ecclesiastical Review,* XVI (January, 1897), 72-80; XVIII (January, 1898), 59-63; XIX (July, 1898), 55-59; XX (January, 1899), 67-74; XXI (July, 1899), 57-61; XXII (January, 1900), 64-59; XXIII (July, 1900), 55-59; XXIV (January, 1901), 59-64; XXV (July, 1901), 53-58; XXVI (January, 1902), 44-50; XXVII (July, 1902), 71-79.

Farrell, John T., "Archbishop Ireland and Manifest Destiny," *Catholic Historical Review,* XXXIII (October, 1947), 269-301.

Heuser, H. J., "Catholic Journalism and the Friars Question," *American Ecclesiastical Review,* XXVII (September, 1902), 266-273.

Hogan, J., "Seminary and University Studies," *American Ecclesiastical Review,* XIX (October, 1898), 361-370.

Holden, Vincent F., "A Myth in 'L'Americanisme'," *Catholic Historical Review,* XXXI (July, 1945), 154-170.

M. S. R., "A Catholic Normal School for High School Teachers," *American Ecclesiastical Review,* XXII (April, 1900), 394-397.

Markoe, Lorenzo J., "Education by the State; or The Evolution of a State Religion," *American Catholic Quarterly Review,* XXVII (October, 1902), 782-812.

McAvoy, Thomas T., "Americanism, Fact and Fiction," *Catholic Historical Review,* XXXI (July, 1945), 133-153.

McDonald, William E., "The Pious Fund of the Californias," *Catholic Historical Review,* XIX (January, 1934), 427-436.

McQuaid, B. J., "Our American Seminaries," *American Ecclesiastical Review,* XVI (May, 1897), 461-480.

Meng, John J., "Cahenslyism: the First Stage, 1883-1891," *Catholic Historical Review,* XXXI (January, 1946), 389-413.

——————, "Cahenslyism: The Second Chapter, 1891-1910," *Catholic Historical Review,* XXXII (October, 1946), 302-340.

Middleton, Thomas C., O.S.A., "Report of the Philippine Commissions (of 1899-1900) on Religious and Educational Matters," *American Ecclesiastical Review,* XXVIII (March, 1903), 262-302.

Mullany, John F., "Some Advantages of the Catholic University," *American Catholic Quarterly Review,* XXVIII (July, 1903), 479-489.

Murphy, John T., "Catholic Secondary Education in the United States," *American Catholic Quarterly Review,* XXII (July, 1897), 449-464.

·"On the Higher Education," *Catholic World,* XII (March, 1871), 721-731; XIII (April, 1871), 115-124.

Poland, William, "Pedagogics: The Ethical Movement in Education," *American Catholic Quarterly Review,* XXIV (April, 1899), 18-40.

"Pontifical College Josephinum," *American Ecclesiastical Review,* XXI (September, 1899), 225-231.

P. R., "Trend of Modern Educational Legislation," *American Ecclesiastical Review,* XXII (January, 1900), 4-31.

"Shall We Have a Catholic Congress?" *Catholic World,* VIII (November, 1868), 224-228.

Shea, John G., "The Rapid Increase of the Dangerous Classes in the United States," *American Catholic Quarterly Review,* IV (April, 1879), 240-268.

Sheedy, Morgan M., "The Catholic Total Abstinence Union of America (History)," *American Ecclesiastical Review,* XII (March, 1895), 183-193.

—————————, "History of the Catholic Summer School of America," *Records of the American Catholic Historical Society,* XXVII (December, 1916), 213-242.

Sr. M. P., "Trinity College," *Catholic Historical Review,* XI (January, 1926), 660-674.

Stang, William, "The First National Congress of Missionaries to Non-Catholics," *American Ecclesiastical Review,* XXV (October, 1901), 331-338.

Thébaud, Augustus J., S.J., "Superior Instruction in Our Colleges," *American Catholic Quarterly Review,* VII (October, 1882), 673-699.

"The University Extension Movement Among American Catholics. A Symposium," I. The Catholic Idea of Popular Summer Schools, Conde B. Pallen. II. The Catholic Summer School and the Clergy, Thomas J. Conaty. III. The Catholic Winter School of America, Thomas O'Hagan, *American Ecclesiastical Review,* XV (July, 1896), 61-87.

Walsh, Louis S., "Unity, Efficiency, and Public Recognition of Catholic Elementary Schools," *American Ecclesiastical Review,* XXV (December, 1901), 481-489.

"What is the Outlook for our Colleges?" *American Catholic Quarterly Review,* VII (July, 1882), 329-336.

Zurcher, George, "Foreign Ideas in the Catholic Church in America," *Roycroft Quarterly,* I (November, 1896), 1-55.

APPENDIX

A

My dear Dr. Conaty:

As I told you Monsy Schroeder called to see me on Tuesday last about the German Chair and left again for Washington that evening. Without giving him any hint how I got the information I went over all the points you had mentioned. 1. As to his visiting saloons in Washington. He answered that he had never entered any saloon. There was one place he visited. McEberts I think the name. He often went there with Stephan or Glaub or Sbarretti. Ebert is a practical catholic. They entered by the family door and went upstairs where they had a glass of beer or wine or lunch in the sitting room of the family — 2. He abused drink—He answered that I had known him for six years—he never in his life had abused drink, was always perfectly clear headed. I can testify also that on every occasion he came to Phila. for the Xmas holidays. I have been with him on these occasions at Father Maus' where he stayed and where there would be a gathering of the clergy but he never abused drink even the slightest and surely then and there, there would have been the temptation to do so. I consider this charge a grave calumny. 3. You go away after dinner and do not return until late at night—He answered that is true—and I go simply for peace sake—I have humbled myself to the dust several times to Shahan and others, but have rec'd nothing but insults; even Prof. Bouquillon acknowledges that their treatment of me is scandalous and infamous. I am accused of the most infamous conspiracy. I am considered the cause of all the trouble and dissensions. I am innocent absolutely and have always used any influence I have in quieting the Germans and keeping the German press from speaking about University troubles. For peace' sake and my own quiet of mind I go every day to Father Glaub's. I have a room there; he has a good library. I take with me such books as I may need and prepare my classes. Surely I have a right to do so. Some of the Professors live in the city and therefore can do as they please. No one criticizes them. I give my classes regularly, why should I be criticized? I know that I am watched always. I have even been informed that a detective has been employed to report on all my actions—4. You have a regular schedule of matter each year in the Year Book, do you carry that out? Answer—I do, that is a Postgraduate course —I take up what I consider the most important questions for my time and treat them fully. It would be absurd to suppose the Professor should treat the matter as it is done in the Seminary. I work out all my lectures— I give the students after each lecture a mimeograph copy of the lecture.

All my lectures being written out I can give them to the Committee on Studies or to the Board and allow them to judge whether I have done my duty or not.

Such Dear Dr. Conaty is in substance the replies of Dr. Schroeder—I told him as his friend it was my duty to tell him all I knew—Of course he felt keenly all these accusations but thanked me for having spoken to him as I had done.

I write this to you for your own *personal* information. Dr. Schroeder is growing disheartened and I fear that if things do not change, he will resign and that would be in my estimation one of the greatest blows the University could receive; for it would inevitably make enemies of the whole German element which is so very powerful in the West and North-west not to speak of the East.

I pray God that your administration will restore peace and harmony. Dr. Schroeder expressed the highest admiration for you and the good you have already done amongst the students of the University.

Sincerely yours in Christ.
✠ Ign. F. Horstmann
Bp. of Cleveland

*ACUA, CHF, Schroeder Case.

B

RECTOR'S REPORT TO THE BOARD OF TRUSTEES*
October 19, 1897

To the Board of Trustees of the Catholic University of America;

From an administrative point of view, after careful consideration covering a period of eight months, I am forced in conscience to report to this Board what I regard as a lamentable domestic condition which seems to be more accentuated as the days go by. The Faculty of Theology and the University Senate by their unanimous action placed the cause of the continuance of this sad condition upon Mgr. Schroeder whom they regard as the stumbling block to that unity and harmony and peace so necessary to the University. My reasons for this conclusion may be summarized as follows:

1. The peace and harmony of the University are now rendered impossible because:
   (a) an irreconcilable character developed toward Mgr. Schroeder and by him toward certain professors by his attacks upon them and the insinuations against their teachings which they attribute to him. (Vide doc. a, and also Faculty reasons, doc. 2.)
   (b) his indirect suggestions of tendency toward heterodoxy and his direct charges of heresy against Dr. Grannan, made to me and others. (Vide doc. a).
   (c) the impression given very assiduously that Dr. Schroeder has been boycotted because of his nationality or because of difference

183

of opinions upon certain questions. (Vide quotations from German Catholic papers and Doc. B).

(d) his unkind and unjust criticism of associates to students. (Vide Doc. H).

(e) his apparent assumption of the role of ecclesiastical censor of their teachings, writings and conversations, reporting these criticisms not to their faculties but to other authorities, notably to Rome and to the former Delegate (Vide doc. H). The frictions that have existed are now in a most aggravated form and seem impossible of remedy in existing conditions. All efforts at peace seem to have failed. Even the students are permeated with the spirit of opposition to him as an element of disturbance to peace and harmony.

2. His desire for ecclesiastical leadership which draws him into polemics that create factionism and dissension;

(a) his weekly or frequent contributions to papers of recognized hostility to the University which engages him as a professor, notable the Review, whose editor, Preuss. [*sic*]

(b) his posing as the one orthodox professor whose presence is heralded as necessary to the faith of the University.

(c) his readiness to rush into print either over his own signature or in articles inspired by him to criticise Church legislation, the utterances of eminent members of the Hierarchy and of this Board, the editorials of papers antagonistic of his peculiar views, thus exciting passions and prejudices and fomenting class and race feuds (Morgan-Journal article) and making national divisions among the people (Vide Doc. A). All this despite the admonitions of the Holy Father. See Doc H, No. 9.

3. His inefficient professorial work—

(a) his apparent inability or unwillingness to go beyond certain tracts in Dogma which seem to be better suited to Seminary than to University work in post-ordination courses.

(b) the constant fault-finding of students made to me and of reported fault found by superiors of religious for too much oratory and not enough teaching.

(c) the apparent difficulty as appears to me for proper preparation, because of newspaper, convention and Church work, assuming at time charge of Forty Hours in a City Church during School Session. I submit that the importance of this matter calls for all his time in preparation of his work. Vide Schedule of work since he came to University. Absence of scientific work such as a professor of Dogma should do. The mere teaching of a lesson is not all that should be expected.

(d) no helpfulness to students many of whom as they have told me attend his classes because it is Dogma and they desire to know it.

4. A criticism in sneering ways of members of this board and notably of the Past Rector. A continuance of newspaper propaganda in spite of promises to the Rector who has labored to take the University out of the newspapers which labor to continue the feuds that tend to scandal. See extracts Doc. B and Doc. I.

5. A certain spirit of defiance which is subversive of all order and authority as has been manifested to me on two different occasions and which appears from the declaration of his friends that because he is a German he can do as he pleases. His threats to tear things from their foundation if any man dare attack him.

6. The financial future of the University.

   (a) the drying up of sources of our revenues Chapel, Divinity, and University funds, as you may see from the report and this is due in large part as I know from personal experience because this man has made himself odious to a large portion of the English-speaking people who are no small portion of the mainstay of this Institution in the two million dollars which it represents.

7. The action of Faculty and Senate which is the legitimate channel of communication on such matters to this Board. Ample opportunity was given to the Senate composed of seven priests and three laymen to discuss and question the matter as it came from the Faculty of Theology. The vote was unanimous as you may see from Senate minutes transmitted in Doc. 3 and based on Faculty reasons, Doc. 2. This action is the highest expression of University action and demands your most serious consideration. The authority of the University is in question, its life is at stake and the Board cannot afford to disregard it, if it wishes to maintain respect for the constitutions which the Holy See has approved and which places rights and privileges within the University by which I have a voice in its corps of instruction. The authority is vested in the Rector to suspend for cause any professor who may be judged as deserving of it—but your Rector has judged better to refer the whole matter to the Board as he feels keenly the vital importance of the question in view of all the circumstances. He regards this as a critical moment in our University life as to whether one man shall rule, either by the press or by his determined attitude and he begs you to bring relief. By this last act of his, I consider that our power of administration, our discipline and government are seriously endangered. Without any evidence of official report he has succeeded in forestalling all judgment or investigation of accusation. How did his friends in Rome know the nature of the accusations standing against him and why should they presume that this Board has neither justice nor prudence in their judgment? An evident misstatement or exaggerated report has been given, fears have been played upon, and as a result this man is placed quasi ex lex, beyond constitutional powers and beyond the jurisdicton of this Board. I feel sure that no such action was

185

intended for by it all authority is nullified and your governing Board and your Rector are powerless; if we have not authority over the entire University. It would be important to know the sources of this action and find the evidence by which the Holy Father has been led to give you this council. Respecting any word that comes from the Pontiff and respecting it as loyal children yet the apostolical constitutions invest you with the right to hear the Report on discipline and report such action as may be judged most prudent.

I have tabulated these charges that you may know how I have arrived at my conclusions. I have considered all sides, weighed all consequences, and I am convinced that the University will never have peace, the young professors will not have that respect for authority or love for this work. The men who have made the University will not have the heart to do their best work unless the one who is regarded as the stumbling block be removed.

I am prepared to give such evidence as has come to me. His life is a constant menace to the character of our professors who value their faith, their reputation as priests and teachers and are always in fear of his insinuations which are taken up by a press friendly to him and made to appear as the acts of semi or whole heresy. The professors have borne this patiently certainly since my advent among them and out of deference to my desires for peace have refrained from acting although he has publicly charged every newspaper report and canard to his associates. There is no hostility to his nationality but to his personality which is known best to those who live with him. I need not remind you of the peculiar circumstances of my nomination which left me absolutely free to act in a most independent manner and hence most impartially and free from prejudice. God knows that I have had no prejudices and have none except that which inclines me to the University. I have tried to bring harmony and to secure a modus vivendi but I have failed because Dr. Schroeder would not do as he had agreed and gave fuel to a press unfriendly to the University upon which it regularly empties the vials of its wrath, while demanding that no one touch him. I was in hopes that its good wishes for me, as the new Rector, would cause revilings to cease, but when on one occasion I refused to grant Dr. Schroeder's request and publicly deny rumors which concerned him and his reported relations with others about which I knew nothing, I was subjected to the vileness of their attacks and in papers for which he writes and with the editors of which he is on most intimate terms. Is such conduct to be tolerated in any professor of the University? Is it becoming above all to the professor of Dogma, the most important position in the University, to enter the field of ecclesiastical politics and in spite of the injunctions of our Holy Father to inflame the passions of men upon questions the settlement of which belongs to the Holy See to pass judgment upon the

186

writings and utterances especially of the University professors. Because I believe not, I am forced to conclude that such a man is not worthy of a place in the University. Peace, order, authority, good example, the proprieties of position as a teacher demand a change and no matter what the misunderstanding may be, the University is worth it all. God will take care of the University. My duty is clear and I fulfil it by this statement. Less I cannot do and be true to the trust confided to me. I have advised with no professor. I have been governed by no set of men. I defy any man to say that he knew what I have just read to you. I have inquired, I have examined. Charges have been made to me at different times and I have always demanded that every charge should be presented in writing and sworn to if it had any bearing on character. I have been my own counselor and confidant because I sought for independence and justice. I have, it is true, spoken to members of this Board, at different times during the year as I met them and I have mentioned my suspicions. I believe that your Rector should have no secrets in his relations with you. I have mentioned my suspicions to Mgr. Schroeder's intimate friend that he might advise him. In my relations I have been frank and I have been impartial. I have warned him about my discussions. I have advised him but warning and advice availed but little. The same impossibility soon manifested itself. In a manly way I told him yesterday of my intended report. I ask you to give relief to the men who are bearing the burdens and heats of the day to realize that your sources of supply are gradually drying up—the diminution of the Divinity, Chapel and University funds—is due to this difficulty as I have heard it on all sides. The friends of the University are sick of this malignant and persistent attack upon its Rectors, its professors, and its Trustees and they ask, How long, O Lord, will a source of supply for this unchristian, inhuman, unamerican attack upon a University established by Leo XIII and maintained by its Bishops be tolerated? I have found such misinformation about the work done and the conduct of men here that I would be ashamed to repeat it and I know that the source is in an evident purpose to destroy the power of the University for good. I am satisfied that there never will be peace and less prospect of it now more than ever unless some action, definite and determined action, to assert once and forever that there is an authority located in this body that will enforce obedience to its will upon every professor. Washington is in a state of ferment and the country is asking if this state of things cannot be changed. Mgr. Schroeder's conduct is discussed among our young men's societies and at lunch rooms of reporters. I believe that the interests of the University demand that you give ear to these reports examine them carefully and act justly but decisively. The University demands that its petition be heard and that you give relief to a situation which is ruinous to religion and to edu-

187

cation. The Board of Senate thinks and places itself on record that the one way to peace among its members is to request the resignation of Mgr. Schroeder and as the Rector, I am in conscience bound to unite with them in this request.

Thomas J. Conaty, Rector.
October 19, 1897.

*ACUA, CHF, Schroeder Case.

C

English draft of the letter sent to Cardinal Rampolla by Cardinal Gibbons in the Schroeder case.

Catholic University of America
Washington, D. C.
November 15, 1897.*

Your Eminence:

As chancellor of the Catholic University of America and acting under a note of the Board of Directors, at the annual meeting held in Washington Oct. 20. I have the honor to transmit a relation of its acts as they refer to the case of Mgr. Schroeder, the Prof. of Dogmatic Theology, as the Board refers the matter to the Holy Father for final decision as suggested by your cablegram of Oct. 16 to Archbp. Martinelli and communicated to me. I am sure your Eminence will appreciate the gravity of the situation which has called for our opinion and I would respectfully submit to the Holy Father some of the reasons that have led us to our recommendation.

. . . . [Here follows the general account of what had been done] . . . .

The reception of Cardinal Rampolla's cablegram had much to do with modifying the action of the Board as out of deference for the Holy Father's implied wish no final action was taken and only an expression of the judgment of the Board was made. It is very probable that if this cablegram had not been received the resignation of Dr. Schroeder would have been immediately demanded. His letter was received and read satisfying the members as to his intention of resigning as may be seen from the letter a copy of which accompanies this relation as Doc.—

While all agreed without discussion that the matter be referred to the Holy Father for final settlement, there can be no doubt as appears from the resolutions that the Board of Directors felt that the interests of the University demanded Mgr. Schroeder's resignation, propter utilitatem Collegii as set forth in Const. Fac. Theo. Cap. III, No. II.

After having made known to His Holiness the results of our deliberations on this matter as Chancellor I may be permitted to call the attention of His Holiness to the following important considerations.

1. The advice of the Rt. Rev. Rector of the University which appears in his Report Doc. A. has in my judgment very great weight. Mgr. Conaty has been called to the responsibility of the Rectorship at a moment of

great difficulty by the unanimous choice of the Bishops, a choice which His Holiness most graciously approved. He governs the University in a manner which commands universal satisfaction. He enjoys the fullest confidence of the Bishops. The loyalty of his character, his recognized impartiality, his perfect freedom from all entanglements, the absence of all prejudice, his straight forward manliness and kindness, his well known devotion to the person of the Holy Father, his freedom from any influence of individuals or parties as seen in his report, all this has convinced us that he is activated by the one motive of the greatest good to the University and to the Church of God. On the other hand, the uprightness of his judgment, his prudence, his knowledge of men and things acquired by long personal experience are a guarantee that he is not deceived when from a conscientious sense of duty he demands the resignation of Mgr. Schroeder from an administrative standpoint as a necessity to the peace and harmony of the University. It is of sovereign importance that the authority of the Rector be publicly recognized and for this he needs the full confidence of the Holy See. My own solemn conviction reached after long and serious consideration coincides absolutely with that of the Rt. Rev. Rector.

2. Another consideration is to be found in the character of the Board of Directors. It is composed of the most eminent and the most distinguished members of the American Episcopate. Their devotion to the University is manifested by the sacrifices of time and expense necessary to attend the meetings, some of them coming six, eight and even a thousand leagues for that purpose. They were familiar with every phase of the situation, they heard the Rector's report, consulted among themselves, examined matters on the ground, weighed matters carefully and without any preconceived ideas or concerted plans arrived conscientiously and with practical unanimity at the conclusions which I have already mentioned. There is great danger that if Dr. Schroeder be allowed to remain that they will be discouraged and become indifferent to the University. I even fear that some of them may be tempted to resign from the Board. It is a most serious moment in the affairs of the University and I certainly agree with them that all our interests demand that Dr. Schroeder retire. Add to this that Dr. Schroeder himself has expressed his desire to withdraw as may be seen from his letter in Doc B. He represents that he awaits but the word of His Holiness for that purpose.

3. A third consideration may come from the feeling of the country at large as may be seen from the expression of public officials and private citizens as also the word of the newspapers and especially what are known to be the judgment of those who are our most liberal benefactors and on whom we must depend in the future for the maintenance of the University. The expression is unmistakably in favor of the vindication and approval of the well known sentiment of the Board. His Holiness may be anxious about the difficulty of supplying the place of Professor

189

of Dogmatic Theology, but I am happy to state that Providence seems to have admirably furnished us with a man eminently fitted to teach and he is Rev. Dr. Shanahan, now teaching in the School of Philosophy. He was a pupil of Cardinal Satolli and Lepicier at Propaganda and was made a Doctor by the Holy Father after a publica disputatio of great merit. He was trained for Dogmatic Theology and for two years past has taught Thomistic Philosophy in the University. He is an enthusiastic Thomist and won great encomiums for his article on the Idea of God against one of the ablest non-Catholic Philosophers who has not dared to answer him. His lectures on the Thomistic idea of God have been given with great success before large bodies of non-Catholic students in one of our largest non-Catholic Universities and all are proud of him as a teacher and a writer according to the idea of St. Thomas.

I may be allowed to add that Mgr. Schroeder is not teaching now as he has requested a leave of absence. Owing to the importance of this matter I have taken the liberty of great explicitness in placing before His Holiness all these reasons that he may know why the resignation is desirable. The Faculty and Senate of the University are the highest expression of its governing power and they unanimously demand it. The Board of Directors is practically unanimous in granting their request and with the Rt Rev Rector and myself as Chancellor unite respectfully in asking His Holiness to sustain our authority and relieve the University of a danger the greatness of which cannot be estimated.

* ACUA, CHF, Schroeder Case.

D

Washington, D. C.
March 3, 1902.*

Rt. Rev. and Dear Dr. Conaty:

By verbal communication, on the first day of the present month of March, you notified me, as I understood it, that one of the decisions reached by the investigating committee which recently met in this city to inquire into the affairs of the Catholic University, was to recommend to the faculty of the University the abolition of the lectureship in Ethics at the institution to take effect at the beginning of the next scholastic year, or on the first of October, 1902. Such action means, of course, that from that time my services will no longer be required at the University.

Precisely what may have determined the distinguished gentlemen who constituted the above mentioned committee to make such a recommendation I do not know. No more do I know by what process they reached the conclusion which preceded that determination. Their attention certainly must have been directed toward the lectureship in Ethics, and toward the work that is being being [sic] done in that branch. But, notwithstanding that I have been doing that work for nearly six years, the gentlemen conducting that enquiry evidently considered themselves able to obtain information sufficient for reaching a rational conclusion without even consulting me. It is, however, of some importance to me to get an idea of the reason of their action, because my own conduct must be guided by such reason; and their method of proceeding makes it necessary for me to try to get at the Knowledge I need by speculation.

To begin with a possibility which I suppose is to be rejected at once, it might be that their action was moved by reasons purely personal with regard to me. I say that this policy is to be rejected because certainly it would be "un-american", it would savour of the "inquisition", it would be "medieval" and "Italian" to act from personal considerations towards a man without hearing him or even intimating to him the intention of acting in a matter of concern to him.

To remain for a moment longer on the borders of personality, it may be that the distinguished gentlemen of the committee concluded that the system of Ethics which I have been teaching is not modern enough, not "up-to-date"—that it is the same old system of scholastic times. Again it would be hard to suppose that those gentlemen could have acted on such considerations, for this much is certain, that the system of Ethics which I have taught is the only one recognized and permitted to be taught by the Roman Catholic Church. It has occurred to me to make this supposition because I have heard it various times in the past that some of the illustrious lay-professors of the University have remarked something of the kind.

Next, it might be imagined that the committee of enquiry, after careful thought, concluded that the lectures in Ethics are not of essential importance in a University course. But it is hard to realize that such could be the opinion of distinguished bishops of the Catholic Church. The spirit and practice of that Church have always been quite the contrary, and it has always considered Ethics as the subject of greatest importance among the natural sciences. The catholic idea is, I think, that in Ethics is to be found the fruit of all the natural sciences, and it is only in so far as they bring forth that fruit that they are of any real service or use to man. Perhaps the committee intends to substitute for the lectureship in Ethics a full professorial chair so that the work in that branch may be strengthened and perfected. In such case—which would imply a most laudable intention—it seems strange again that the committee should have felt no need of consulting the only person connected with the University who had paid the least attention to that work and concerning the means of providing for its future development—without consulting the only person who has ever taught Ethics in the University, and who has taught it there for six years. Moreover, I can scarcely conclude that there is any serious intention of continuing the teaching of Ethics under more perfect and favorable conditions, since to do so would more than double the expense, and I have been given to understand that the purpose for which the committee of enquiry was appointed by the board of trustees was precisely to find means of reducing expenses and avoiding so large an annual deficit.

This brings me to the last hypothesis of which I can think. I can see no reason for the action of the committee other than an economic one. The expenses of the University must be reduced and one of the luxuries most easily dispensed with is of course Ethics. I realize that this supposition presents some difficulties; but, everything considered, it seems to be the most probable of all. If it be true, then of course there is nothing to be said about the substance of the decision, since economic determinations are of a peculiarly personal nature. The manner in which the committee puts its decision into effect, however, is a thing which I feel I have a right to criticise. I have given conscientious service to the University for six years in the class room, and outside the class room I have, during the same time, done for it many things which have tended to promote its interests. Consequently, I feel that the committee of enquiry owed it to me to consult me before taking action affecting the course in Ethics. If the committee determined that these lectures should cease, it ought to have abolished them itself. I refuse absolutely to permit the question to be brought before the faculty and discussed there so long as I am lecturer in Ethics.

Therefore my determination is that this present communication shall contain my resignation as Lecturer in Ethics at the Catholic University of America, and thus save the faculty the trouble of acting in the matter. Furthermore, if the finances of the Institution are in such a desperate condition that the committee of investigation was constrained to take such action and to take it in such a way, I am willing that you should consider this resignation as taking effect at once, so that the amount which would be due me were I to continue my work for the rest of the academic year may be saved to the University.

With sentiments of highest esteem and profound respect, thanking you for your own universal courtesy toward me, I remain,

Most faithfully yours,

Frederick Z. Rooker.

* ACUA, FBT, Envelope 28, XXVIII Meeting, November 1902, in typescript.

E

Rigi-Scheidegg, Switzerland
August 20, 1902.*

Your Eminence:

I have just returned from Rome, whither I went on business connected with the Biblical Commission. While there, I learned with surprise, that the keenest interest is felt in the condition of the University; that they possess an unusual amount of accurate and detailed knowledge about it; that the impression prevails in the minds of many that it is in a precarious condition; that some drastic measure is needed; that, above all, a change of administration is imperiously demanded as the only means of restoring confidence, now lost; that the reappointment of Dr. Conaty would be disasterous [*sic*]; and that the Board should provide, not for Dr. Conaty, but for the University. In particular, this is the oft expressed opinion of Cardinal Satolli, who, perhaps, because he is prefect of the Congregation of Studies, as well as for other reasons, is sure to be consulted in the matter when the time comes. He has very accurate information, is outspoken in his opinion, and says positively that we must either change or perish: "Bisogna o cambiare o morire." He says it was he who first suggested the insertion of the clause limiting the Rectorship to a term of six years, and that this was done on set purpose so as easily to get rid of a Rector, when he is a failure, as in the present case. He also adds that the term of six years is about to expire; that the reappointment of Dr. Conaty would be disasterous [*sic*]; and that a new slate should be submitted to the Holy See by the Trustees next November. He says that the time limit was made to cover just such cases; and that if it is not applied to this case, it has "no raison d'etre." He then went on to tell me that he has a candidate who would meet perfectly the conditions of the University, — Monsignore Denis O'Connell, former Rector of the American College at Rome. He is convinced that Dr. O'Connell has the intelligence, the courage, the integrity of character, and the prudence, — to succeed, where others have failed. It is also his opinion and his hope that the Bishops, the Priests, the Faculties of the University, and the laity of the country would welcome Dr. O'Connell to Washington. As that is largely my own opinion, I could not but agree with him, at least in the main.

But, as I said above, it was not I who suggested the changes; it was Cardinal Satolli himself who first suggested them. He also informed me that, for weeks and even months past, he has advocated the same changes both by word of mouth in Rome itself, and by letter in some quarters in America. He has also requested some others to make it known as his opinion. In fact, it seems to me that Cardinal Satolli has gone so far in insisting on the early retirement of Dr. Conaty, whether he gets a diocese or not, and has advocated so earnestly the appointment of Dr. O'Connell as his successor, that it would now be impossible for the Cardinal to retire from the position he has taken, even if he were at all inclined to do so. That he has not the remotest idea of retracing his steps, is evident from this, that as time goes on he becomes more and more convinced that he is right and that what he wants will go through. It seems, from what I have heard elsewhere in Rome, that the above views are not confined to Cardinal Satolli; but are shared by many others, some of whom will have a vote in the matter, when the time comes. Your Eminence perhaps is not aware that Dr. O'Connell is growing in favor in the Eternal City, all the more so as the conviction is spreading that he has not been properly treated, and that some public satisfaction is due him.

That a change of Administration at the University is felt at Rome to be demanded as the only means of restoring confidence in the stability of the Institution, is the opinion of at least two other Cardinals, both of whom told me they had heard, with surprise, that a member of the Board of Directors, while admitting that Dr. Conaty's administration was a failure, nevertheless thought that, in view of the new dignity conferred upon him, he might be reelected, — just to save his feelings. One of the Cardinals characterised such conduct and such motives in a Director as "perfidious" and the other called it "Treason against the Church." Both these gentlemen added that the Directors should provide, not for Individuals, but for the Institution. Both also favor a change of administration.

I had a long private & separate audience with the Holy Father, of which I have nothing to say.

I have deemed it my duty to communicate the above facts to your Eminence, as Chancellor of the University, in order that you may know the lie [sic] of the ground, and have some idea of the sentiments prevailing in higher ecclesiastical circles in Rome. You may thus shape your actions in any emergency that might arise.

The sudden change of temperature between Rome and the mountains of Switzerland gave an inflamation of the lungs, of which I was laid up for repairs in the Sisters Hospital at Ingenbohl for two weeks. I am now out and around. I sail from Rotterdam on the 19th prox.

With best wishes,

I am yours in Xto,
Chas. P. Grannan.

* BCA, 99-W-5.

F

Rotterdam
Sept. 18, 1902*

Dear Doc: [Denis O'Connell]

I suppose Sat. [Satolli] will tell many a one about the information which I gave him verbally and in writing. It will also reach the ears of Americans. Here is my defense: I have come to Europe eleven times in thirteen years, and this is the first visit to Rome in twenty two years, except a day going to, and a day returning from the Orient, on which occasion I saw nobody but only rested. So no one can accuse me of too much Romanising. Even this time I did not go of my own accord. Last June I submitted the question to the Academic Senate. They told me to follow instructions from the Biblical Commission. I submitted to them the pros and cons, and they even fixed a date for me to appear in Rome. Once there, and by no active initiative of my own, I simply answered such questions as competent authorities put to me. 1) I might have shrugged my shoulders, played the ignorant and answered nothing. But that would be too thin, too diaphanous, as they say. I am not so stupid, or deaf, or

194

blind as not to know what is going on around me. 2) I might have lied and denied the facts; but that would not do; because the Romans knew the facts already and could not be deceived; and also because I was taught in my younger days that it is always wicked to lie, notwithstanding the example of many distinguished ecclesiastics to the contrary.

3) So there was no alternative but for me to tell the truth. And I told the truth, the whole truth (at least as far as time would permit,) and nothing but the truth, and I make no secret about it. I thought only of the Institution, and had not a particle of concern for the persons implicated. I had no interest either to exaggerate or to minimize the conditions; I had no interest either to emphasize or palliate the faults committed. I was responsible for the accurate *statement* of facts and not for the *facts* themselves. As to the facts let those answer who committed them or permitted them, with their eyes wide open, and contrary to the plainest dictates of common sense, & common honesty.

This is my defense and I would like to see the man who says "nay" to it.
. . .
Anything about the Biblical Commission will be of interest to me. I think we win.

With best wishes.

Jeshurun. [Charles P. Grannan]

[P.S.] Did you hear that the Kaiser has appointed Schroeder Rector Magnificus of the new University of Munster?

Riordan either knew or took it for granted that I met you, and his demand was so direct that I had to confess that we met on the Rigi. I am not sure that he goes to Rome, but even if he does, it should not be mentioned beforehand.

[P.P.S.] Dear Doc.

On further consideration I decided to run over to the Hage [*sic*], and lunch with Abp. Riordan. I am glad I did. I found him in good humor and left him in better humor. Though the international tribunal was in session and his case was under discussion, still he had time to hear me, at least in outline. The outline contained everything ad rem. I need not rehearse it to you.

He told me that George Montgomery has been appointed his coadjutor, and Farley Abp. of N. York. Both O.K. Now let J.L.S. [Spalding] go to Chicago and the work is largely done. All that will then remain to be done is for D. J. O'C. [O'Connell] to go to Washington and may the good Lord and our friends bring it about. Keep me posted on all the veerings of the ecclesiastical weather cock in the "eterna citta".

Aufwiedersehen.

Jeshurun.

over

195

I have just written to Sat. [Satolli] before sailing, to tell him how much I am pleased with the appointment of Farley, and to tell him that, after revolving in my mind the probable action of the Directors of the University, I calculated that two, at most, Ryan and Horstmann, would at first be against you, because of their friendship with Corrigan. Then, after some remarks about the dead being soon forgotten, I add that Ryan will, in the end, go with the majority, as soon as the way the wind is blowing is known to him, and that Horstmann now counts for little, as he is often sick, and sometimes absent from the meeting of the Directors, as he was last time.

* Richmond Diocesan Archives.

INDEX

Compiled by Margaret M. Donahue

BECKER, THOMAS A., Bishop
   Univ. protagonist, 2
   rumored for rectorship, 6
BENEDICTINES
   at Univ., 92
BERNARD, BRO., 103
BIBLICAL COMMISSION
   Grannan appointment, 134
BIOLOGICAL SCIENCES, School of; *see*
   Faculty of the Biological Sciences
BISHOPS' MEETING, New York, 1893, 143
BISHOPS, Province of Dubuque
   meeting, 131
BISMARCK
   Cath. opposition to, 158
BOARD OF GOVERNORS, Faculty of Philosophy; *see* Faculty of Philosophy
BOARD OF INSTRUCTION IN TECHNOLOGY;
   see Technology, Board of Instruction
BOARD OF REGENTS, New York, 20, 114
BOLLING, GEORGE M.
   replaced Quinn, 36, 107
BOSTON COLLEGE
   Harvard controversy, 73n, 75
BOUQUILLON, THOMAS
   adviser to Conaty, 83
   McGlynn commission, 11
   report on religious as Univ. professors, 33
   rumored dismissal, 10
   school controversy pamphlets, 142
BRANDI, SALVATORE M., S.J.
   O'Connell's dismissal, 145
BRANN, H. A.
   proposed for rectorship, 8
BRANNEGAN, FRANK H., 126
BRIGGS, EDMUND B.
   asked support of Corrigan, 126
   desired to be reinstated, 127
   life, 126
   reappointment, 50
   resigned from Univ. for Philippines, 125
BROSNAHAN, TIMOTHY, S.J.
   Catholic and non-Catholic colleges, 73
BROWNE, ROBERT
   first mention of a Catholic university, 1
Bulletin
   Investigating Committee, 135
   Schroeder's contribution requested, 151
   Shahan, interest in, 134
   Univ. finances, 59
BYRNE, THOMAS S., Bishop
   Conaty's appointment to Univ., 23
CAHENSLY, PETER PAUL
   feared attacks on Pohle and Schroeder,
   150

praised by Schroeder, 149
   presented memorial to Pope, 148-149
CAHENSLYISM
   condemned, 151
   effect of, 4
   effect of Schroeder's resignation, 157
   St. Raphael's Society, 149
CALDWELL, ELIZABETH
   established scholarships, 2, 111
   site for Univ., 2
CALDWELL, LINA; *see* Caldwell, Elizabeth
CALDWELL, MARY GWENDOLINE
   Caldwell Hall Chapel, gifts to, 111
   established scholarships, 111
   library gift, 111
   site of Univ., 2, 3
   urged Spalding to Washington, 41
   visit to Univ., 110
CALDWELL HALL
   faculty residence, 32
   see also Divinity College
CALDWELL HALL, Chapel
   gift to, 111
   opening of, 3
   use of, 50
CALIFORNIA, UNIVERSITY OF; *see* University of California
CAMERON, FRANK K.
   resignation, 35
CANDIDATES FOR MATRICULATION
   definition, 48
CAPTIER, A., S.S., 31
CARR, SIMON J.
   resignation, 35
CATHEDRAL OF THE ASSUMPTION, Baltimore
   Conaty's consecration, 113
CATHOLIC ACADEMY OF MÜNSTER; *see*
   Münster, Catholic Academy of
CATHOLIC ALUMNI ASSOCIATION
   honored Conaty, 23
CATHOLIC CENTER PARTY, Germany
   opposition to Bismarck, 158
CATHOLIC COLLEGES, Association of
   formation, 68-70
   meetings of, 76, 79-80
   purpose, 70
   state in education, 76
   success reported, 72
CATHOLIC COLLEGES, Conference of
   Conaty organized, 168
CATHOLIC EDUCATIONAL ASSOCIATION
   formation, 69
   groups of, 80
CATHOLIC HIGH SCHOOLS
   archbishops' aid, 79

Catholic Home and School Magazine, 18
CATHOLIC INSTITUTE OF PEDAGOGY; *see* Institute of Pedagogy
CATHOLIC MISSIONARY HOUSE, 87
CATHOLIC MISSIONARY UNION, 87
CATHOLIC SUMMER SCHOOL, Cliff Haven
chartered, 20
Conaty, organizer of, 9, 19
Conaty lectured (1901), 113
Corrigan, 152
Institute of Pedagogy, 85
purpose, 19
CATHOLIC SUMMER SCHOOL, New London, Conn., 19
CATHOLIC TOTAL ABSTINENCE UNION OF AMERICA; *see* Temperance
CATHOLIC UNIVERSITY; *see* University
Catholic University Bulletin; *see Bulletin*
CATHOLIC WINTER SCHOOL, New Orleans
Conaty, 20, 108
CHAIR OF GAELIC; *see* Gaelic, Chair of
CHAIR OF PEDAGOGY; *see* Pedagogy, Chair of
CHANCELLOR OF UNIVERSITY; *see* Gibbons
CHAPEL, CALDWELL HALL; *see* Caldwell Hall Chapel
CHAPELLE, PLACIDE L., Archbishop
Schroeder case, 153, 155
CHARLESTON, South Carolina, 1
CHICAGO, World's Parliament of Religions, *see* Religions, World's Parliament of
CHRISTIAN BROTHERS
Institute of Pedagogy, 84
CHURCH AND STATE
Jannet's statement, 158
Testem Benevolentiae, 162
CHURCH OF THE SACRED HEART, Worcester
Conaty, first pastor, 15
farewell to Conaty, 27
CHURCH OF ST. PAUL, New York
first meeting of Board of Trustees, 3
"*Chumps*"; *see*: Grannan; O'Connell; Pace; Shahan
CITY AND SUBURBAN RAILWAY
moved from Univ. grounds, 51
CLIFF HAVEN SCHOOL; *see* Catholic Summer School, Cliff Haven
CLIFF HAVEN CATHOLIC SUMMER SCHOOL; *see* Catholic Summer School, Cliff Haven
COLLECTION TOURS, 56; *see also*: Beaven; Conaty; Harkins; Keane
COLLEGE
basis of sem. and univ., 67

COLLEGE, LOUVAIN; *see* American College, Louvain
COLLEGE OF ST. FRANCIS XAVIER, New York; *see* St. Francis Xavier College, New York
COLLEGE OF THE COMMISSARIAT OF THE HOLY LAND; *see* Franciscan Monastery
COLLEGE OF THE HOLY CROSS; *see* Holy Cross College, Worcester
COLUMBIAN EXPOSITION (1893), Chicago
World's Parliament of Religions, 143
COLUMBIAN SUMMER SCHOOL, Madison, Wisc., 19
COMMISSARIAT OF THE HOLY LAND, COLLEGE OF; *see* Franciscan Monastery
COMMITTEE ON TECHNOLOGY, 53
CONATY, ALICE LYNCH
Mother of Thomas, 14
CONATY, BERNARD
represented brother at Holy Cross, Worcester, 21
CONATY, PATRICK
at son's consecration, 115
father of Thomas, 13
CONATY, THOMAS J.
accused of Nestorianism, 110
administrative policy, 32-33
analysis of a college, 71
analysis of a university, 71
Ancient Order of Hibernians, 123
appointed titular bishop, 113
appointed to rectorship, 13, 25
army's looting Philippine churches, 129
Association of American Universities, 82-83, 168
Association of Catholic Colleges, 60, 70, 72, 76-79, 80
Briggs, reinstatement, 127
business ability, lack of, 135
candidate for rectorship, 22
Catholic chaplain appointed for Navy, 129
Catholic Church in Cuba, 128
"The Catholic College of the Twentieth Century," 76
Catholic Educational Association, 80
Catholic Home and School Magazine, 18
Catholic Summer School, 19-22, 24, 113
Catholic Total Abstinence Union of Amer., 15
Catholic Winter School, New Orleans, 108
"Celtic Influence on English Literature," 26
Characterization, 13, 23-24, 107
Chicago bishopric, 112

Church of the Sacred Heart, Worcester, 15, 27
class schedule, 32
collecting tour, 34
Columbus bishopric, 42, 111-112
Committee on technology, 53
Conference of Catholic Colleges, 168
cooperation with O'Connell, 171
degree from St. Joseph's College refused, 113
Dept. of Pedagogy, 86
departure from Univ., 171
domestic prelate, 103-104
Dominican affiliation with Univ., 93-94
Dudleian Lectures, 108
education, purpose of, 72
educational integration, 70
educational standards of, 65
entrance requirements, 64
evaluation as rector, 63
Father Mathew Chair, 15
Garrigan, praise of, 130
German-American opinions of, 152
Gibbons support of, 169
Grand Army of the Republic, 18
Grand Seminary, 14
Grannan affair, 131-133, 167
Guam, 127
Harvard invitation, 108-109
Henebry case, 118, 120, 122
Holy Cross College, Worcester, 14
honorary degrees, 18, 26
honors proposed for, 26
idea of a university, 60
inauguration to rectorship, 28
inter-faith movements, 18
interest in Philippines, 125
Investigating Committee, 133
Irish affairs, interest in, 16-17, 114, 120
Irish background, 152
Irish National League of Mass., 17
Keane, support from, 13n
Knights of Columbus Chair, 46
Land League, 17
law professors, 50-51
lecture tours, 108, 111
life, 9, 13
Los Angeles bishopric, 170-171
McKinley, addressed by, 51
McKinley, interview, 128n
manual for students, 37
New Testament Studies, reviews of, 109-110
orator, 24
ordained, 14
Parnell Fund, 17
patriotism, 17
Petit Seminaire de Montreal, 14
"Plea for Teachers," 74
political influence in Washington, 129
professors, securing of, 33

proposed for rectorship, 8
public lectures for students, 33
Quinn, 104
reception by French and Austrian ships, 108
rector's report (1897), 34
rectorship, choice of, 22
relationship with Sulpicians, 31
resignation, 61, 171
Roosevelt influence, 130
St. John's Parish, 14
Schroeder case, 35, 153
science and religion, 71n
second term, 136-137
seminaries and the Univ., 67
seminary presidents, 65, 67, 168
Shahan's opinion of, 29
Springfield bishopric, 18
Springfield, Diocese of, 14
Springfield Diocesan Temperance Union, 15
state and education, 76
Stoddard retirement, 124
temperance, 15-16, 18, 24, 108, 115
temperance rally, Worcester, 16
terna for third rectorship, 170
testimonial banquets for, 26
Titular Bishop of Samos, 102, 113-115, 168
Trinity College, foundation of, 63, 95, 100
value of teachers, 72
women in education, 100
Worcester Free Public Library, 14
Worcester School Board, 14
Concilionisti
friendly to O'Connell, 146
interest in Amer. democracy, 159
CONFERENCE OF CATHOLIC COLLEGES; *see* Catholic Colleges, Conference of
CONFERENCE OF COLLEGES AND SCHOOLS; *see* Association of Catholic Colleges, Parish School Conference
CONFERENCE OF SEMINARY PRESIDENTS (1898); *see* Seminary Presidents, Meeting of
CONGREGATION OF PROPAGANDA; *see* Propaganda, Congregation of
CONGREGATION OF STUDIES; *see* Studies, Congregation of
CONGREGATION OF THE HOLY CROSS; *see* Holy Cross College, Wash., D. C.
CONSERVATISM
and the Univ., 140
Board of Trustees, 9
Father Aiken's sermon at Univ., 101
CONSERVATIVE PARTY
supporters of, 139
see also Conservatism

DUMONT, FRANCIS L., S.S.
  president of Divinity College, 31
DUNN, JOHN J.
  replaced Henebry, 119-120, 122
DUNWOODIE; *see* St. Joseph's Seminary,
  New York
ECCLESIASTICAL REVIEW; *see American Ecclesiastical Review*
EDES, ELLA B.
  acting for Corrigan and McQuaid, 141
EDUCATION
  integration, 78
  purpose of, 72
  standards, 65, 69; *see also* University
  state control of, 77
  see also: American Universities, Asso-
    ciation of; Catholic Colleges, Asso-
    ciation of; Catholic Educational As-
    sociation
EDUCATION, Dept. of
  foundation of, 58; *see also* Institute of
    Pedagogy
EDUCATIONAL CONFERENCE OF SEMINARY
  FACULTIES
  joined Assoc. of Catholic Colleges, 68-69
EDUCATIONAL STANDARDS; *see* Education,
  University
EGAN, MAURICE FRANCIS
  Corrigan, assurances to, 10
  opposition to Henebry, 122
ELDER, WILLIAM H., Archbishop
  nominations for Bishop of Columbus,
    112
ELIOT, CHARLES W.
  Catholic Alumni Association meeting, 23
  Pres. of Association of American Uni-
    versities, 82
ELLIOTT, WALTER, C.S.P.
  identity of French attackers, 160
  Life of Father Hecker, 159
  mission house, 87
ELLIS, JOHN TRACY, *The Formative Years
  of the Catholic University of America*, 1
ENGINEERING; *see* Technology, Board of
  Instruction
ENGINEERING, SCHOOL OF; *see* Technology,
  Board of Instruction of
ENVOYS, Irish
  reception for, 114
EUPHRASIA, SISTER, S.N.D.
  Trinity College, 95, 99
EXECUTIVE COMMITTEE; *see* Board of Trus-
  tees, Executive Committee
FACULTY
  definition of, 4n

FACULTY OF BIOLOGICAL SCIENCES
  depts. in, 49
FACULTY OF LAW
  depts. in, 50
  formed, 33, 50
  proposed in Chicago, 59
  requirements for degrees, 50
  resignations from, 125
FACULTY OF LETTERS
  depts. in, 49
FACULTY OF MEDICINE, 58
FACULTY OF PHILOSOPHY
  Board of governors, 124
  depts. in, 4, 19
  entrance examinations, 64
  Henebry, opposition to, 122
  Henebry's contract, 118
  requirements for degrees, 49
  Social Science, 33
  Stoddard contract terminated, 124
  students' residence, 31
FACULTY OF PHYSICAL SCIENCES
  depts. in, 49
FACULTY OF SOCIAL SCIENCES
  depts. in, 4
  placed under Faculty of Philosophy, 33
FACULTY OF TECHNOLOGY
  finances, 54
  Senate Committee report on, 54
  see also Technology, Board of Instruc-
    tion, 54
FACULTY OF THEOLOGY
  depts. in, 4, 49
  requirements for degrees, 49
FALCONIO, DIOMEDE, Archbishop
  life, 60n
  new Apostolic Delegate, 60
FARIBAULT, Minn.
  school controversy, 142
FARLEY, JOHN M., Bishop
  Faculty of Medicine, 58
  Keane's resignation, 7
FATHER MATHEW CHAIR, 15
FEEHAN, PATRICK A., Archbishop
  Assoc. of Catholic Colleges, 70
FITZGERALD, EDWARD H., 127
FITZGERALD, J. P.
  baccalaureate sermon, 34
FOLEY, WILLIAM E.
  student of Satolli, 21
FOUNDERS' DAY
  origin of, 110
FRANCE
  Ireland's lectures on government, 159
FRANCISCAN HOLY LAND COLLEGE; *see*
  Franciscan Monastery

203

GREEK, Dept. of, 104-106
GREENE, EDWARD L.
    rumored resignation of, 105-106, 134
GREIFSWALD, University of
    Ph.D. to Henebry, 117
GRIFFIN, JOHN J.
    Committee on Technology, 53
GUAM
    Catholic Church in, 128
    Conaty's activities in, 127
HAGUE TRIBUNAL, Pious Fund; see Pious
    Fund
HALE, EDWARD
    regretted Conaty's refusal to Harvard,
    109
HALL, G. STANLEY
    Association of American Universities, 81
    Catholic Alumni Association, 23
    Keane, praise of, 27
HARKINS, MATTHEW, Bishop
    collection tours, 43
HARPER, WILLIAM R.
    Conaty accepted Association of Ameri-
    can Universities' invitation, 82
HARTNEDY, M. M. A.
    Nominated for Bishop of Columbus, 112
HARVARD-BOSTON COLLEGE controversy,
    73n, 75
HARVARD UNIVERSITY
    Dunn trained in Gaelic, 119
    invited Conaty to preach, 108-109
    non-acceptance of Catholic college stu-
    dents, 73n
HECKER, ISAAC, C.S.P.
    Americanism, 164
    doctrines of, 159
    papal letter on teachings promised, 161
HENEBRY, RICHARD
    Ancient Order of Hibernians opposed
    dismissal of, 119
    appointment not renewed, 115, 118
    contract expired, 118
    dismissal of, 120
    Gaelic Chair, 38, 116
    leave of absence, 117
    Ph.D. from Univ. of Greifswald, 117
    president of Gaelic League of America,
    117
    professor at Maynooth College, Ireland,
    116
    replaced by Dunn, 119
    salary, 117-118
    statement on dismissal, 121-123
HERBARIUM COLLECTION, 50
HIBERNIANS, Ancient Order of
    change of attitude on Henebry case, 123
    conference in Denver, 123

Gaelic Chair, 116, 120-121
    opposed Henebry's dismissal, 119
HIGH SCHOOL
    in Catholic educational system, 77
HISTORY CHAIR; see Knights of Columbus
HOGAN, JOHN, S.S.
    affiliation of St. John's Seminary, 66
    "Seminary and University Studies," 68
HOAR, GEORGE F., 26
HOLY CROSS COLLEGE, Washington, D. C.
    dedication of, 91-92
HOLY CROSS COLLEGE, Worcester
    Conaty, alumnus of, 9
    testimonial to Conaty, 26
HOLY FATHER; see Leo XIII, Pope
HOLY GHOST COLLEGE, Pittsburgh, 65
HOLY SPIRIT
    direct action of, 159
HONORARY DEGREES
    Univ. adverse to, 113
HORSTMANN, IGNATIUS F., Bishop
    Conservative Party, 139
    Peries' resignation letter, 165-166
    Schroeder case, 153-155
HOUSES OF STUDY, religious, 87
HUDSON, DANIEL
    correspondence with Spalding, 12
HUSY, P. M.
    nominations for Bishop of Columbus,
    112
HYVERNAT, HENRI H.
    rumored resignation of, 105-106, 133-134
ICARD, H. J., S.S.
    Sulpician contract, 31
ICARD-KEANE CONTRACT; see Keane-Icard
    contract
Imprimatur, 161
INDIVIDUALISM
    Hecker's doctrine of, 159
    Testem Benevolentiae, 162
INSTITUTE OF PEDAGOGY
    origin of, 79
    Univ. extension, 86
INVESTIGATING COMMITTEE; see Trustees,
    Board of
IRELAND, JOHN, Archbishop
    Abbelen plan, opposition, 148
    agrees with Grannan's views on Univ.,
    133
    Conaty to Los Angeles, 170
    Corrigan's treatment of Paulist, 162
    counter-charges to Rome against, 144
    democratic efforts in France, 159
    Faribault-Stillwater plan, 142
    governmental political activity of, 127

KNIGHTS OF COLUMBUS
  Chair of History, 22, 46
KRAUS, F. X.
  O'Connell, relationship with, 158
LAND LEAGUE
  convention (1880), Buffalo, 17
  convention (1881), Chicago, 17
LAVAL UNIVERSITY, Toronto
  honorary doctorate to Conaty, 26
LAVELLE, MICHAEL J.
  Catholic Summer School, Cliff Haven,
  28
LAW SCHOOL; see Faculty of Law
LAWSUIT, Riverside Drive property, 60
LENIHAN, THOMAS M., Bishop
  death of, 131
LEO XIII, Pope
  affiliation of Catholic schools to Univ.,
  63
  Conaty, appointment to rectorship, 25
  constitution of Univ., 63
  democracy, 145
  favors Univ., 26
  Grannan's opinion of, 132
  Hecker's doctrines, 161
  Ireland requested to lecture in France,
  159
  jurisdiction of Univ. changed, 170
  Keane, audience with, 145
  Keane, welcome to, 11n
  Keane's resignation, 4-5
  Keane's return to America, 40, 42
  O'Connell, resignation requested, 145-
  146
  pleased with conduct of Univ., 111
  removal of professors, 11
  rumored removal of professors, 148
  Schroeder and German Chair, 152
  Schroeder's resignation, 154, 156
  Testem Benevolentiae, 162-164
  titular bishopric for Conaty, 103, 113
  "*tolerari potest*" for Ireland's school plan,
  143
  Trinity College, 98
  Univ., letter on, 55-56, 132
  Univ., support of, 3, 5
LEPIDI, ALBERT, O. P.
  congratulated by Corrigan, 163
  imprimatur protested, 161
  imprimatur to Maignen, 160
  Testem Benevolentiae, 163
LETTERS, SCHOOL OF; see Faculty of Letters
LIBERALISM
  Aiken's sermon at Univ., 101
  and Univ., 140
  Board of Trustees, 9
  Conaty, wary of, 109
  effect of Schroeder's resignation, 157

McQuaid's opinion of, 144
professors' dismissals, 10
Protestant opinion of, 139
Schroeder, opposition to, 149
supporters of, 139
LIBRARY
  Banigan's gift to, 38n
  Caldwell gift to, 111
  lack of funds, 45
LICENTIATE DEGREE; see Degree, licen-
  tiate
LONG, JOHN D.
  Catholic chaplain for Navy, 129
  visit to Univ., 51
LOUVAIN, AMERICAN COLLEGE; see Ameri-
  can College, Louvain
LUCERNE MEMORIAL
  presented to Pope, 148
LUDDEN, PATRICK A., Bishop
  opinion on University, 10
McAVOY, THOMAS T.
  "Americanism, Fact and Fiction", 138
McDONALD, JAMES A.
  Law appointment, 38
McGLYNN, EDWARD
  doctrine of, 11
  Keane's intervention for, 141
  life, 11n
  single tax theory, 11n
McGUIRE, HUGH
  Association of Catholic Colleges, 70
McKINLEY, WILLIAM
  attitude toward Catholic Church, 128-
  129
  visit to Univ., 51
McMAHON, JAMES, Monsignor
  Aiken's sermon at Univ., 101
  gift to Mary Gwendoline Caldwell, 110
  see also, Riverside Drive, New York
McMAHON, JOSEPH, Monsignor
  Cathedral Library University Extension
  Centre, 83
  collecting tour, 44, 57
  Conaty associated with, 28
  Institute of Pedagogy, 84-85
  Special Collector of Univ., 136
  temperance, 28
McQUAID, BERNARD J., Bishop
  Briggs, defense of, 126
  Catholic Summer School, Cliff Haven,
  21
  Conservative Party, 139
  defeated as condidate for Regents, 144
  Ireland, 144, 172
  Keane's resignation, 6, 147
  O'Connell, 145
  opposition to Univ., 3, 140

206

SANTA MARIA CHURCH, Trastevere, 146
SATOLLI, FRANCESCO, Cardinal
  Catholic Summer School, 20
  Conaty's appointment, 23, 152
  Congregation of Studies, 147, 169, 170
  Conaty's report on McKinley's attitude,
    128
  Keane in Rome, 148
  Keane's resignation, 6, 8n
  McQuaid admonished, 144
  O'Connell opposed by, 146
  partisanship, 140, 147
  school controversy, 143
  statement on rumors of dismissal, 10
  Trinity College, 97
  World Parliament of Religions, 144
SBARRETTI, DONATUS, Bishop
  Univ., 92
SCHILLING, GODFREY, O.F.M., 88-90
SCHOLARSHIPS
  granting of, 33
  School of Divinity, 111
SCHOLASTICISM
  rebirth of, 3
SCHOOL; see Faculty
SCHOOL CONTROVERSY OF 1890's, 4, 142-
  143
SCHROEDER, JOSEPH, Monsignor
  attack on feared, 150
  Bulletin, 151
  Cahenslyism, 149-151
  charges against, 153
  Corrigan praised by, 149
  dismissal campaign, 104
  dismissal effect, 119
  forces against, 153
  German Chair at Univ., 152
  Ireland's comment on resignation, 157
  Keane's dismissal, 147, 151
  Münster appointment, 156
  newspaper publicity, 154
  opposition to, 144, 155-156
  papal support of, 154
  Pohle defended, 151
  Quinn's resignation, effect of, 104
  resignation, 35-36, 148, 153-156
  school controversy, 142
  temperance, 149
  tenacity, 150
  Trinity College, opposition to, 96
  Union of German Roman Catholic
    Societies, N. Y., convention of, 151
SCIENCE AND RELIGION, 71n
SCRIPTURE, DEPT. OF, 46, 49
SEARLE, GEORGE M., C.S.P.
  mathematics and astronomy, 33
  resignation, 35

SECOND PLENARY COUNCIL, Baltimore; see
  Plenary Council, Baltimore, Second
SECRETARY GENERAL
  instituted in Univ., 44
SECRETARY OF STATE, Papal; see Rampolla
SEMINARIES
  affiliation with Univ., 65, 69n
SEMINARY PRESIDENTS, meeting of, 65
  see also Educational Conference of
    Seminary Faculties
SENATE, ACADEMIC; see Academic Senate
SETON HALL COLLEGE, South Orange, N. J.
  Briggs, alumnus of, 125-126
  Corrigan, interest in, 140
  intended location of Univ., 3
  McQuaid's interest in, 140
SHAHAN, THOMAS, Bishop
  advisor to Conaty, 83
  Bulletin, 134
  Catholic Summer School, lectures, 21
  "The Chumps," 131
  Conaty, opinion on, 29
  Conaty's consecration sermon, 114
  dismissal rumored, 10
  Gaelic Chair, 116
  Henebry case, 122
  Institute of Pedagogy, 58, 85
  Investigating Committee, 134
  McGlynn commission, 11
  Schroeder case, 155-157
  terna for third rectorship, 170
SHANAHAN, EDMUND T.
  substitute for Schroeder, 36
  translations of constitutions and docu-
    ments, 36
SHEA, DANIEL W.
  Association of American Universities, 81
  committee on technology, 52-54
  elected General Secretary, 44
  resignation offered, 54
SHEEDY, MORGAN M.
  Association of Catholic Colleges, 70
  Conaty's temperance work, 15
SHIELDS, THOMAS EDWARD
  services denied to Univ., 45
SIMEONI, JOHN, Cardinal
  Keane-McGlynn, 141
SIOUX CITY
  erection of a diocese, 130-131
SISTER M. EUPHRASIA, S.N.D.; see
  Euphrasia, Sister, S.N.D.
SISTER M. JULIA, S.N.D.; see Julia, Sister,
  S.N.D.
SISTERS OF NOTRE DAME DE NAMUR
  Trinity College, 95

SKINNER, CHARLES RUFUS
educational policy attacked, 79
SMYTH, H. P.
question of coadjutor of Chicago, 112
SOCIAL SCIENCES, SCHOOL OF; see Faculty of Social Sciences
SOCIETY OF MARY; see Marists
SOCIETY OF SAINT SULPICE; see Sulpicians
SOCIOLOGY, 4
SOUTH ORANGE, NEW JERSEY, SETON HALL; see Seton Hall College, South Orange, N. J.
SPAIN, treaty with U.S., 128
SPALDING, JOHN LANCASTER, Bishop
Conaty's inauguration, 29
dedication of Holy Cross College, Wash., D. C., 92
finances of Univ., 135
fund raising for Univ., 40-41
Institute of Pedagogy, 84
Investigating Committee, 131, 133-134
Keane's removal, 12
Keane's return, 41
lecture, 41
O'Connell as rector, 169
Progressive Party, 139
proposed for coadjutor of Chicago, 112
rectorship, 3, 6
temperance, 15n
Univ. protagonist, 2
SPALDING, MARTIN J., Archbishop, 1
SPANISH-AMERICAN WAR
veterans' privileges, 36
SPECIAL COMMITTEE; see Trustees, Board of, Investigating Committee
SPECIAL STUDENTS, 48
SPRINGFIELD, Diocese of
Conaty, 9, 14
SPRINGFIELD DIOCESAN TEMPERANCE UNION
Conaty, president of, 15
SPRINGFIELD DIOCESAN TOTAL ABSTINENCE UNION, 16
STATE AND CHURCH; see Church and State
STEINHUBER, ANDREAS, Cardinal
interference for Schroeder, 155
Keane's removal, 151
Schroeder's return to Univ., 154
STILLWATER, MINN.
school controversy, 142
STODDARD, CHARLES WARREN
denied rumored resignation, 106
English dept., 51
resignation, 129, 133
rumored resignation, 105

STUDENTS
classification of, 48
enrollment (1900), 47, 48n
STUDIES, CONGREGATION OF
Satolli, Prefect of, 169
Univ. jurisdiction, 61, 170
SUBJECTS; see Faculty
SULPICIANS
authority of Caldwell Hall, 31-32
Conaty, educated by, 9
English-speaking, for president of Divinity College, 136
procurator, 31-32
St. Austin's College, 92
see also Divinity College
SUMMER SCHOOL; see Catholic Summer School
SUMMER SCHOOL, Maryland, 20
TAUNTON, Massachusetts
Conaty's birthplace, 14
TAYLOR, HANNIS
rumors over postponed lecture, 107
TEACHING BODY
requirements for, 74
size (1900), 47-48
TECHNOLOGY, BOARD OF INSTRUCTION
degrees, 50
reorganization of, 52
see also Faculty of Technology
TECHNOLOGY, SCHOOL OF; see Faculty of Technology
TEMPERANCE
Catholic Total Abstinence Union of America, 35
Conaty, 16, 78, 108
German opposition to, 149
Schroeder opposed, 149
see also; Catholic Total Abstinence Union; Father Mathew Chair; Springfield Diocesan Temperance Union
Terna for rectorship, 8-9, 170
Testem Benevolentiae
body of, by Lepidi and Mazzela, 163
date of, 163n
proposed outline, 162
reception of, 163n, 164
THEOLOGY; see Faculty of Theology
THIRD PLENARY COUNCIL, Baltimore; see Plenary Council, Baltimore, Third
TRINITY COLLEGE, Wash., D. C.
establishment of, 63
foundation of, 95
opening, 99-100
purpose of, 96
TRUSTEES, BOARD OF
Dept. of Pedagogy at Univ., 84-86
Dominican affiliation, 95

211

educational standards, 65
endowment fund, 57
examining conditions at Univ., 131
Executive Committee, 35, 107
General Secretary elected, 44
Grannan's comment on meeting, 133
Henebry case, 115, 117-118, 121
Institute of Pedagogy, 84-85
Investigating Committee, 57, 133, 135, 168
Keane's dismissal, 7
organization, 47
Quinn's resignation, 107
Schroeder's resignation, 154
statement of unity on elections, 9
supervisory authority over religious houses of study, 86
UNION OF GERMAN ROMAN CATHOLIC SOCIETIES OF NEW YORK; *see* German-Americans
UNITARIAN CHURCH
conference of, 18
UNIVERSITY ACADEMIC SENATE; *see* Academic Senate
UNIVERSITY
admission of women, 96, 98
Association of American Universities meeting, 81, 83
collection for, 34, 38-39, 40-41, 43-44
conditions of, 132-133
constitutions of, 36
educational standards of, 64
entrance requirements, 64
extension; *see* Institute of Pedagogy
finances, 38, 46, 53, 57, 59, 124, 135-136
Founder's Day, 110
Franciscans, 88-90
Germanic Literature, Chair of, 152
governing body; *see* Academic Senate
honorary degrees, adverse to, 113
jurisdiction over Univ. changed, 61, 170
Negroes, 98
officers of, 47
opposition to, 140, 145
organization of, 47
purpose of, 5
regulations for residence, 30-32
sabbatical leave, 124
Secretary General of, 44
see also: Academic Senate; *Bulletin;* Caldwell Hall; Faculty; Faculty of Biological Sciences; Faculty of Law, etc.; graduate school; Keane Hall; Leo XIII, Pope; Library; Professors; Scholarships; Students; Trustees, Board of
University Bulletin; see Bulletin
UNIVERSITY OF ATHENS; *see* Athens, University of

UNIVERSITY OF CALIFORNIA, 81
UNIVERSITY OF GREIFSWALD; *see* Greifswald, University of
UNIVERSITY OF THE STATE OF NEW YORK, REGENTS; *see* Board of Regents, New York
VANNUTELLI, SERAFINO, Cardinal
O'Connell, relationship with, 146
Testem Benevolentiae, 162
VANNUTELLI, VINCENZO, Cardinal, 146
VELD, RABBI
Catholic Summer School, 20
VICE-RECTORSHIP, 12
VISITATION CONVENT, Georgetown; *see* Georgetown Visitation Convent
VOWS
Hecker's doctrine of, 159
Testem Benevolentiae, 162
WAGGAMAN, THOMAS E.
finances of Univ., 135
"WAR OF 1897," 148, 153; *see also* Schroeder
WATERSON, JOHN A., Bishop
death of, 111
WHITE BILL, New York, 76
WILLIAMS, JOHN, Archbishop
Chair, 43
Conaty, 23
Investigating Committee, 135
neutrality of, 14
opinion of Conaty, 23
Schroeder case, 153
WINTER SCHOOL OF NEW ORLEANS, 20
WOMEN
admission to Univ., 96, 98
WORCESTER FREE PUBLIC LIBRARY
Conaty member of board, 14
WORCESTER SCHOOL BOARD
Conaty member of, 14
WORLD'S PARLIAMENT OF RELIGIONS; *see* Religions, World's Parliament of, 143
YORKE, PETER
opposition to Univ., 124
ZAHM, JOHN A., C.S.C.
Holy Cross College at Univ., 91
ZARDETTI, OTTO, Bishop
praised by Schroeder, 149
ZEDTWITZ, VON, BARONESS; *see* Caldwell, Elizabeth
ZEDTWITZ, WALDEMAR CONRAD
scholarship, 111
ZURCHER, GEORGE
temperance, 149n

212